D0890559

An Islamic Response to Imperialism

An Islamic
Response
to Imperialism

Political and Religious Writings
of Sayyid Jamāl ad-Dīn "al-Afghānī"

by N I K K I R . K E D D I E

Including a Translation of
the *"Refutation of the Materialists"*
from the original Persian
by Nikki R. Keddie and Hamid Algar

University of California Press
Berkeley, Los Angeles, London

University of California Press
Berkeley and Los Angeles, California

University of California Press Ltd.
London, England

© 1968, 1983 by The Regents of the University of California
Library of Congress Catalog Card Number: 68-13224

First Paperback Printing 1983
California Library Reprint Series 1983
ISBN 0-520-04774-5 paper
       0-520-04766-4 cloth

Designed by Wolfgang Lederer
Printed in the United States of America

1   2   3   4   5   6   7   8   9

Additional Note on Transliteration

Since there is some variation in systems of marking different consonants that are pronounced in the same way in Persian, the following chart is given. Only in the notes and bibliography are the Persian diacriticals used.

Arabic	Persian
ẓ	ẓ
ḍ	z̤
dh	z̲
ṣ	ṣ
th	s̲
w	v

With the exception of ḍ, dh, th, and w, consonants are transliterated the same way in Persian as in Arabic.

In the modern Turkish Romanization, letters are pronounced very much as spelled, except that *c* equals Arabic and English *j*. Thus the name of Jamāl ad-Dīn in Turkish begins with *C*.

To
Gustave E. von Grunebaum

with gratitude

Preface to the 1983 Edition

For the new edition I have made minor changes in the text and have added a new introduction indicating Afghāni's relationship to later trends in Islamic thought and activity. When footnotes in this book refer to my articles for futher details, the reader should now rather refer to Nikki R. Keddie, *Sayyid Jamāl ad-Dīn "al-Afghānī": A Political Biography* (Berkeley and Los Angeles: University of California Press, 1972). The work on the new edition was done while I held Rockefeller Foundation and Woodrow Wilson Center fellowships in 1982 and thanks are due to both of them for giving me the time and assistance to complete this work. Naturally, neither is responsible for what I have written.

Preface to the 1968 Edition

Since the summer of 1964 I have been engaged in a study of the life and writings of Sayyid Jamāl ad-Dīn al-Afghānī,* best known as an ideologist of pan-Islam and of Islamic reform. One product of this study has been a detailed biography of Afghānī, of which an almost complete draft now exists. Portions of this long biography have appeared in preliminary form as articles, which are listed in the bibliography and footnotes of the present book.

In the course of this study of Jamāl ad-Dīn it became clear that some of the numerous misconceptions current about him were due to a failure to refer to his Persian-language writings and to heavy reliance upon Arabic articles in his newspaper al-'Urwa al-Wuthqā, which represent only one phase of his thought and activity. It seemed useful, therefore, in order to make available a more complete picture of Afghānī, to analyze some of his more neglected writings, particularly those written in Persian, and to translate some of the most illustrative of them. In analyzing Afghānī's thought I have found it particularly important to indicate his relationship to unorthodox traditions of Islamic rationalist philosophy. A very brief version of Afghānī's biography makes up the first chapter of this book, as background to the analysis of his thought.

The study of Jamāl ad-Dīn al-Afghānī's life and activities also necessitated reference to the Persian original of his most famous work, known in the West under the title of its Arabic translation, the "Refutation of the Materialists." It immediately became apparent that the Persian text was quite different from the Arabic text, which is a paraphrase rather than a translation. The Arabic translation was done by Muḥammad 'Abduh, who knew no Persian but got

---

* Although, as the following pages show, Sayyid Jamāl ad-Dīn was born and brought up in Iran, not Afghanistan, I have continued to use the name "Afghānī" under which he is known everywhere outside Iran, rather than follow the technically accurate but unfamiliar Iranian practice of naming him after his native village of Asadabad.

the sense of the original from Afghānī's Persian servant, Abū Turāb. Since the latter was not a learned man, the discrepancy between the original and the Arabic is not surprising. Until now the only Western translation of the "Refutation" has been from the Arabic, and hence shares 'Abduh's deviations from the original text. (This is Jamāl ad-Dīn al-Afghānī, *La Réfutation des matérialistes*, trans. A. M. Goichon [Paris, 1942], a volume that brings together much useful material.) Although the general sense of the Arabic text is similar to the Persian original, it seemed useful to provide an English translation of this widely cited work which was based on an accurate text. An idea of the difference between the Persian and Arabic texts may be obtained by taking almost any substantial section of the English translation herein and comparing it to Mlle. Goichon's French translation from the Arabic. In general, the Arabic is a somewhat longer paraphrase of what Afghānī is presumed to have meant. When his Persian text is ambiguous or obscure, as it frequently is, words or phrases are often added indicating what the translators thought Afghānī meant. Since there is no evidence that Afghānī approved or corrected the Arabic translation, it seemed better to try to avoid reliance on the paraphrases of the Arabic version when doing the present translation. I have not tried to duplicate Mlle. Goichon's most useful detailed annotations of the persons and schools referred to by Afghānī; those interested should refer to her work.

I did the original translation of the "Refutation" from a recent Tehran edition, but subsequently obtained from the Majlis Library in Tehran a microfilm of the original Indian lithographed edition. Hamid Algar of the Near Eastern Languages Department, University of California, Berkeley, did the difficult work of checking my entire translation against these rather illegible photographs and made various revisions, many of which were based on correcting errors in the more recent edition. Dr. Algar also checked, and suggested revisions for, the translation of "The Benefits of Philosophy."

For the translations of articles it was not possible to refer to first editions, but the editions used contained none of the obvious errors found in the Tehran text of the "Refutation." The Persian articles were translated from *Maqālāt-i jamāliyyeh* (Tehran, 1312 h. solar/1933); "The Materialists in India," from the Cairo, 1958, edition of *al-'Urwa al-Wuthqā*; and the "Answer to Renan," from Mlle. Goichon's translation of the "Refutation," referred to above.

Although Afghānī's writing is often obscure, particularly where, as in "The Benefits of Philosophy," he is discussing technical questions of traditional Islamic philosophy, I have preferred not to burden the text or notes with a heavy scholarly apparatus or possible alternate meanings. On the points that I am most concerned to illustrate—Afghānī's political and religious views—there are no major ambiguities or obscurities in the texts. In general, the translations follow the pattern of being as literal as is consistent with smooth English usage. This has meant breaking up long sentences; providing clear antecedents for the ubiquitous *it's* and *he's* of Arabic and Persian; but retaining much of the rhetoric and reiterations of synonomous phrases so characteristic of Afghānī's style.

Transliteration in a text that deals with Arabic, Persian, and Turkish words and works presents peculiar problems, for which every author will have his own solution. Mine has been to use the modern Turkish Romanization for Turkish; the standard system adopted by the UCLA Near Eastern Center for Arabic; and a modification of this Arabic system for Persian, whereby the vowels are transliterated in the Arabic system, while consonants are given their Persian pronunciation without the diacritical marks that distinguish between different letters pronounced in the same way. In the notes and bibliography, however, I have added standard diacriticals to the Persian consonants as an aid to anyone who might wish to look up an author or work in Persian. Place-names and words whose position in English is attested by their inclusion in recent unabridged dictionaries are presented without diacriticals, although the sign for *'ain* is retained in the middle of such words: as ulama, Shi'i, Isma'ili, Babi, Muhammad. *Neicheri* is spelled in a way that has become common in English.

My work on Afghānī has been almost a group project, so much have I called on the generous help of others. For the material included in this book I would like to record heartfelt thanks to Mrs. Homa Pakdaman of Paris, who has shown me her thesis on Afghānī, which includes numerous important and excellent translations. I want to thank her particularly for allowing me to refer to her translations of the "Lecture on Teaching and Learning," and "Commentary on the Commentator." My translations were done directly from the Persian, but reference to her translations sometimes helped clarify dubious points. Also deserving profound thanks is Elie Kedourie of the London School of Economics, who first suggested I undertake a biography of Afghānī and has made numerous useful suggestions, not only regarding the completed text, but at all stages of my work. Although our views on Afghānī are not at all identical, Professor

Kedourie has been unstintingly generous in forwarding my study. My colleagues Amin Banani and Moshe Perlmann have also given most generously of their time and knowledge in answering numerous questions about translations from Persian and Arabic. Professor G. E. von Grunebaum, director of the Near East Center at UCLA, has also encouraged my work from the beginning, and has read the entire work and made useful suggestions for changes. The work, in an earlier stage, was also generously read and commented on by Hamid Algar and Ira Lapidus of the University of California, Berkeley, and by Benjamin Schwartz of Harvard, Aziz Ahmad of the University of Toronto, and Muhsin Mahdi of the University of Chicago. Errors and deficiencies that remain are, of course, mine alone. Useful suggestions have also come from conversations and correspondence with Professors H. A. R. Gibb; Bernard Lewis of London; Albert Hourani of Oxford; Niyazi Berkes of McGill, Montreal; Joseph R. Levenson and William Brinner of the University of California, Berkeley; Maxime Rodinson of Paris; and Iraj Afshār, Asghar Mahdavī, ʿAbd al-Husain Zarrinkūb, Sayyid Hasan Taqīzādeh, Muhīt Tabātabāʾī, Mojtaba Minovi, and Sifātallāh Jamālī (Afghānī's grandnephew) in Tehran. Dr. Zarrinkūb, in particular, gave freely of his time and help when I was in Iran and suggested a number of ideas about Afghānī and his Persian followers which are fundamental to the present work. Those whose help contributed mainly to the longer biography include my colleagues Andreas Tietze and Janos Eckmann and various acquaintances in Cairo and Istanbul, who will be thanked more adequately in that work. My research assistants, Miss Shannon Stack and Mr. Gene Garthwaite, and my editor, Kathleen Jasonides, have also helped above and beyond their duties.

The study was helped financially by grants from the John Simon Guggenheim Foundation, 1963–1964; the American Philosophical Society, summer, 1965; and the University of California Humanities Foundation, summer, 1966; to all of whom thanks are due.

I should like to conclude this preface in a heterodox way, by appealing to my readers for comments, criticisms, and corrections. Since my longer biography of Afghānī remains to be concluded and published, it should be possible to incorporate corrections and suggestions into that work.

N. R. K.

Los Angeles
April, 1967

From Afghānī to Khomeini

It is now just a century since Jamāl ad-Dīn "al-Afghānī," the leading defender of his day of the Muslim world against the incursions of the West, was in his prime. His political and educational activities in Egypt in the late 1870s, his writing in India from 1880 to 1882 of most of the works translated in this volume, and his editing with Muḥammad ʿAbduh of the pan-Islamic newspaper al-ʿUrwa al-Wuthqā in 1884 mark high points in his productivity and influence. Since his death in 1897 he has had a growing reputation in the Muslim world, with numerous books and articles being written about him, and his name appears in textbooks, in the media, and elsewhere. Today he is taken by some to be a precursor of the "Islamic Revival" of our time, although many of the more orthodox ulama still do not accept his interpretations of Islam. He is a precursor not so much of those ulama as of a line of ideological modernizers—mostly laymen who often had some religious training—who have tried to interpret Islam in new ways to inculcate in Muslims the virtues of reform and self-strengthening, in order to change and build up the Muslim world and insure its independence.

Except in a few clear cases of immediate disciples or persons who have left evidence of a strong direct influence by Afghānī, it is difficult to measure his influence. He in large part expressed a mood and viewpoint that was in any case beginning to come to the fore in the Muslim world during his lifetime—a mood of many who did not wish simply to continue borrowing from the West or bowing to growing Western domination, but wished rather to find in indigenous traditions, both Islamic and national, precedents for the reforms and self-strengthening they wanted to undertake. Such an outlook has continued, with some interruptions, to grow in the Muslim world—in some periods taking the more nationalist form that Afghānī stressed before the 1880s and in others the more Islamic revivalist form he stressed thereafter.

The line of Afghānī's influence is chiefly traced through two men, greatly influenced by him but in many ways different from him and from each other, both in ideology and in temperament: his chief Egyptian disciple Muḥammad ʿAbduh, and the latter's disciple, also mostly active in Egypt, Rashīd Riḍā. After collaborating through 1884 with Afghānī in ways described in this volume, ʿAbduh later broke with him, saying he had too violent a temper and had done good work only in Egypt (where Afghānī was chiefly an educator). ʿAbduh abandoned his early interest in Afghānī's plans for violent and sudden action in favor of slower educational and legal reforms, which he was able to introduce from his position of Grand Mufti of Egypt and reformer of the traditional al-Azhar university. Despite this change, and ʿAbduh's pointed silence when Afghānī died, Afghānī's influence may be seen even in ʿAbduh's career and writings as a moderate gradualist reformer. Afghānī's introduction of ʿAbduh to Islamic philosophy, with its rationalist view of Islam, was one aspect of such influence. Also, it would seem that ʿAbduh retained a practice not exclusive to Afghānī, but especially associated with him, of talking or writing one way for the elite and another for the masses. Although many have doubted Lord Cromer's published surmise that ʿAbduh was really an agnostic, one may infer that he spoke to some in ways that could lead to this supposition, though he did not speak or write to most Muslims in these ways.

While no evidence seems yet to exist that ʿAbduh acquired his frequently noted "neo-Muʿtazilite" ideas from Afghānī, this is possible, especially since the Twelver Shiʿi school of doctrine in which Afghānī grew up and was educated was Muʿtazilite in theology, not Ashʿarite as were nearly all Sunni theologians. Among the relevant differences between the two schools were that the Muʿtazilites, calling themselves partisans of the Unity and Justice of God, raised Justice to a general principle and said that God must act in accord with it, while the Ashʿarites, believing in the inscrutable omnipotence of God, said that whatever He did was just, and Justice had no independent existence as an abstraction separate from God's acts. In addition, most Muʿtazilites came to believe that God acts via secondary causes, according to regular laws of causation, whereas Ashʿarites saw this as a limitation on the absolute (or arbitrary) power of God. Many of the Ashʿarites extended the idea that God acts only directly in the world to the conclusion that He recreates and reactivates the universe every moment as He wishes, with no secondary causes, apparent regularities being due only to his mercy toward mankind. The Muʿtazilite position, although not originally a Shiʿi one, came to dominate Twelver Shiʿi theology; it was closer to the natural-law, virtually deistic, notions of many of the Islamic philosophers than was Ashʿarism, which came to dominate Sunni thought. Muʿtazilism was the earlier school, overtaken in Sunnism, but not in Shiʿism, by Ashʿarism, and some have seen a tie between the rise of Sunni absolute and arbitrary rulers, the decline of philosophical and scientific speculation, and the dominance of Ashʿarism. Some of the rationalist ideas called neo-Muʿtazilite by commentators on ʿAbduh might have come to him from the Muslim philosophers, whose influence on Afghānī and ʿAbduh is documented. Nonetheless, Afghānī's Shiʿi education was surely influenced by Muʿtazilite ideas, and he probably passed on some of these in his education of his closest disciple, ʿAbduh. It is known that ʿAbduh sometimes spoke badly of Shiʿism, but it should be noted that there is no necessary connection between Muʿtazilism and Shiʿism: when Twelver Shiʿism began it was not Muʿtazilite, but became so later, and when Muʿtazilism began it was not expounded by Shiʿis. Further, there is no evidence that Afghānī's background made him think of himself, or speak of himself outside Iran, as a Shiʿi.

Muʿtazilism believes in free will for humans, while Ashʿarism says everything that occurs is willed by God. While both free will and predestination have in various places and times been used to support activism, it would seem that in modern Islam Ashʿarite predestination was associated with a nonactivist clinging to old ways, while an implicitly Muʿtazilite belief in free will was more characteristic of activists and reformers.

If ʿAbduh used some of Afghānī's intellectual tools to begin to build a kind of gradual-reformist "bourgeois" Islamic liberalism, ʿAbduh's disciple Rashīd Riḍā (1865–1935) moved especially toward another aspect of Afghānī's legacy, the religious reform of Islam that would bring it into accord with the ways of the earliest Muslims. This had already been a practice of the eighteenth-century Wahhabis of Arabia, who wished to rid Islam of mystical (Sufi) and superstitious accretions and revive the original Islamic (especially Koranic) punishments, taxes, and so forth. The Wahhabis, however, were an indigenous movement that could hardly have been seriously affected by the Western impact, while the nineteenth- and twentieth-century figures discussed here were much affected by the West. The idea of a return to true early Islam as a means of reform had already been put forth by Afghānī and some others. Such an idea, elaborated and explained by Riḍā, shares with similar Western and other "protestant" reforms the virtue of allowing the reformer to clear away whatever he dislikes from the religion's later periods as "superstitious accretions," "foreign borrowings," "un-Islamic" and the like. What remains from the early period may be interpreted by the reformist according to his own interpretation, which is influenced by the modern world and ideas he knows. This is a basic difference between Riḍā and the rather conservative reformist Salafiyya movement that followed him on the one hand and the Wahhabis on the other. The latter really want to revive (and in Saudi Arabia have largely revived) early Islamic taxes, punishments, and rules, whereas Afghānī, ʿAbduh, Riḍā, and many others were pursuing their versions of the "true" Islam, which in their time included few literal revivals of early Islamic prescriptions, but introduced various degrees of modern liberalism, interpreted as being what was really meant by such things as Koranic "consultation," and early Islamic consensus of the community. Riḍā often supported the Saudi Arabian Wahhabis, but his interpretations of early Islam were mostly different from theirs.

Among the problems created by the Western impact on Eastern societies was cultural fragmentation, in which to the existing cultural and class diversities were added radical new ones, without the old ones disappearing. On the whole, among those in the upper and upper middle classes with close ties to Western powers or businesses there was a widespread adoption of Westernized ways once these became available. This included Westernized education, travel, fashions, and a more equitable treatment of women, without much concern for literal Koranic injunctions. The Islamic reform and activist notions of men like Afghānī and Riḍā, on the other hand, tended to appeal to those it is fashionable to call "petty bourgeois." They may also, and perhaps better, be defined by their partial ties to the old culture and economy—ties that were greater than those of the first, generally wealthier groups, but not great enough to turn them away from Western ideas in their search to rebuild their societies, which were seen as weak and backward by comparison to the increasingly menacing West. This dual role of Western countries as menace and model meant that there was a growing need to present ideas derived from the West, or at least first thought of because of the Western challenge, in Islamic ways. Afghānī was a pioneer in this method, and it is not accidental that his work came at a time when the Western menace was acutely felt in conquests in the Ottoman Empire, Tunisia, Egypt, and elsewhere. Purely Westernizing responses were associated, naturally enough, with those who collaborated with the West, and, indeed, of the three men discussed above, the most Westernizing, Muḥammad ʿAbduh, was also the one who collaborated most with the westerner—in his case as an appointee of the British rulers of Egypt.

Reformers, including the ones discussed, rarely appealed to what inadequately may be called the "traditional classes"—urban and rural masses in largely traditional occupations or the majority of the ulama, who were conservative. When the masses were swept into movements with reforming and/or anti-foreign elements, these were nearly always militant messianic or Sufi-led movements, not movements sparked by modernizers. Examples include the long Sufi-led resistance movements of Abdel Qadir in Algeria against the French, Shamyl in the Caucasus against the Russians, the Libyan Senussis against the Italians and the Mahdists in the Sudan. In all these we find largely traditional forms of organization and ideology mobilized for partly new aims. Few modernizers have tried to mobilize the masses, and many have actually antagonized them. The Salafiyya movement, strongest in North Africa, and taking some inspiration from Riḍā, ʿAbduh, and Afghānī, for example, was notable, as were some other Muslim reformists, for its attacks on "unIslamic superstitions" characteristic especially of the popular Sufi orders. To such purists, attacks on saint-worship, music, dancing, and various Sufi practices might seem a class-neutral attempt to regain the rational Islam of its founding fathers, but to the popular classes it probably seemed that Salafis or others who attacked the religion they practiced were taking away their only consolations and pastimes without providing any satisfactory substitute. In other words, most of the religious reformists pressed for a kind of religion that had little emotional appeal to the popular classes, who continued to look either to the leaders of their orders, or to the more "old fashioned" clergy. This ideological class split among the Westernized rich, the partially Westernized and partially reformist middle group, and the masses, who are more apt to turn to apocalyptic religious movements than to Western-influenced reformist practices, has continued to develop down to the present.

For a long time, however, the reaction of the popular classes and the ulama were largely ignored (although Afghānī to a degree appreciated their importance), and the second ideological group, the reformers, seemed to be growing constantly in strength. The twentieth century up to World War II has aptly been called the Liberal

Age—a period in which reformers grew in strength, and parliamentary liberalism came to the fore in the newly liberated states of the Arab East, while Iran and Turkey had governments which if despotic were also secularist, reformist, and Westernizing. A number of reformists throughout the Muslim world invoked the name of Afghānī in this period, while the Afghans, who during his lifetime gave him little notice, and wrote of him first in a World War I newspaper, now made him into a national hero. They began to agitate to get his body back in the 1930s, and although an eyewitness could only find one Turk who claimed to know his unmarked grave, this was enough to have the body dug up and honored in Arab territory *en route* and even more in Afghanistan, where a large monument was eventually built for him. Drowned out were the complaints of several Iranians, who insisted—with evidence—that Afghānī was Iranian; Reza Shah was not interested.

In the interwar period, as at other times, Afghānī's example could plausibly be invoked for a variety of causes and policies, but at this time he was used largely to support Islamically-tinged liberal reformism, which had become popular with a growing and increasingly Westernized middle class. As Western influences and education spread in the Middle East, so too did the kind of apologetic writing that claimed that all modern virtues were found in Islam (especially early Islam) if only it were properly understood. This kind of claim is also found in Afghānī, but it is important to note that it served a very different purpose for him, writing before Westernized ideas had spread widely among Muslims, than it did for those writing well into the twentieth century, when modern Western ideas were widely taught in schools and elsewhere. Afghānī was addressing people whose primary commitment was to Islamic values, and in saying modern Western virtues were to be found in Islam he was trying to attain Muslim acceptance of those modern ideas. By the 1930s, however, Islamic liberals were writing for an audience educated in Western ways, and when they conflated Islam and Western values they were trying to reinstate Islam with that audience, and to build a type of Islam that their hearers would find as acceptable as they did Western values. Or else they were speaking to people torn between Islam and secular Westernized loyalties, and trying to indicate that their newer ideas could be reconciled with Islam. Afghānī was primarily calling people to action, not to an admiration of Islam. Those doing the latter are largely those characterized by Wilfrid Smith in his *Islam in Modern History* as apologists: people who wish to build pride and admiration regarding Islam, while the underlying standards by which they interpret it are really modern and Western. For them, unlike Afghānī and recent Muslim revivalists, Islam is an object for approval and new interpretations to combat alienation rather than a force for action.

At the height of this apologetic Islamic liberalism in the 1930s, however, a type of Islam that represented a continuation of a different side of Afghānī's writings and activity began to be important. This took the form of militantly Islamic activist mass movements, represented first by the Muslim Brotherhood, which began in Egypt in 1928. These movements appealed largely to the urban popular classes, particularly the petty bourgeoisie in traditional jobs or with partly traditional backgrounds, including students and civil servants. These people were less Westernized and less tied to Westerners than were the liberals, and their education and/or economic role gave them less interest in Westernizing their society, and a stronger resentment against the Western influence on and modernization of their economy and nation. They hence felt much less need than the liberals for apologetics showing them that Islam was worthy of modern approval, and were more open to appeals that asked them to mobilize against the growth of Western control of their economy and society in defence of Islam. The new movements thus incorporated Afghānī's anti-Western activism, but they departed from him in their devotion to older Islamic ways and rejection of liberal interpretations of Islam. Their Islam generally stressed socioeconomic justice, not parliaments and legal reform. During World War II such militant Islamic movements gained strength from Indonesia through the Arab world. In India militant popular Islam helped change the idea of Pakistan from an improbable dream to a reality within a very few years in the 1940s.

Important political events in the growth of militant Islam were the growth of Zionism and of pro-Zionist commitments by the West, the formation of Israel, and the series of losing wars fought by the Arabs thereafter. Muslims throughout the world identified with the Arab cause, and Israel was seen as a colonial enclave in the Arab world, splitting that world in two and humiliating the Arabs. Partly because of Israel, many in the Arab world and even in the Muslim world felt themselves to be still fighting an imperialist West. This generalized hostility to the West was for many, and in particular for the popular classes strongly tied to Islam, associated with the defense of Islam more than the defense of particular nations. There is, however, a problem in associating the Palestine question with Islam, as Palestinians include a large number of Christians, some of whom head constituent parts of the Palestine Liberation Organization. In addition both the P.L.O. and many Palestinians and Arabs have made a special point of calling Israel a theocratic state and saying that *their* Palestine would be secular and treat all religions equally. In the 1970s and 1980s, however, the Palestinian movement has seen a growth of Islamic revivalists in its ranks, and the worldwide Islamic revival spills over into the struggle over Palestine.

Just as liberalism and apologetics represent only one side of Afghānī's life and activities, and negate another side, so the same is true for the Islamic Revival, which has roots as far back as the 1930s, but became most prominent beginning in the 1970s. Afghānī, like the revivalists, wished to mobilize Muslims to fight against Western control and conquest and to strengthen Muslim countries. He did not, however, stress strict Koranic or early Islamic laws and practices, as most revivalists do, and he did not support the traditional ulama as many revivalists do. He was concerned to show that Islam was compatible with reason, freedom of thought, and other modern virtues. In context, Afghānī's Islamic appeal may be seen as more "progressive" than that of the modern revivalists—more open to new ideas and not concerned with reinforcing the Islam of the past.

Contemporary Islamic revivalism shares with Afghānī a belief in anti-Western activism, but the various movements labeled Islamic revivalist differ not only from him but from one another. Excluding the "traditionalists" of the Arabian peninsula, we may point to Islamic revivalist organizations in several countries often led by minor intellectuals, including the Muslim Brotherhood and smaller, usually more extreme, Muslim groups in Egypt, the Muslim Brotherhood in Syria and elsewhere, new Sufi Orders like the Nurcilar in Turkey, and Islamic organizations in Indonesia, Pakistan, and elsewhere. The most dramatic example is Iran, which had two main streams: the ulama-led movement appealing chiefly to the bazaaris and subproletarian urban migrants, mainly represented by Ayatollah Khomeini, and the radical stream represented by Ali Shariati and the Mojahedin-e Khalq. Iran has been somewhat special in having leaders of the ulama represented in all its rebellious and revolutionary movements since the late nineteenth century. This can be traced to special features of Iranian Shiʿism as compared to Sunnism, including a history of growing independent economic, ideological, and political power and claims for the Shiʿi ulama. With their greater political and economic independence and their partial role as protectors of the masses against the government, the Iranian ulama were able to produce individuals who plausibly claimed that they, not the illegitimate shahs, had the right to rule. Ayatollah Khomeini's claim to direct rule by the ulama, led by one of their number, was not in accord even with past Shiʻi doctrine, but was for some a plausible development of that doctrine. This went far beyond anything Afghānī had asked for; in his writings he is often very critical of the ulama of his time for being lost in trivial traditional questions instead of entering the great struggles of the time. When Afghānī found ulama entering such struggles he worked with them, however, and it is impossible to say where he would have stood in relation to the various stages of the Iranian revolution. Probably, like many others, he would at first have supported Khomeini, but would later have been disillusioned by the killings and the attempts to enforce the strictest interpretation of Islamic punishments and to impose arbitrary punishments unconnected with Islam.

Also generally considered part of the Islamic revival are Col. Muammar Qadhafi of Libya—who, however, has his own populist interpretation of Islam that bears little resemblance to any orthodoxy—and Zia ul-Haqq of Pakistan—who has mostly grafted a few elements of Islamic law and punishments onto a dictatorial military rule. More significant may be movements of masses of people, whether now in organizations or not, who have been disillusioned because Western-style modernization, liberalism, nationalism, and in some cases "socialism" seem to have given them little, and hence they are turning to populist Islamic politics. The victories of Iran in the second year of the Iran-Iraq war gave strength to this trend, though defeats and difficulties could reverse this.

Today both liberals and Islamic revivalists find appeal in Afghānī, and publication of biographies of him and books by him has been part both of a continuing apologetic tradition and of a newer revivalism, in Iran and elsewhere. Although some of Afghānī's themes are restated in both movements, as well as by persons who belong to neither movement, it seems also that both movements could have arisen without his influence. Despite this, it is important to realize how far back many themes of contemporary writers and leaders go— at least as far back as Afghānī. His stress on Islam as a force to ward off the West and to strengthen Muslim peoples through unity, his call for reforms and changes under the banner of Islam, and his attack on those who side with the West or otherwise split the Muslim community are all themes that found a long and continued succession after him. Although Afghānī, for his own time, was far more a reformer than a reviver of the Muslim past, he was even more a self-strengthener against the encroaching West, and this is a theme that has continued with undiminished force among subsequent leaders and thinkers. His activist, anti-imperialist version of Islam is one that still has a great appeal among a wide variety of Muslims.

Contents

1

The Life and Thought
of Sayyid Jamāl ad-Dīn

1 The Life of Sayyid Jamāl ad-Dīn al-Afghānī

Sayyid Jamāl ad-Dīn al-Afghānī, 1838/9–1897, one of the most dramatic figures of nineteenth-century Middle Eastern history, has in recent years attracted increasing attention in both the Middle East and the West. Afghānī was one of the first influential figures to try to restate the Muslim tradition in ways that might meet the agonizing problems brought by the growing encroachments of the West in the Middle East. Rejecting both unthinking traditionalism and blind imitation of the Christian West, he began what has been a continuing reinterpretation of Islam, emphasizing values vitally needed for life in the modern world, such as activism, the freer use of human reason, and political and military strength. By seeking these values within the Islamic tradition instead of openly borrowing from the heretical West, Afghānī was able to attain an influence on believing Muslims which was not shared by those who simply appropriated Western ideas. As the first "Neo-Traditionalist" whose influence spread beyond the borders of a single Muslim country, Afghānī is in some sense the parent of various later trends that reject both pure traditionalism and pure Westernism. Although Afghānī was, during his period of greatest influence, primarily an ideologist of pan-Islam, his style of thought has some affinity with numerous other trends in the modern Islamic world. These range from the Islamic liberalism associated particularly with Afghānī's most prominent disciple, Muḥammad 'Abduh, to the more conservative Islamic revivalism of the Egyptian Rashīd Riḍā and the Muslim Brethren, and include pan-Arabism and various other forms of Middle Eastern nationalism. Although Afghānī's direct influence on all these movements is frequently exaggerated, his mode of reinterpreting the Islamic past in modern and nationalist terms displayed a temper of thought that was to become increasingly popular in the Middle East.[1] That Afghānī has been chosen as a hero by so many Middle Easterners gives him an importance that withstands all evidence that his influence during his lifetime was often small.

Afghānī has also attracted interest because of the mysteries and controversies surrounding his life. The two most controversial questions about him concern his nationality and his religious orthodoxy. Afghānī and his chief Arab disciples maintained that he was born and brought up in Afghanistan, which would have made him, as he claimed to be, a follower of the majority, Sunni, branch of Islam. Yet even during his lifetime there were many Iranians who said he was born and raised in Iran and educated in the minority, Shi'i, branch of Islam that was Iran's state religion. The argument has continued until today, with the Arabs and Afghans generally making him an Afghan Sunni, and the Iranians producing ever more proofs that he was an Iranian Shi'i. The nationality question is tied to the orthodoxy question, which has, however, more dramatic elements. Throughout his life there were incidents pointing to Afghānī's unorthodoxy, and sometimes even irreligion, which his Muslim followers have been at pains to explain away. For example, in 1870 he was expelled from Istanbul at the request of the highest religious officer, the Şeyhülislam, on the grounds that he had given a heretical and unbelieving speech; later disciples attributed to him skeptical views; and he himself wrote a religiously skeptical article in French in 1883, his "Answer to Renan."[2]

In addition, many other points of Afghānī's biography have remained unclear until now. The entire first thirty years of his life have been shrouded in mystery, and even his later life has been enveloped in a mythology fostered by him and his disciples. Afghānī's contacts with governmental leaders during his far-flung travels in

---

[1] An excellent summary of the later trends in the Muslim world embodied in Afghānī is found in Wilfred Cantwell Smith, *Islam in Modern History* (Princeton, 1957), pp. 47–51. Smith notes that Afghānī seems to have been the first to stress the "Islam-West" antinomy and the first important figure with "nostalgia for the departed earthly glory of pristine Islam." Smith further notes that Afghānī stressed both internal reform and external defense, encouraged both nationalism and pan-Islam, and advocated borrowing from the West and a new vitalistic activism.

[2] These incidents are discussed in more detail below. The most complete gathering of evidence and indications pointing to Afghānī's unorthodoxy or unbelief is found in Elie Kedourie, *Afghani and 'Abduh: An Essay on Religious Unbelief and Political Activism in Modern Islam* (London, 1966).

Afghanistan, the Ottoman Empire, Egypt, India, Paris, London, Iran, and Russia have been disproportionately magnified, partly by Afghānī and partly by his admiring biographers.

In view of recent interest in Afghānī, it is somewhat puzzling that greater efforts have not been made to construct an accurate picture of either his life or his thought. His thought has often been treated merely by summarizing his words, removed from the context of the particular Islamic traditions to which he was heir, and from that of his biography and political goals.

Nearly all later biographies stem directly or indirectly from two closely related sources, both written by Arab admirers of Afghānī, and based on what Afghānī wished the public to believe about him. These are a biography by Afghānī's disciple, Muḥammad 'Abduh, and a biographical article by Jurjī Zaidān, written shortly after Afghānī's death.[3] The 'Abduh biography was written specifically to refute charges of irreligion made against Afghānī, and both his and Zaidān's accounts glorify their subject. Concerning everything before Afghānī's trip to Egypt in 1870, and much thereafter, both depend entirely on Afghānī's own word. Since it is easy to prove that Afghānī frequently made up stories about himself, the only sound principle for a biography of Afghānī would seem to be a search for primary sources that are independent of Afghānī's word. The main outlines of such a biography follow. (Hereafter the usual account will be called the " 'Abduh-Zaidān account" or the "standard biography.")

There is now abundant evidence that Afghānī was not, as he usually claimed, born and brought up in Sunni Afghanistan, but rather in Shi'i Iran. The confusion on this point rests on an acceptance of Afghānī's stories about himself; ignoring the Persian-language proofs of Afghānī's Iranian origin; and relying on Arabic accounts that depend ultimately on Afghānī's own word. Especially

---

[3] 'Abduh's article was first prefaced to his Arabic translation of the "Refutation of the Materialists," and then to a new edition of al-'Urwa al-Wuthqā; it was translated into French in Jamāl ad-Dīn al-Afghānī, Réfutation des matérialistes, trans. A. M. Goichon (Paris, 1942), pp. 31–57. Zaidān's admiring obituary notice was first published in his periodical al-Hilāl in 1897 and later in his Tarājim mashāhīr ash-sharq (Celebrated Men of the East). Internal evidence shows that these two apologetic articles are the chief sources of the biography in E. G. Browne, The Persian Revolution of 1905–1909 (Cambridge, 1910) and, partly via Browne, of many other Western accounts of Afghānī's life.

since the recent publication in Iran of a catalog, with reproductions of Afghānī's documents,[4] and the unearthing of Government of India documents showing that Afghānī appeared in Afghanistan *for the first time* in 1866, there should be no more question about his nationality. Following is a brief review of some of the evidence proving Afghānī's Iranian birth and upbringing.

First, there is no early account of an Afghan birth and upbringing that does not rest on Afghānī's own word. Whereas several Iranian contemporaries have recorded their knowledge of Afghānī's family and childhood in Iran, there is nothing analogous for Afghanistan. The first Afghan account of Afghānī's life apparently dates from 1916, and is a paraphrase of the 'Abduh-Zaidān story. Only after that did the Afghans begin to add childhood details, with no contemporary sources cited.[5]

Second, there are several early Persian accounts that give particulars about Afghānī's birth and childhood in Iran, the most detailed of which comes from Afghānī's nephew Lutfallāh, who grew up in Afghānī's own village of Asadabad near Hamadan in northwest Iran. Letters to Afghānī from Lutfallāh and other members of Afghānī's family in Asadabad, photographs of which appear in the recent Persian *Documents* volume, confirm many essential points of Lutfallāh's story. The same volume contains several passports issued to Afghānī by the Iranian government listing him as a Persian subject, but no comparable document from the Afghan government.[6]

Third, documents from Afghanistan for the years 1866–1868 show

---

4 Īraj Afshār and Aṣghar Mahdavī, *Documents inédits concernant Seyyed Jamāl-al-Dīn Afghānī* (Tehran, 1963). This source is henceforth referred to as *Documents*.

5 The 1916 account is in the Afghan newspaper *Sirāj al-Akhbār*, VI, nos. 3 and 5. A more detailed account is in the review *Kābul* (Dec. 1939–Jan. 1940), and is summarized in Ettore Rossi, "Il centenario della nascita di Gemal ud-Dīn el-Afghani celebrato a Kabul," *Oriente Moderno*, XX, 5 (1940), 262–265. More details on this and other aspects of Afghānī's youth are in Nikki R. Keddie, "Sayyid Jamāl al-Dīn al-Afghānī's first Twenty-Seven Years: The Darkest Period," *Middle East Journal*, XX, 4 (Autumn, 1966), 517–533 (henceforth cited as Keddie, *MEJ*). Where this earlier article disagrees with the present account, however, the latter, which is based on new information, should be considered the more accurate.

6 *Documents*, pls. 68, 69; photos 149 and 150. Mīrzā Luṭfallāh Asadābādī, *Sharḥ-i ḥāl va āṣār-i Sayyid Jamāl ad-Dīn Asadābādī maʿrūf bi "Afghānī"* (Tabriz, 1326/ 1947–48), chaps. i–v, pp. 13–24.

that these were the years of his first (and only) trip to Afghanistan. In these years the Government of India's representative was concerned about the appearance of a mysterious foreign sayyid in the counsels of the Amir of Afghanistan, and set out to find out about this man. The man's given name was Jamāl ad-Dīn; he was accompanied by his lifelong servant, named Abū Turāb; and the dates for his stays in Qandahar, Ghazni, and Kabul correspond exactly to the dates independently documented in the Persian *Documents* volume. There is thus no doubt that Afghānī is the man involved, particularly since the standard biography puts Afghānī in Afghanistan as an adviser to the Amir during these years, and has him expelled from Afghanistan by the next Amir, Shīr 'Alī, in 1868, as do these documents.

The Government of India's investigations show that Jamāl ad-Dīn in 1866–68 made no claim to be an Afghan, and was known to everyone as a foreigner, unknown in Afghanistan until his entry in 1866. He could hardly have been brought up in Afghanistan, as it was reported that he "talks Persian *like an Irani (Persian)*." He claimed in this period to be a Turk from Istanbul.[7]

Finally, both the British Foreign Office and the U. S. Department of State at different times launched independent investigations to determine the question of Afghānī's birthplace, and both decided unequivocally that he was Iranian.[8]

As to Afghānī's childhood, there is again no documentation beyond his own word that it was spent in Afghanistan, while his appearance as a foreigner in Afghanistan in 1866, speaking with an Iranian accent, seems proof that he was not brought up in Afghanistan. There are somewhat conflicting Iranian accounts of his child-

---

[7] Great Britain, Commonwealth Relations Office, Government of India, Foreign Department, *Narrative of Events in Cabul from the Death of Dost Mahomed to the Spring of 1872. . . . Cabul Précis 1863–74* (Simla, 1874) pp. 46–48, 65; *Proceedings of the Government of India in the Foreign Department, Political* (Calcutta, 1869); "Cabul Diary," Dec., 1868, pp. 54 ff., and Jan., 1869, pp. 417–418 (both sources confidential prints, available in the Commonwealth Relations Office library).

[8] See numerous documents in the British volume on Afghānī, F.O. 60/594, which was compiled largely to decide the question of Afghānī's birthplace and nationality. The American investigation was seen by Elie Kedourie and is described by Sylvia Haim in *Arab Nationalism* (Berkeley and Los Angeles, 1962), p. 7 n. 4.

hood, derived from acquaintances and family. So far the documentation tends to confirm the chronology of the account given by Afghānī's nephew, Lutfallāh Asadābādī, despite the fact that Lutfallāh's biography contains adulating mythological elements.

Lutfallāh says that Jamāl ad-Dīn was born in Asadabad, near Hamadan, into a family of sayyids (descendants of the Prophet). He was educated at home until his tenth year, after which he went to school in Qazvin and later in Tehran, where he had the usual Shi'i Islamic religious education.[9] The same account was given in a brief biography of Afghānī published in 1889, after Afghānī's first mature trip to Iran, by the Iranian minister of press.[10] After this, Lutfallāh says, Afghānī went to the Shi'i holy cities in Ottoman Iraq, where he continued his religious education with the leaders of Shi'i Islam. That Afghānī was educated in the shrine cities appears to be confirmed both by a correspondent in the *Documents* who remembered studying there with Jamāl ad-Dīn, and by the investigations of an Iranian scholar, Muhīt Tabātabā'ī, who found an Iranian religious scholar who remembered studying in these cities with Jamāl ad-Dīn.[11]

These Iranian accounts and later reports by acquaintances indicate that Afghānī received a thorough grounding in the traditional Islamic disciplines, plus considerable knowledge of the Islamic philosophers and of Islamic mysticism, or Sufism. The *Documents* show that he read and taught philosophical and Sufi works, and showed an interest in various esoteric and heterodox subjects, such as mystical alphabets, numerical combinations, and esoteric treatises.[12]

There is much in Afghānī's later life and thought that seems to reflect both traditional Iranian influences and the particular religious and political climate of Iran in the mid-nineteenth century. Twelver Shi'ism, the Iranian state religion, holds that the twelfth Imam, or hereditary infallible leader, disappeared more than a thousand years ago, but will return as messiah, or mahdi, to institute

---

9 Lutfallāh, *op. cit.*, pp. 18–21.

10 Muḥammad Ḥasan Khān I'timād aṣ-Ṣalṭaneh, *al-Ma'āṣir va al āṣār* (Tehran, 1889), p. 224.

11 Interview with Muḥīṭ Ṭabāṭabā'ī and Ṣifātallāh Jamālī Asadābādī, Tehran, September, 1966. *Documents*, pp. 100–101, letters from Āqā Shaikh Muḥammad Ḥasan from Qum. In these letters the author says he had known Jamāl ad-Dīn at Najaf for years, and names their teachers there.

12 *Documents*, pp. 17–20, and numerous documents in Afghānī's early notebooks, now in the Majlis Library, Tehran.

the millennium. The messianic strain in Twelver Shiʻism is a more central element than it is in the Sunni orthodoxy of other Muslim countries. Pending the return of the twelfth Imam, his will is interpreted by religious leaders who exercise *ijtihād* (individual judgment or endeavor) to interpret this will in religious and legal questions. Whereas for the Sunnis the door of ijtihād was closed in the early centuries of Islam, the Twelver Shiʻis legitimize variation in the interpretation of law and doctrine. Although the practical difference in rates of change in law and custom between Shiʻis and Sunnis has been small, Shiʻi doctrine provides a better theoretical basis for the introduction of innovation than does Sunnism. Both Afghānī's later messianic tendencies and his advocacy of reinterpreting religious doctrine seem to have a basis in Iranian Shiʻi traditions.

Another characteristic of Afghānī, documented below, was his practice of *taqiyya,* or precautionary dissimulation of his true beliefs, and his use of quite different arguments to an elite audience of intellectuals and to a mass audience. These related features are found in various Iranian cultural traditions. Shiʻism, which began as a minority, persecuted religion, early legitimized precautionary dissimulation. The Sufi mystics and the Hellenized philosophers also practiced dissimulation, partly for precautionary reasons, and both believed that men could be divided into an elite of the initiated and a mass for whom unquestioning literalist orthodoxy was most useful.[13]

Judging from his library and teachings, the Islamic philosophers were a major influence on the young Afghānī. Unlike the Arab and Turkish world, where most Greek-inspired philosophers had for centuries been suppressed as heretics and removed from the school curriculum, Iran had a living philosophical tradition, some books of Avicenna and later Iranian philosophers being taught even in religious schools. The rationalist interpretation of religion favored by many of these philosophers influenced Afghānī, and some of the ideas for which he was attacked as a heretic in the Sunni world come straight from the philosophers.

In addition, Afghānī was later well acquainted with, and probably influenced by, the religio-political ferment experienced by Iran in the late eighteenth and nineteenth centuries. A significant new

---

[13] See chap. ii of the present study, and Nikki R. Keddie, "Symbol and Sincerity in Islam," *Studia Islamica,* XIX (1963), 27–63.

school of Twelver Shi'ism, the Shaikhi sect, was founded in the late eighteenth century, and its influence spread in the Shi'i areas of Ottoman Iraq and in Iran. Without presenting its doctrines in detail, one may note that it involved both a more philosophical interpretation of religion and a stronger search for infallible religious leadership than does the usual Twelver Shi'i doctrine.[14]

In 1844, encouraged by other Shaikhis, the young Sayyid 'Alī Muhammad of Shiraz declared himself to be the *Bāb*, or gate, to the twelfth Imam whom some of the Shaikhis were expecting. In later years his claims increased until he said he was the twelfth Imam himself, bringing a new religious dispensation that superseded the law and teachings of the Koran. He and his disciples quickly gained a wide following throughout Iran for their new dispensation. Babism was somewhat egalitarian regarding social classes and the sexes, favorable to economic enterprise, and in general more in tune with the demands of modern society than the traditional religion, even though it contained mostly traditional elements. Probably the popularity of messianic Babism was tied to the economic and social dislocations brought by the early Western impact in Iran.[15]

Babi struggles and uprisings occurred in Iran during Jamāl ad-Dīn's boyhood there, and a great persecution and emigration of Babis came in 1852 after a group of them had made an attempt on the life of the young Shah, Nāsir ad-Dīn. According to Lutfallāh's biography, made more precise on the basis of further research by his son, Sifātallāh, Afghānī lived in Tehran at this time, and left for the shrine cities in about 1852. Although an attempt to tie the young Jamāl ad-Dīn or his father to Babism would be speculative, it seems clear from his later writings and words that Afghānī was well acquainted with both Shaikhi and Babi doctrine. The *Documents* show that among his early possessions was a treatise by Shaikh Ahmad Ahsā'ī, the founder of Shaikhism, and parallels may be found

---

14 On the Shaikhis, see Alessandro Bausani, *Persia religiosa* (Milan, 1959), pp. 403–407; A. L. M. Nicolas, *Essai sur le Cheikhisme* (Paris, 1910–1914); H. Corbin, "L'École Shaykhie en Théologie Shi'ite," École Pratique des Hautes Études, Section des Sciences Religieuses, *Annuaire 1960–1961* (Paris, 1961), pp. 3–59; G. Scarcia, "La 'guerra tra Šeiḫī e Bālāsarī,'" *Annali del Istituto Universitario Orientale di Napoli*, n.s. XIII (1963), 195–238.

15 On Babism as a social movement, see Nikki R. Keddie, "Religion and Irreligion in Early Iranian Nationalism," *Comparative Studies in Society and History*, IV, 3 (April, 1962), esp. pp. 267–274, and the sources cited there.

between Shaikhi doctrine and the ideas Afghānī expressed in his best-known talk in Istanbul in 1870.[16] During his adolescent years in the Shi'i shrine cities in Iraq, and perhaps before, Afghānī was probably exposed to discussions of these new religious doctrines. He grew up in an environment where religious arguments and doctrinal innovation were more in the air than they were in most of the Sunni world, and this probably affected his own propensity to innovate. The politically activist and meliorist ideas of the Babis may have contributed to Afghānī's revision of Islam in these directions. Babism was one of several activist religious movements that Afghānī had a chance to witness in the Muslim world, and which probably contributed to his understanding of the power of religious appeals to the Muslim masses.

All sources agree that Afghānī went to India in his late teens. An authentic Iranian personal reminiscence regarding his stay in the southern port city of Bushehr on his way to India dates this stay in 1855/6, when Jamāl ad-Dīn was 17 or 18.[17] Although the standard biography says that Afghānī stayed in India "a year and some months," there is no totally convincing account of where he spent the following seven years, and it may be that he spent more time in India than he told his biographers. However long he stayed, there seems, judging from his later life and activity, an inescapable inference that this Indian stay had a profound and traumatic effect on Afghānī which his biographers have not noted. From the time of his first appearance in Afghanistan in 1866 Afghānī was a champion of Muslim struggle against British imperialist encroachments and a violent critic of British rule over Muslims. Such ideas scarcely could have obsessed him in northern Iran or in the shrine cities of

---

16 *Documents*, pl. 7, photo 19, has the end of a treatise by Shaikh Aḥmad Aḥsā'ī, copied by Jamāl ad-Dīn "Istanbūlī" in Baghdad, though he has written over the word "Baghdad," perhaps showing a desire to hide the fact that he was there in his youth. The resemblance between Afghānī's Istanbul words and Shaikhi doctrine was pointed out to me by Homa and Nasser Pakdaman. Many sources cite Afghānī's close knowledge of Babism, and Buṭrus Bustānī in his Arabic encyclopedia cites Afghānī's words as his major source in his article on Babism. After conversations with Afghānī's grandnephew Ṣifātallāh Jamālī and others in the summer of 1966, I no longer think it likely that Afghānī's family were Babis.

17 *Kāveh*, II, 9 (1921), p. 11. The reference is discussed in detail in Keddie, *MEJ*, p. 526.

Iraq, where British influence was hardly felt, but could have easily arisen from a stay in India in the period right before, and probably during, the Indian Mutiny of 1857.

In India the British were replacing the former Muslim ruling classes, and there was a feeling among Muslims, which had some basis in fact, that they were being discriminated against in education, religious institutions, and government jobs. The mutiny was endorsed by many Muslim leaders as a holy war, or jihad, against the British. Even before the mutiny, a state of chronic socio-religious revolt had existed among Muslims of Bengal and the Northwest Frontier. This jihad movement was an offshoot of a move for Muslim religious purification begun by the great eighteenth-century reformer, Shāh Walī Allāh of Delhi. Although we do not know whether Afghānī had any contact with this reform movement or its jihad offshoot, his later advocacy of both religious reform and armed struggle against the British may show some such influence; and he was probably affected by Muslim response to the mutiny. More certain is the inference that it was in India, and specifically from contacts with Indian Muslims under British rule, that Afghānī first developed his lifelong hatred of the British. Afghānī's later expressed belief that the British were out to undermine Islam and substitute Christianity was, for example, a belief that had wide currency in the Indian Muslim community.[18]

The standard biographies tell us that it was in India that Afghānī had his first contact with Western learning. It seems possible that this contact was more traumatic than this bare statement would suggest. Coming from an Iranian and Iraqi Shi'i environment where unorthodox religious and philosophical ideas were being widely discussed, Afghānī now entered a country that had not only some parallel religious novelties, but also some contact with Western science and ideas. There is one account in Arabic of what Afghānī came to believe in India, written by a man who knew him in the 1870's in Egypt, Salīm al-'Anhūrī. 'Anhūrī thought that Afghānī continued to hold these beliefs, and there is so much resemblance between the ideas he ascribes to Afghānī and those occasionally expressed by Afghānī to an elite audience, notably in his "Answer to Renan," that it seems appropriate to translate 'Anhūrī's account.

'Anhuri says that while Afghānī was in India:

---

[18] See Keddie, *MEJ*, pp. 526–532, and the sources cited there.

He excelled in the study of religion, until this led him to irreligion *(ilḥād)* and belief in the eternity of the world. He claimed that vital atoms, found in the atmosphere, formed, by a natural evolution, the stars we see which revolve around one another through gravity, and that the belief in an omniscient Prime Mover was a natural delusion that arose when man was in a primitive state of evolution and corresponded with the stage of his intellectual progress. This meant that when man was a pure savage and primitive he used to worship the lowest things in existence, like wood and stone, and when he had progressed on the ladder of civilization and knowledge, his objects of worship rose correspondingly, and he began to venerate fire, then clouds, then the heavens and their celestial bodies. Man went on progressing on the scale of knowledge and deriving light from the lamp of science. Taking the natural course, he elevated the object of his worship and raised it in degree of loftiness until he said: "It is free from quality and quantity, free of beginning and end, boundless and incomprehensible, filling everything and in everything, seeing all while none see it." However, man's intellectual capacities progressed after that until they reached the knowledge that all these [beliefs] are kinds of delusions and confused dreams, originating from man's fear of death and his desire for immortality. This made him build from air castles of faith and towers of hope, such as had taken root in his imagination to the point that they almost became a fixed belief.

Man began by saying that he would pass on after death to an eternal life, and that the wood or the stone were what would lead him to this highest place if he showed reverence to it and showered devotion upon it, and there arose from this worship liberation from the bitterness of thought about a death with no life after it. Then it occurred to him that fire was more powerful and greater in benefit and harm, so he turned to it. Then he saw that clouds were better than fire and stronger, so he adhered to and depended on them. The links of this chain, wrought by the two tools of delusion and desire together with the instinct and nature of man, continued to increase until he [man] culminated at the highest state. The result of natural laws was a reaction leading to the conviction that all the above is idle talk that originates in desires, and that it has no truth and no definition.[19]

Afghānī's later life and words give ample evidence that he was at least profoundly skeptical about positive religions and that he held an evolutionary view of religion, believing that a simpler prophetic religion was useful for less advanced peoples, and a more rational reformed religion was what the masses needed later. His Iranian and Iraqi childhood and his Indian experience both probably contributed to these views.

After the first Indian stay, all sources have Afghānī next take a leisurely trip to Mecca, stopping at several points along the way. Both the standard biography and Lutfallāh's account take Afghānī's word that he entered Afghan government service before 1863, but since documents from Afghanistan show that he arrived there only in 1866, we are left with several years unaccounted for. The most probable supposition seems to be that he may have spent longer in India than he later said, and that after going to Mecca he traveled elsewhere in the Ottoman Empire. When he arrived in Afghanistan in 1866 he claimed to be from Istanbul, and he might not have made this claim if he had never even seen the city, and could be caught in ignorance of it.

The first date recorded by Afghānī in the *Documents* is the fall of 1865, when he left the "revered place," (*makān-i musharraf*), probably the Iraqi Shi'i shrine cities, and proceeded to Iran, arriving in Tehran in mid-December of 1865 and staying there until the late spring of 1866, after which he went to Herat via the northeastern Iranian city of Mashhad. The Lutfallāh biography also says that after his trip to Mecca Afghānī went to the Iraq shrine cities, then to Iran, and then to Afghanistan, although it pushes back the dates of this trip.[20]

Although much remains dark about Afghānī's first twenty-seven years, it seems certain that he was born in Asadabad, and received his basic education in Iran. Lutfallāh's story that Afghānī got his higher education in the Iraq shrine cities now appears also to be

---

[19] Reprinted in Rashīd Riḍā, *Tārīkh al-ustādh al-imām ash-shaikh Muḥammad 'Abduh*, I (Cairo, 1931), 43–44.

[20] Lutfallāh, *op. cit.*, pp. 22–23; *Documents*, date table, p. 156.

confirmed, and there is no reason to doubt the trip to India. A subsequent trip to Mecca and the Shi'i shrine cities seems highly probable, and a visit to Istanbul may also be inferred. It is only in 1866, however, that one finds written documentation of exact dates and activities. These activities turn out to be startlingly different from those claimed by the standard biography.

The standard biography says that Afghānī returned to his Afghan homeland after his trips to India and Mecca in time to participate with the famous Amir Dūst Muhammad Khān in his seige of Herat in 1863. It also states that in the civil wars that followed Dūst Muhammad's death, Afghānī gave active assistance to one of the princes, A'zam Khān, and advised him on reform and modernization. This story is disproved both by the recently published Persian *Documents* volume, and by documents emanating from the Government of India's newswriter and its representative at Kabul. These documents, quoted at greater length elsewhere, show that Afghānī came to Afghanistan for the first time in 1866, and was known to be a foreigner.[21] While in Afghanistan he claimed to be a Turk, while afterward in Turkey he claimed to be an Afghan—in both cases evincing concern to deny his Iranian background. He entered into intimate relations with A'zam Khān while the latter was military ruler in Qandahar, and then came with him to Kabul just before he took over as amir. Afghānī's advice to the new Amir, as recorded in the British documents, was not for modernization or reform, but rather to encourage him to ally himself with the Russians and fight the British. His recorded words already have the fiercely anti-British tone that was to characterize most of his life. The British and some Afghans believed Afghānī (or, as he then called himself, Sayyid Rūmī or Istanbūlī) to be a Russian agent, and he evidently asserted at the end of his stay that he was such, though there is no positive evidence for this beyond his own word. In any case, his first well-documented appearance on the stage of history was as a man with purely political, anti-British aims, and there is no evidence that he appeared then either as a religious figure or as a reformer.

Late in 1868 A'zam Khān was defeated in battle by his half-brother Shīr 'Alī Khān. A'zam Khān fled to Iran, where he died, and his nephew 'Abd ar-Rahmān went to Bokhara. Afghānī did not attempt

---

[21] For the whole story, including documentation, see Nikki R. Keddie, "Afghani in Afghanistan," *Middle Eastern Studies*, I, 4 (July, 1965), 322–349.

to accompany them, but rather tried to ingratiate himself with the new Amir. Shīr 'Alī, who seems first to have promised Afghānī a post, later became suspicious of him and ordered him expelled from the country, refusing his request to be allowed to go to Bokhara (a city Afghānī already cites as his goal in a poem written before he reached Afghanistan). Afghānī was escorted out of the country, leaving Qandahar in December, 1868. From there he went to Bombay and thence to Cairo and Istanbul, where he was to be found in the autumn of 1869.[22]

The standard biographies speak of Afghānī as a famous man by the time he reached Istanbul, but in view of the newly uncovered documents about his Afghan stay, the story of his fame must be discounted. He could hardly have been renowned in high Istanbul circles as a man who while in Afghanistan had claimed to be from Istanbul, but now convinced everyone that he was an Afghan. It does seem true that Afghānī now, as at other times in his life, was able to use his magnetic personality to become intimate with some fairly high personages. It is known that he had contact with Westernizers and secularists, men of the *Tanzimat* reforms, such as Münif, president of the Council of Education, and Tahsin, the scientific-minded director of the new university. Afghānī, with his religious training, may have been useful to such men in giving a religious coloring to their Westernized educational projects, which were opposed by the local ulama. In any event, Afghānī was chosen to give one of the speeches at the opening of the new university, early in 1870. In this speech he praised Westernizing reforms, urging Muslims to awaken from their long sleep of neglect and to emulate the "civilized nations" of the West.[23] This first recorded talk by Afghānī evinces his lifelong concern with Muslim self-strengthening, here expressed in the Westernizing language of the Tanzimat.

Later in 1870 Afghānī was appointed to the reformist official Council on Education, and still later in the year he gave a public lecture that caused his expulsion on grounds of heresy. This incident, embarrassing to Afghānī after he took on more orthodox coloring, has been distorted by 'Abduh and other biographers. First, the talk was not, as they say, a great public event, but simply one of a series

---

22 *Documents*, p. 156, and the documents referred to there.
23 The speech is quoted from the official journal in Osman Keskioğlu, "Cemâleddin Efgânî," *İlâhiyat Fakültesi Dergisi*, X (1962), 96–97.

of annual public lectures organized by the university. An advance newspaper story announced the topics for the series, which had to do with modern science and industry, and asked for volunteers to give the lectures. Through his connection with the head of the university Afghānī was in a good position to volunteer. Although no text of the talk seems to exist, 'Abduh's version being incomplete and possibly doctored, enough can be reconstructed from various sources to indicate the source of the trouble. Instead of confining himself to a scientific discussion of his topic, industry and the crafts, Afghānī introduced themes from the Islamic philosophers, comparing prophecy and philosophy as the highest of crafts. If Afghānī had spoken of the virtues of modern industries, as was surely the intent of the topic assigned, he would have been walking the well-trodden path of numerous Tanzimat reformers and caused no trouble. By introducing philosophical ideas long condemned as heretical in Western Sunni Islam, however, he gave the Ottoman ulama an ideal handle with which to attack their real targets—the expanding Westernized educational system, and particularly the university. It seems clear that the essential charge made by the ulama, including the top religious figure, the Şeyhülislam, that Afghānī had called prophecy a craft, was true. Afghānī's expulsion from Istanbul was demanded, and was granted by the secular authorities. His talk was also one reason for the immediately subsequent dismissal of Tahsin as head of the university, and became one pretext for the later closing of the university. In all this, Afghānī was essentially an incidental figure who had enabled the ulama to get at their real target—the university and what it represented. Later stories that the Şeyhülislam or others were jealous of Afghānī's growing influence in Istanbul are improbable and without documentary support.[24]

After his expulsion from Istanbul Afghānī returned to Cairo, where he remained from 1871 until his expulsion in August, 1879. He apparently went at the invitation of the prominent Egyptian politician Riyāḍ Pāshā, on whom he had made a favorable impression. Riyāḍ offered him a regular stipend, which appears to have come from official rather than personal funds. Afghānī achieved political prominence in Egypt only in the last year or so of his stay. Up to that time he was primarily engaged in informal teaching, and his magnetic personality and wide range of knowledge attracted

---

[24] For the first accurate discussion of this whole incident see Niyazi Berkes, *The Development of Secularism in Turkey* (Montreal, 1964), pp. 180–188.

many of the most intelligent young men of Cairo to his sessions. Chief among his disciples was the young Muḥammad 'Abduh, who later distinguished himself as an educator and legal reformer. Other Egyptians and Syrians who became prominent in writing or politics were also among his circle.

Aside from Afghānī's personal magnetism and charisma, which helped evoke among his followers an attitude toward him very much like worship, there seems to have been at least one other important reason for his popularity among young Egyptian intellectuals. This was his strong emphasis in Egypt on the study of the Islamic philosophers, as notations on his personal book collection confirm.[25] The relevance of medieval Muslim philosophy to the problems of Egypt in the nineteenth century may not be immediately apparent, but it can be explained. Egypt was, in the 1870's, going through a crisis brought about by increasing indebtedness to, and dependence on, European bankers and capitalists, and there were the first stirrings of a nationalist reaction against the policy of Egypt's rulers and their Western creditors. The young intellectuals wished to reform and strengthen Egypt and to free it from Western domination. There were some who urged a wholehearted adoption of Western methods, but there was a natural psychological barrier to the thought of jettisoning all one's own tradition, particularly in favor of that of the Western oppressors.

In this situation the time was ripe to try to find an *indigenous* ideology that could bring about the reform and self-strengthening that the intellectuals desired. In many ways, medieval Muslim philosophy could provide the basis for such an ideology. First of all, it exalted reason above literalist revelation, and had always been used to attack the pretensions of the religious classes to the truest knowledge. Second, it argued for a nonliteral interpretation of those parts of revelation and tradition that seemed least rational. This system of interpretation, used by the Muslim philosophers to advocate Aristotelian rationalism, could equally be used to try to show that the Koran and Muslim Traditions actually enjoined modern science, parliaments, and powerful national armies; and Afghānī and many of his followers did argue in this way. In addition, the Muslim philosophical tradition held that it was necessary to vary one's words

---

[25] *Documents*, pp. 17–20; and Rashīd Riḍā, *Tārīkh*, I, 79. Riḍā notes, probably accurately, that Jamāl ad-Dīn's outlook was a mixture of ancient and modern philosophy and mysticism. He also notes the proximity of Afghānī's views and methods to those of the esoterics (*bāṭinīs*).

and arguments according to whether one was addressing the intellectual elite or the masses. This method of using one argument for an elite of close followers or Western audiences and another for the general public characterized Afghānī throughout most of his life. His expulsion from Istanbul on religious grounds must have warned him to be more circumspect in his public presentation of philosophical ideas, and he subsequently was more careful to dissimulate his philosophic tendencies when dealing with the general public.

The idea of using one argument for the elite and another for the general public was particularly useful for those who wanted to arouse the masses against Western encroachments, as Afghānī and his followers often did. The masses' traditional and religious sentiments could be inflamed by stressing the Western threat to Islam, or to local traditions, while the elite discussed the reform of religion and society on more rational bases. Despite their different ideological approaches, both elite and masses could unite in a struggle against Western domination. Islamic philosophy, as presented by Afghānī, thus provided something in the indigenous tradition, something not borrowed from the Western oppressors, which might form a basis for building a more independent, rational, and reformed society.

Afghānī's followers tell us it was he who encouraged them to set up newspapers in the late 1870's and to discuss in them the political issues of the day. In these years political interest on the part of Egyptians rose dramatically. The deepening crisis of Egyptian finances, the growing burden of taxation, proposals to extend the power of the Egyptian parliament, and the Russo-Turkish war, which saw Egypt's suzerain defeated by a Christian power, all added to such interest. In this period Afghānī came to the fore as a political figure, particularly in two ways: first, by trying to make an Egyptian Freemasonic lodge a vehicle for political intrigue and change; and second, by his influence as a popular orator.[26]

---

26 The main primary sources on Afghānī in Egypt are the Arabic biographical notices gathered in Riḍā, Tārīkh, Vol. I; the quotations from 'Abduh in his Rissalat al Tawhid, trans. B. Michel and M. Abdel Razik (Paris, 1925), introduction; the materials on this period in the Documents; and various Egyptian newspapers of the 1870's. Also useful on Afghānī and his circle in Egypt are Kedourie, op. cit.; Jacob Landau, Parliaments and Parties in Egypt (Tel Aviv, 1953) and "Prolegomena to a Study of Secret Societies in Modern Egypt," Middle Eastern Studies, I, 2 (Jan., 1965), 135–186; Wilfrid S. Blunt, Secret History of the English Occupation of Egypt (New York, 1922); and Irene L. Gendzier, The Practical Visions of Ya'qub Sanu' (Cambridge, Mass., 1966).

The story of Afghānī's Masonic activities is particularly obscure, since there are conflicting eye-witness reports. The new *Documents* volume proves that he applied for membership in a Masonic lodge as early as 1875, and that he remained a Mason for the rest of his stay in Egypt.[27] Afghānī appears to have been expelled from one lodge because of his attempt to use it for political purposes, but he was, in early 1878, elected head of the preexisting Eastern Star Lodge.[28] It was apparently this lodge that he converted into a political instrument, attracting into it men of position who were interested in political change. Afghānī at this time favored the deposition, and even the assassination, of the Khedive, Ismā'īl, who had done so much to mortgage Egypt to private European interests; and Afghānī seems to have had ties to the heir apparent, Taufīq. When Ismā'īl was actually deposed in 1879, however, his fall was brought about by the British and French, who then became the powers behind the throne of Taufīq. Whatever promises of reform and personal influence Afghānī may have had, or thought he had, from Taufīq came to nothing.

In 1878 and 1879 Afghānī also began making fiery public speeches, directed particularly against the British and in favor of the preservation of Egyptian independence. He thus got a considerable reputation as a popular leader and orator. Since some of his friends and followers were active in politics at this time, and continued to be so after Afghānī's expulsion from Egypt, he can be credited with some influence on these early phases of Egyptian nationalism. The stories that credit Afghānī with inspiring the nationalist movement among Egyptian officers which culminated in the 'Urābī movement are, however, not based on fact. The officers' movement began in alliance with Khedive Ismā'īl, whom Afghānī was hoping to have deposed; Afghānī's followers were at first hostile to the 'Urābī movement, joining it only after it had gained power.[29] 'Abduh and other disciples of Afghānī did have some influence in 'Urābī's government, but they were never leaders in this movement.

---

[27] *Documents*, pp. 24–25, and the photographed documents to which these pages refer.

[28] *Documents*, pl. 17, photo 41, is a letter to Afghānī announcing his election. This confirms the reports of some of his Arab followers.

[29] Kedourie, *op. cit.*, pp. 26–27, 31–34. The distance of the 'Urābī movement from Afghānī's disciples is also discussed in a series of letters from them to Afghānī early in 1883, catalogued and reproduced in the *Documents* volume.

In late August, 1879, the new Khedive, Taufīq, suddenly ordered Afghānī expelled from Egypt. The expulsion was probably based on Afghānī's inflammatory antiforeign speeches and on his political intrigues. Afghānī's statements that this and subsequent expulsions were caused by British pressure may have been based on a genuine conviction, but the documents do not support this view. It is clear from the private report home of the incident by the British consul that the latter was informed of the event by Taufīq, and knew nothing of it beforehand.[30] Afghānī's Egyptian followers continued to be active in politics after his expulsion, and several of them worked for the 'Urābī government after it took power, being subsequently exiled after the British victory and occupation of Egypt in 1882.

From Egypt Afghānī went via Bombay to the Muslim-ruled princely state of Hyderabad, in South India, where he remained for two years. Here he apparently spent most of his time writing and teaching. The only contemporary documentation of this stay states that while in India Afghānī associated chiefly with modernizing reformists, especially followers of the westernized Sir Sayyid Ahmad Khān. Such associations were consistent with his life up to that time; in Istanbul his known ties were with thorough Westernizers, and in Egypt also he dealt mostly with modernizing reformists. Yet, according to one contemporary document, despite the kindness of Sayyid Ahmad Khān's followers to him, he turned against them and wrote a book to discredit their beliefs.[31] This book was entitled *The Truth about the Neicheri Sect and an Explanation of the Neicheris*, which was translated into Arabic as "The Refutation of the Materialists." The *neicheris* were the followers of Ahmad Khān; the word was a new coinage, meaning followers of nature. In this book Afghānī presents himself as the passionate defender of religion in general and Islam in particular against the attacks of the neicheris and the unorthodox, including in his attack the men of the Tanzimat who had befriended him in Istanbul. An analysis of the "Refutation" is made below, but here it is pertinent to ask why Afghānī precisely at this point in his life chose to present himself in a new guise, as an impassioned defender of religion.

The post-1881 "religious" Afghānī has become so enshrined in

---

[30] FO 78/3003, Lascelles to Salisbury, no. 498, Cairo, Aug. 30, 1879.

[31] FO 60/594, printed memorandum on Afghānī by the Government of India, Thagi and Dakaiti Department, 1896. This is quoted, and other evidence given, in chap. ii, p. 70, where doubts about the document's accuracy are also noted.

the later biographies that it is important to realize it was apparently only beginning with the "Refutation" that Afghānī presented himself to the public as a great defender of religion. Until that time nearly all religious references to Afghānī tie him to irreligion and heresy. In Egypt Afghānī was more cautious about the public expression of unorthodox beliefs than he had been in Istanbul, but he did not appear as a great defender of religion. Why, in 1881, did Afghānī begin to present himself as a defender of Islam, and soon after, of pan-Islam, the unification of the Muslim world against the West?

That Afghānī underwent a genuine religious conversion at this time seems improbable, especially in view of the fact that the unorthodox "Answer to Renan" was written two years *after* the "Refutation." Yet he was probably affected by some of the same currents that were changing such men as the reformist Young Ottoman writer Namik Kemal into defenders of Islam and pan-Islam. The rise of pan-Islamic sentiment had followed very closely on the heels of Western Christian conquest of Islamic territory. The first appeals for aid to Mecca and Istanbul came in the first half of the nineteenth century from Indian Muslims subject to British attack. The appeals to Istanbul made by Turks from Central Asia during the Russian conquests of the 1860's apparently turned Ottoman rulers to the idea of asserting more strongly than they had hitherto their claims to a universal Muslim caliphate. The Russo-Turkish War was followed with interest not only by Muslims in the Ottoman Empire but also by those in India, some of whom contributed funds to help the Ottoman side. Increased British and French pressure on Egypt and North Africa also aroused feelings of Muslim defensive solidarity. On the intellectual side, Namik Kemal and some of the other Young Ottomans had already begun to write in favor of pan-Islamic solidarity in the early 1870's. Ottoman pan-Islamism, already promoted under Sultan Abdülaziz, got a strong boost from the new, anti-Western Sultan Abdülhamid, who acceded to the throne in 1876.[32]

At the same time as pan-Islamic sentiment was rising, there was disillusionment with the West as a model and a revulsion within the Ottoman Empire toward Westernizing reformers. All the vaunted innovation of the men of the Tanzimat had not saved the empire

---

[32] Berkes, *op. cit.*, pp. 261–270; Bernard Lewis, "The Ottoman Empire in the Mid-Nineteenth Century: A Review," *Middle Eastern Studies*, I, 3 (April, 1965), esp. pp. 291–294; and Albert Hourani, *Arabic Thought in the Liberal Age: 1798–1939* (London, 1962), pp. 103–107.

from defeat by Russia, from rising discontent among the very Christian subjects to whom the greatest concessions had been made, or from growing economic enthrallment to the West. In Egypt there was a similar reaction against Westerners, and it was hard to dissociate Western ideology from Western exploitation. Afghānī, who throughout his life opposed the British and their encroachments in the Muslim world, was ready to use this traditionalist and pan-Islamic reaction in order to strengthen the unity of the Islamic world against foreign, and particularly British, incursions.

The Indian situation at this time particularly encouraged Afghānī to make an appeal against Westernizers like Sir Sayyid Ahmad Khān and his followers, since they were the primary advocates of Muslim cooperation with British rule in India. As a violent opponent of such cooperation, Afghānī would have wished to use any means possible to discredit Ahmad Khān and his school.[33]

At the time of the crisis of the 'Urābī movement in 1882 Afghānī left Hyderabad, where he had spoken of his intention of going to France to work against British policy in Egypt.[34] He was apparently kept under surveillance by the British in Calcutta, perhaps until

---

[33] These points are elaborated in the next chapter, where it is also shown that for all its expedient character, the "Refutation" is not in fact so much a defense of religion as it has usually been taken to be.

[34] FO 60/594, Syed Husein [Bilgrāmī] to Cordery, June 20, 1883, enclosed in Cordery to Grant, June 25, 1883. This reads in part:

"About three years ago a man came here from Egypt who alleged that he had been turned out of the country by the orders of H.H. the new Khedive Towfik Pasha for preaching doctrines distasteful to the authorities. I gathered from his conversations that he was a freethinker of the French type, and* a socialist, and that he had been got rid of by the authorities in Egypt for preaching the doctrine of 'liberté, fraternité, egalité' to the students, and the masses in that country. I found him to be a well informed man for a Herati (he is a Herati by birth) though rather shallow in his acquirements. He c[oul]d 'hold forth' in Persian and Arabic with great easiness and purity of idiom. He talked a little French and used to say that it was his purpose to go and make Paris his headquarters for some time in order to get justice out of Towfik through the French.

". . . [In Hyderabad Afghānī spent] his time in teaching and in philosophical discussions. When, however the imbroglio in Egypt made a stir in the papers, the Sheikh, Jamal-ud-din (for such was his name) suddenly disappeared from Hyderabad, I . . . felt quite sure . . . that either Cairo or Paris was his destination.

"Some months ago I was startled by having an Arabic periodical sent to me from Paris, and on opening it I found that it was conducted by no other than the quondam philosopher of Hyderabad. . . ."

*[I have used "and" for the sign +, the form used in this letter.]

after the British defeat of 'Urābī, which began the British occupation of Egypt. He left India for Europe late in 1882. He spent a short time in London at the very beginning of 1883, and then went to Paris, where he joined Arab journalist friends and wrote newspaper articles in Arabic, with an anti-British and pan-Islamic emphasis. It was in 1883 that he entered into the journalistic discussion with Renan, analyzed below. In this discussion, writing for a Western audience, Afghānī strongly criticized the Islamic religion for stifling science, free thought, and progress. Renan wrote of him in great admiration as an enlightened freethinker who reincarnated the virtues of the medieval Muslim philosophers.[35]

In 1884 Afghānī and Muḥammad 'Abduh, who had joined him in Paris, published the pan-Islamic Arabic newspaper *al-'Urwa al-Wuthqā* (*The Strongest Link*—a reference to the Koran). In it they continued to castigate the British, particularly for their policy in Egypt, and they also presented more philosophical articles. The newspaper was banned in Egypt and in India by the British, but whether this is what discouraged further publication after less than one year, or whether their unknown source of financial support was suddenly withdrawn, is unclear. Along with the "Refutation," *al-'Urwa al-Wuthqā* was the greatest basis of Afghānī's reputation in the Islamic world, fitting in, as it did, with the growing defensive and pan-Islamic mood of the time.

In 1884 and 1885 Afghānī became involved in schemes of the philo-Arab Englishman Wilfrid Blunt to try to negotiate with the British government a settlement of the Egyptian question and of the Sudanese Mahdi's rising. Perhaps sensing in Blunt's concern a means once more to move into high political circles, Afghānī claimed to be the European agent of the Mahdi, a claim for which there is no shred of documentary evidence. When the Conservatives over-threw Gladstone's government in 1885, partly on the Sudanese issue, Blunt brought Afghānī to England to meet his important governmental friends Randolph Churchill, now Secretary of State for India, and Sir Henry Drummond Wolff. Wolff was soon to go on a mission to Istanbul and Cairo to try to negotiate the withdrawal of British forces from Egypt on terms satisfactory to the British government. Whereas Blunt had failed to convince Gladstone to make use of Afghānī's services, he almost convinced Wolff to take Afghānī along

---

35 See the quotations in the next chapter.

to Istanbul, but Wolff changed his mind at the last minute.[36]

The only significant result of this series of intrigues, a result that has come to light only with the publication of the recent Persian *Documents* volume, was to put Afghānī in touch with Sultan Abdül-hamid II. Two Egyptians who entered the Sultan's service were also involved in Blunt's and Afghānī's schemes, and through them Afghānī communicated with the Sultan. It was probably a few years earlier that Afghānī wrote to the Ottoman rulers a long petition offering his services as a kind of wandering pan-Islamic messianic emissary. (Afghānī specifically makes the analogy to Abū Muslim, whose messianic propaganda in the East helped bring on the triumph of the Abbasid dynasty.)[37] In 1885 the Sultan asked Afghānī to stay put for the present, and no contact between them is recorded between 1885 and 1892, when the Sultan invited Afghānī to Instanbul. The standard biographies speak of the Sultan as the initiator of the first overtures to Afghānī, but the new documents make it clear that Afghānī was trying very hard to ingratiate himself with the Sultan and, hopefully, to obtain a position from him. Considering Afghānī's gravitation toward men of power and high-level intrigue, it is possible that the "Refutation" was written partly to please the Sultan, to whom he later presented an authorized Turkish translation of the work. In this translation he adds a sentence justifying the Sultan's punishment of two of the Tanzimat leaders who are mentioned only obliquely in the original.[38] *Al-'Urwa al-Wuthqā*, with its specific

---

[36] Wilfrid S. Blunt, *Gordon at Khartoum* (London, 1912), *passim*.

[37] See Nikki R. Keddie, "The Pan-Islamic Appeal: Afghānī and Abdülhamid II," *Middle Eastern Studies*, III, 1 (1966), 46–67.

[38] Berkes, *op. cit.*, p. 267, says that Abdülhamid: ". . . must have rejoiced to see the author refer, as usual anonymously, to Midhat Paşa and Süleyman Paşa as men who, like all *nacharis*, had sold their country to its enemies for petty gains. He had just court-martialled both, and had sentenced one to death and the other to permanent exile; but even he had not gone to the extent of accusing them of treason. Afghani's boldness must have made him feel almost a coward! Although Afghani gave no proof to substantiate his accusation, his authority must have helped to relieve the Caliph's conscience. The Turkish version of the *Refutation* contained the following clause, which does not appear in the original: 'And these traitors met their deserved punishment by the justice-enforcing hand.' In this fashion Afghani earned the favours of the Caliph. It was a strange way of paying his debt to the 'men of modern ideas' to whom he owed his life under the Tanzimat, when the Şeyhul-Islâm would gladly have signed a *fetva* for his execution."

praise of the Sultan and of pan-Islam, is even more tied to Afghani's efforts to ingratiate himself with Sultan Abdülhamid II.

Afghānī's turn toward Abdülhamid is paralleled by that of several other erstwhile Muslim revolutionaries. To a later generation, which saw in Abdülhamid the incarnation of reactionary and oppressive rule, such ties to this sultan might seem paradoxical. But for Afghānī they are not really surprising. First, Abdülhamid's reassertion of traditional Islamic values and repudiation of the West corresponded to a growing mood in the Muslim world. The acts that later marked him as a reactionary occurred mostly after the mid–1890's, and even then they were not marked by the kind of hostile reaction that developed in force within the empire only in the last years of his reign. Also, pan-Islam was a movement in many ways analogous to nationalism, uniting different classes and bringing conservatives and reformers together in order to defend the homeland. The original ideologists of pan-Islam were reformist Young Ottomans, and Afghānī was to a large degree carrying forth and expanding on their ideas and methods. As the strongest independent ruler of the Muslim world, and the only one with a claim to the loyalty of all Muslims, the Sultan was the logical focus for sentiments favoring Islamic unity in order to ward off the encroaching West. Finally, Afghānī throughout his life gravitated toward men of power—the Amir of Afghanistan, the leading politicians of Egypt, the Shah of Iran, and others—hoping that they would adopt his schemes and give him a position of influence. Abdülhamid was to him an obvious choice for a leader in a movement to unite the Muslim world against Western advances.

When his appeal to Abdülhamid came to nothing, and when he despaired of influencing British policy in the direction of the evacuation of Egypt, Afghānī, after being asked by his host, Blunt, to leave his home, traveled eastward again in 1885. For some months his whereabouts are unclear, but early in 1886 he landed in Bushehr, a South Persian port where his books had been sent from Egypt. Afghānī was apparently planning to go to Russia, after picking up his books; he had been invited to Russia from Paris by Katkov, the prominent Russian chauvinist editor and publicist. Afghānī spent some months in Bushehr, stopping apparently because of ill health. While there he received an invitation to Tehran on behalf of the Shah from the Iranian minister of press, who had translated al-ʿUrwa al-Wuthqā for the Shah. Afghānī then went to Tehran, stopping off in Isfahan where he saw the Shah's most powerful son, the Zill as-Sultān, and perhaps discussed with him schemes for the Zill to succeed to the throne when the Shah died instead of the recognized crown prince. In Tehran the Shah was soon disillusioned with Afghānī, possibly after an interview in which Afghānī reportedly offered himself as a sword to be used against the Shah's foreign enemies.[39] Afghānī's violently anti-British ideas could not fail to alarm Nāsir ad-Dīn Shāh, who, with some reason, feared doing anything to offend either the British or the Russians. The Shah soon asked Afghānī's Tehran host to suggest that he leave the country, and he departed for Moscow in 1887.

Afghānī now spent two years in Russia, devoting himself to trying to influence the Russian government to start a war against Great Britain, which Afghānī saw as a means of encouraging Muslim and Indian revolts against British rule. Afghānī had come to Russia on the invitation of Katkov, who had evidently promised to introduce him to important governmental figures. Katkov died soon after Afghānī's arrival, however, and Afghānī had to make his way alone to St. Petersburg. In the course of his stay he managed to see some important governmental figures, including Pobedonostsev, the Procurator of the Holy Synod. He had several interviews with Zinoviev, head of the Asiatic Department of the Ministry of Foreign Affairs, in which he tried without success to convince Zinoviev of his scheme for a Russian war against Britain. The Russians may have seen in Afghānī a nuisance value against the British in Asia, which may explain such heed as they paid him.[40]

In 1888 and 1889 the British were making advances in Iran to counter the steady growth of Russian influence in that country. During this period the ubiquitous Sir Henry Drummond Wolff was sent on a special mission to Iran, and he succeeded in getting the Shah to open the Karun River in the South to navigation and to grant a concession for a national bank, with attached mining con-

---

[39] 'Abbās Mīrzā Mulk Ārā, a brother of the Shah who was then at court, records this interview: *Sharh-i hāl-i 'Abbās Mīrzā Mulk Ārā*, ed. 'Abd al-Husain Navā'ī (Tehran, 1946–47), pp. 111–112. The Amīn ad-Dauleh, a liberal minister of the time, recalls rather that the Shah's displeasure at the first interview was due to Afghānī's speaking of the need for order, reform, and law: *Khātirāt-i siyāsī-yi Mīrzā 'Alī Khān-i Amīn ad-Dauleh*, ed. Hafez Farman-Farmaian (Tehran, 1962), p. 128.

[40] For a more detailed account, with documentation, of Afghānī's activities 1886–89, see Nikki R. Keddie, *Religion and Rebellion in Iran: The Tobacco Protest of 1891–1892* (London, 1966), pp. 15–27, and the sources cited there.

cessions, to a British subject. The Russians were angry at these concessions and brought pressure on the Iranian government to change its policies. In 1889 the Shah took his third trip to Europe, going by way of St. Petersburg, where Afghānī managed to see some of his friends among the Iranian ministers in the Shah's entourage. Afghānī rejoined the Shah's party briefly later in Munich, where the Shah, probably thinking that it might help appease Russian anger, invited him back to Iran. Before going there Afghānī returned to St. Petersburg, apparently in the belief that he had been given a mission by the Iranian prime minister to try to smooth over Russo-Persian relations. The prime minister denied any such mission and refused to see Afghānī after his return to Iran at the end of 1889.

Once Afghānī realized he was to have no influence on the Iranian government, he evidently began gathering around him a group of Iranian disciples to whom he preached the necessity of a change in government and a firm stand against foreign, and particularly British, encroachments. As had been the situation in Egypt, the time was ripe for such an appeal, since the growth of concessions to foreigners and the absence of any governmental reform were causing hostile reactions among Iranians, particularly of the merchant and intellectual classes. Alarmed at Afghānī's influence, the Shah was about to exile him far from Tehran, but Afghānī apparently got wind of this plan and took sanctuary at a shrine a few miles south of Tehran, where he continued his preaching and agitation.

In January, 1891, alarmed at a leaflet directed against both the government and foreign concessions which was circulated in Tehran, the Shah violated Afghānī's sanctuary and had him rapidly and forcefully escorted from the country in the middle of winter. This unusual and degrading treatment, especially for a sayyid in holy sanctuary, contributed to Afghānī's desire for vengeance upon the Shah. Afghānī went first to Baghdad and then to Basra, and from there to London. While in Basra and Baghdad he wrote letters to many of his followers and to prominent ulama, complaining on religious grounds against the Shah's policy of granting concessions to foreigners.[41]

Iran at this time was an ideal ground for Afghānī's tactic of using religious appeals in order to stop foreign enchroachments. For many reasons, including the fact that their leadership was located in Iraq,

---

[41] *Ibid.*, pp. 46–49, 69–73.

beyond the Shah's control, the Iranian ulama increasingly in the nineteenth century became a center for opposition to the Shah's policies. The issue of concessions to Christian foreigners was one on which religious leaders, nationalists, and reformers could unite in opposition to the government. Afghānī's use of religious appeals to unite all segments of the population against government policies, and his training of disciples in the methods of oppositional organization and propaganda, helped encourage a significant mass protest that took place in Iran in 1891.

In 1890 the Iranian government had given a British subject a concession over the purchase, sale, and export of all tobacco grown in Iran. Such foreign control over an item of daily use and commerce brought forth a mass movement against the concession which spread to many cities in Iran during 1891. The leaflet that had caused Afghānī's expulsion from Iran had already mentioned the tobacco concession among the many signs of growing foreign power. When a protesting sayyid was expelled from the southern city of Shiraz, he went to see the head of the Shi'i ulama in Iraq, and on his way saw Afghānī in Basra. As a result, Afghānī wrote his famous letter to the head of the Shi'i ulama, asking him to intervene and protest the sale of Iran to unbelievers. This letter was one of the factors influencing the Shi'i leader later to issue a decree calling for the boycott of the sale and use of tobacco by Iranians—a decree that helped bring about the cancellation of the concession. After he reached London in 1892, Afghānī printed up his letter and sent it to Iran for circulation, as he did with two appeals to the Iranian ulama to depose Nāsir ad-Dīn Shah. Although Afghānī's role in the successful tobacco movement was much smaller than is suggested by some of his admiring biographers, he did play some part in encouraging both active opposition to the government and the alliance of religious and radical leaders that helped bring about the movement's success.[42]

In London Afghānī joined Malkam Khān, an Iranian reformer of Armenian background and European education, in propaganda and attacks on the Iranian government as an oppressive autocracy. At this point Sultan Abdülhamid conveyed to Afghānī an invitation to come as his guest to Istanbul; Afghānī, after holding out for some guarantees of his personal position and safety, agreed. Although Afghānī was undoubtedly hoping that the Sultan would use him

---

42 *Ibid., passim.*

as a top adviser in pan-Islamic and anti-British plans, it is very doubtful that the Sultan ever had any such intention. Indeed, there is now evidence that the Sultan associated Afghānī with Wilfrid Blunt's schemes for an Arab caliphate, which would have hurt the Sultan's own claims, and that he was inviting Afghānī largely in order to control him and keep him under surveillance.[43] The Sultan's suspicions of Afghānī as a supporter of the British and of an Arab caliphate probably date from Afghānī's scheming with Blunt and the British in 1885, and according to Blunt and other sources, Afghānī did at least occasionally toy with the idea of such an Arab caliphate.

In Istanbul Afghānī was at first well-treated by the Sultan, but was never given major responsibilities. The Sultan had him work with a group of Persians in Istanbul who were to send letters to the Shi'i ulama in Iran and elsewhere asking them to support the Sultan's pan-Islamic claims. The Iranians working with Afghānī in Istanbul included schismatic Babis and men who had left Iran because of their political or religious radicalism. They were now moved to support pan-Islam even though many of them were not

---

[43] The letters from the Sultan's chief religious adviser, Abū al-Hudā, to Afghānī in London trying to persuade him to come to Istanbul already imply the Sultan's suspicions of Afghānī: *Documents*, photographs 213–215. Many thanks to Elie Kedourie for translating these for me. An Iranian, Khān Malik Sāsānī, has unearthed the reports sent home by the Iranian Minister to Istanbul concerning Jamāl ad-Dīn. These show that the Sultan wanted to bring Afghānī to Istanbul in 1891, when he was in Basra, because he feared that if Afghānī went abroad he would cause trouble for the Sultan. After Afghānī's arrival in Istanbul, the Iranian minister wrote home, basing his comments on what he had heard from the Ottoman government:

"For some time the English government has been of the opinion that they should undermine the Sultan's caliphate and dissuade people from believing in it. With this aim they have incited the Arab shaikhs and brought them to the point of revolt. The British are giving them the idea of choosing the caliph themselves and placing it in Mecca, or else recognizing the Sharīf of Mecca who is a descendant of Zaid ibn 'Alī. One of the means of the activity of the English was the presence of Jamāl ad-Dīn who published some articles in London encouraging and inciting the Arab shaikhs, and making them stand firm in rebelliousness against the Ottoman government; and making the common people disrespectful of the Sultan, whom they recognized as the caliph of the earth. The policy which the Ottoman government followed to repel this danger was to write to their Ambassador in London in order to lure and tempt Jamāl ad-Dīn and bring him to Istanbul . . ." (quoted in Khān Malik Sāsānī, *Siyāsatgarān-i daureh-yi Qājār* [Tehran, 1338/1959–60] pp. 193–194).

even Muslims. In addition to the anti-imperialist sentiments that led some radicals to support pan-Islam, the Iranian pan-Islamists were probably moved by a desire to weaken Nāsir ad-Dīn Shāh. The letters sent out to the Shi'i ulama by Afghānī and his followers were accompanied by gifts and promises of further favors; possibly for this reason, they received some positive response. But Afghānī was prevented by the Sultan from carrying out any directly hostile propaganda against either the Shah or the British. The Shah was, however, further aroused against Afghānī and his followers by their activities favoring the Sultan's pan-Islamic claims.[44]

A series of events lost Afghānī the confidence of the Sultan within a few years of his arrival. The Sultan's Arab religious confidants grew hostile to Afghānī and denounced him to the Sultan as a heretic and a deceiver. When the new Khedive of Egypt, 'Abbās Hilmī, came to visit Istanbul in 1895, he secretly went to see Afghānī, and the Sultan believed, possibly correctly, that they were discussing an Arab caliphate under the control of the Khedive. The Armenian struggles and the rise of a Turkish opposition also made the Sultan more suspicious, and he sent out spies to follow Afghānī. In 1895 Afghānī tried to leave Istanbul by getting a British visa, claiming he was an Afghan subject and hence protected by Great Britain, but the Sultan's surveillance was evidently strong enough to stop him.[45]

Soon after this, one of Afghānī's Iranian followers, a cloakmaker named Mīrzā Rizā of Kirman who had been imprisoned for years for his oppositional activities, came to Istanbul to see Afghānī. Afghānī,

---

[44] For Afghānī's activities in Istanbul, see Nikki R. Keddie, "Religion and Irreligion in Early Iranian Nationalism," esp. pp. 283–289, 292–295.

[45] FO 60/594, Currie to Salisbury, Dec. 12, 1895, no. 923. This letter says: "It would appear that the Sheikh was deeply implicated in a movement among the softas hostile to the present Sultan and that his bitter enemies the Sheikh Abal Huda and Ahmed Essad availed themselves of this to bring about his downfall. He was subjected to the strictest espionage and practically made a prisoner in his house." The enclosed letter from Jamāl ad-Dīn says: "I have passed a great part of my life in the Orient with the single aim of uprooting fanaticism, the most harmful malady of this land, of reforming society and establishing there the benefits of tolerance." He notes that he has been unjustly accused of participation in recent events, and that the Armenian disturbances have aroused the Sultan's suspicions. The reasons for the Sultan's estrangement from Afghānī are discussed by various witnesses; see the appendix to my "Religion and Irreligion." Shakīb Arslān, Hādir al-'ālam al-Islāmī, (Cairo, 1924–25), I, 202–203, notes that Abū al-Hudā accused Afghānī of unbelief and heresy, and discusses Afghānī's meeting with 'Abbās Hilmī.

who often spoke of the necessity of killing Nāsir ad-Dīn Shāh, probably encouraged Mīrzā Rizā to carry out this deed. Mīrzā Rizā returned to Iran and in May, 1896, shot and killed Nāsir ad-Dīn Shāh at a shrine near Tehran. On the demand of the Iranian government, three of Afghānī's Iranian followers who were already being held in prison at Trebizond were extradited to Iran by the Ottoman government and executed, as was the assassin. The three had no connection with the assassination, but Afghānī, who had, was kept in Istanbul by the Sultan despite repeated Iranian demands for extradition. The Sultan used as his excuse Afghānī's claim to be an Afghan, not a Persian, but it is likely that his real grounds for hesitation were that Afghānī knew too much about what was going on at the Sultan's court, and particularly about his pan-Islamic activities.[46]

In his last years in Istanbul Afghānī was reduced to political impotence. Like a caged lion he growled to foreigners against his enforced confinement and spoke bitterly of his dashed hopes for reform in the Muslim world. Outside a circle of Istanbul disciples he now had little influence and was evidently permitted to publish nothing. Indeed, he seems to have been fading from the consciousness of both Easterners and Westerners until the Shah's assassination brought on a brief flurry of articles and references. From the reminiscences of those who saw him in Istanbul we know that his contact with reality was growing ever weaker, as he regaled them with tales of his huge influence on various governmental leaders and of his persecution by the British and others.[47]

In 1897 Afghānī died of cancer of the chin. At the time and there-

---

46 Sāsānī, op. cit., pp. 194–220, has the fullest documentation of the unsuccessful Iranian efforts to extradite Afghānī.

47 Muḥammad al-Makhzūmī, Khāṭirāt-i Sayyid Jamāl ad-Dīn Asadābādī, trans. into Persian by Murtaẓā Mudarissī Chahārdihī (Tabriz, 1328/1949–50), records what Jamāl ad-Dīn told him in Istanbul. It is full of stories of Afghānī's great importance to the Shah of Iran and other high governmental figures, including the Tsar of Russia. The Shah is said to have given Afghānī the Ministry of War on his first trip to Iran, and to have done nothing without his advice. An interview with the Tsar is also described, which almost surely never occurred. Then, it is said, in Munich the Shah asked Afghānī's pardon, and on his return to Iran asked him to codify the laws in accordance with the times, but got angry when he saw that Afghānī was working for a constitutional government and legislative assembly (pp. 50–56). If Makhzūmī's report is accurate, Afghānī was departing widely from the facts.

after rumors circulated in the Muslim world that he had been poisoned by the Sultan, but his illness and the fact that he underwent operations for it are well attested by witnesses. Some of the more fanciful reports speak of the Sultan's surgeon injecting him with venom, but these tales are almost surely of a piece with the many myths about Afghānī. At the time of his death he was apparently attended by only one person, a Christian servant, and his death brought no great reaction in either the East or West. Only later, when his pan-Islamic, apologetic, and anti-Western ideas began to be picked up by a growing body of Muslim writers, was he once again eagerly and widely read, and regarded as a modern Muslim hero.

In describing Afghānī's personal character, his acquaintances often noted his boldness, single-minded devotion to a cause and indifference to worldly goods. The evidence also suggests certain peculiar qualities that have not been discussed by his biographers—delusions of grandeur, distortions of reality, and an expressed hostility toward relations with women.

Afghānī's personal magnetism was evidently quite extraordinary, and he had an unusual ability to find his way into high governmental circles; however, he almost always lost the favor of the powerful very quickly. This loss of favor seems to have been due largely to two things: his propensity to plot for reform or revolution at the same time as he was dealing with governmental figures, and his advocacy of grandiose and unrealistic anti-foreign schemes. His personal bluntness, quick temper, and lack of deference to the powerful also played a part. He was primarily a man with a taste for quick and violent action; assassinations, wars, intrigues, or revolts were means to his ends. In the nineteenth century there was not enough of a popular movement and social conditions were not ripe to make such methods effective against Western encroachments except in brief instances, but in the twentieth century some of these means, backed by new realities, could be employed to much greater effect.

Afghānī's fabrication of stories about himself seems to go beyond the purely expedient use of fact sanctioned by some of the heterodox traditions in Islam. He apparently really saw himself as an unsung messiah of pan-Islam who was hounded from country to country by the British, whose imperialist policy he personalized. His stories about his own influence and his unjust persecutions, particularly those recorded near the end of his life, have the ring of those told by persons who do not completely distinguish truth from fantasy. As for the sexual aspect of the pattern, it may be noted that there is only one woman who is known to have had any attachment to him, and it is not at all clear that this was a sexual attachment. When the Sultan offered (or threatened?) to give Afghānī a wife, Afghānī said if the Sultan did so, he would cut off his own sexual organ.[48] Letters from his younger disciples are filled with adoring phrases, and while there is no evidence that Afghānī was a homosexual, he rejected ties to women. His avoidance of contact with his family, even when he came to Iran, and his denial of his origins and upbringing are also of some significance. The connection between the unusual family and sexual pattern and Afghānī's public life is unclear, but might be worth competent analysis, if only to get a fuller picture of Afghānī than is yet available.[49]

Afghānī's psychology would matter little were there not ties between his ways of perceiving the world and those of many other modern Muslims. The increasing power of Westerners, and especially the British, over Muslims, whom they often mistreated, brought forth defensive reactions not only from Afghānī but from much of the Eastern world. Assertiveness about the virtues of Islam (which often masks insecurities about the worth of the militarily defeated culture); violence of temperament; paranoia about British machinations which overrates diabolical cleverness and underrates military and economic power as the roots of British strength—all of these "Afghānīan" features and others are still found in the Muslim Middle East.

Yet it would not be fair to end on this negative note. For all his faults and lack of realism, Afghānī surely contributed something of

---

[48] Muḥammad al-Makhzūmī, *Khāṭirāt Jamāl ad-Dīn al-Afghānī* (Beirut, 1931), p. 111. Other acquaintances also record his statements against ties to women. A love letter from a European woman is, however, in *Documents*, plates 66–67.

[49] For all their difference in cultural background, one is struck by the similarities in psychology between Afghānī and the political agitators analyzed by Harold Lasswell in *Psychopathology and Politics* (new ed.; New York, 1960). Lasswell analyzed several agitators personally and found among them hyperactivity, high verbal ability, a desire to control others and sway crowds, and delusions of grandeur and of persecution, which Lasswell related to their latent homosexuality or fears of impotence. Such pyschological discussions suggest parallels, although these cannot be definitive in a man whose childhood is as little known as Afghānī's, and should not be taken as denial of either the sociohistorical roots or the value of what he said and did.

positive value to the modern Muslim. After a century of denigration by the West, he helped present those parts of the Muslim tradition that might be worthy of pride, and suggested that reform could and should take place within the boundaries of Islam. By his extraordinary personal boldness on many occasions he gave courage to those who felt there was no alternative to submitting to the existing power structure. He helped organize and disseminate such tools of modern political action and education as the journal of opinion, the leaflet, and the secret political society, all of which have been important in changing the face of the Muslim world. Though his desire for self-strengthening outweighed his desire for reform, his followers assert that he did preach to them the need of parliamentary and constitutional reforms, and of ending autocratic governments. Had he concentrated more on his organizational and educative activities and given himself less to high-level and inevitably unsuccessful intrigues, his legacy would have been less ambiguous than it now appears.

Afghānī initiated the partial transformation of Islam from a generally held religious faith into an ideology of political use in uniting Muslims against the West. As Sylvia Haim has noted:

> What al-Afghani did was to make Islam into the mainspring of solidarity, and thus he placed it on the same footing as other solidarity-producing beliefs. His political activity and teaching combined to spread among the intellectual and official classes of Middle Eastern Islam a secularist, meliorist, and activist attitude toward politics, an attitude the presence of which was essential, before ideologies such as Arab nationalism could be accepted in any degree. It is this which makes al-Afghani so important a figure in modern Islamic politics.[50]

It is to an analysis of Afghānī's use of Islam as ideology and his original contributions built up from an Islamic philosophical base that attention is now turned.

---

[50] Sylvia Haim, *op. cit.*, p. 15. This book contains an excellent discussion of Afghānī's ideological role and influence.

2

Sayyid Jamāl ad-Dīn's Ideas

A Summary
of Afghānī's Aims
and Methods

THAT Sayyid Jamāl ad-Dīn's life was full of obscure and complex intrigues has long been known, and if anything, the picture of complication and even confusion in his activities has been reinforced by important new material, such as that unearthed by Elie Kedourie, and the recent publication in Iran of newly discovered sources about his life. Some of the same contradictions that run through his political activity can be found in his ideas and writings, and to a degree the source of these contradictions is the same. Just as he appealed during his life to the most various people to help him fulfill his goals—in the Islamic world to the ulama, to heretics and freethinkers, to rulers and men of government, and sometimes to the masses; and in the Western world to the Russian, English, and possibly French governments at different times, and to both reactionaries and liberals—so his writings seem sometimes to be the work of several different men, differing not only in ideas but even profoundly in style and in type of thought, depending on the audience he was addressing. When speaking to a Western audience, not only in the famous "Answer to Renan," but also in other talks and newspaper articles addressed to a French or British public, Sayyid Jamāl ad-Dīn could be almost the image of logic, clarity, and rationality, appealing to the liberal sentiments of his audience in a way that would be impossible for a man who had not a fairly sympathetic acquaintance with modern Western ideas. When writing a book or articles intended for mass circulation in the Muslim world, such as "The Refutation of the Materialists" or his '*Urwa al-Wuthqā* articles, his words are often full of such rhetorical exaggeration and factual imprecision as to make Westerners wonder why intelligent Muslims had such a generally high regard for his intellect.[1] A clue to this question is found, however, in reports of his private teachings and in some of his letters, as well as in a few articles and speeches to Eastern audiences, where once again is found a more rational, scientific mode of argument and a different set of emphases.

Must one conclude, then, that Jamāl ad-Dīn was a pure opportunist, concerned only to say what he thought appropriate to his goals at a given moment, without any clear principles or ideas? This would seem unlikely in view of the strongly positive intellectual impression he made not only on intelligent and sophisticated Easterners like Malkam Khān, but on at least equally intelligent and sophisticated Westerners like Ernest Renan. In fact, quite consistent syntheses of his doctrines, as culled from his major writings, have recently been made, in detail in Sharīf al-Mujāhid's McGill University thesis, and with much subtlety and attention to Afghānī's Islamic philosophical background, in Albert Hourani's *Arabic Thought in the Liberal Age*.[2] The following discussion owes much to these syntheses, which, however, do not seem adequately to deal with the antireligious implications of such documents as the "Answer to Renan" or the reports and activities recently stressed by Elie Kedourie and Sylvia Haim.[3] To draw a really consistent picture of Afghānī's ideas which takes into account his contradictory statements it seems necessary to posit four fundamental points, which are discussed in more detail below.

1. Afghānī was profoundly influenced by the tradition, particularly strong among the Islamic philosophers, that it was correct and proper to use different levels of discourse according to the level of

---

[1] The difference between Afghānī's style in Arabic (and Persian) and the reports of his words in Western languages arises in part from the different modes of expression favored by Middle Eastern and Western languages. On the discursiveness of Arabic, as compared to Western languages, see the words of Aḥmad Amīn translated in Anouar Abdel-Malek, *Anthologie de la littérature arabe contemporaine*, II (Paris, 1965), 91–94.

[2] Albert Hourani, *Arabic Thought in the Liberal Age: 1798–1939* (London, 1962), chap. v; Sharīf al-Mujāhid, "Sayyid Jamāl al-Dīn al-Afghānī: His Role in the Nineteenth Century Muslim Awakening" (unpublished M.A. thesis, McGill University, Montreal, 1954).

[3] Sylvia Haim, *Arab Nationalism: An Anthology* (Berkeley and Los Angeles, 1962), pp. 3–15; Elie Kedourie, *Afghani and 'Abduh: An Essay on Religious Unbelief and Political Activism in Modern Islam* (London, 1966), *passim*.

one's audience. Like the philosophers, he believed that the masses, *'āmma*, were not open to rational philosophical argument. A literalist scriptural religion that stressed a day of judgment would keep them loyal to the community and moral in their actions, and would discourage the formation of sects that would split the community. As seen below, his attacks on those who spread doubt among the masses and encourage sectarianism virtually echo those of Averroes. Unlike the philosophers, he probably hoped the masses would improve somewhat. On the other hand, it is clear that Afghānī always was surrounded by an elite, the phrase *khāṣṣa* is often used, to whom he suggested ideas very different from literalist orthodoxy, employing the usual method of Islamic philosophers, oral teaching. Although Afghānī particularly stressed the philosophers in his teaching, he was probably also influenced by Sufi and other heterodox traditions of levels of discourse, which were also strong in Iran.[4]

2. When in writings like the "Refutation of the Materialists" Afghānī used the word "Islam" in a strongly positive sense, and praised Islam for its tolerance, scientific spirit, and so forth, he was think of an idealized "Islam," different not only from the Muslim religion or civilization of his own day, but from any he imagined to have existed for more than a millennium. In accord with the first point, he usually did not make this distinction explicit, but he did give enough hints so that those who had eyes to see would see. The positive "Islam" of Afghānī is examined in more detail below. Suffice it to say here that this "Islam" included: *(a)* An idealized picture of the Age of the Prophet and the first four caliphs, whose appeal to Afghānī was based largely on its aggressive military success, which contrasted so vividly with the recent Western military defeats of Islam; *(b)* The idea, taken from the Islamic philosophers but also found in many religious modernists, that when scripture apparently contradicted reason or science, scripture must be reinterpreted; this Afghānī extended to include modern science and philosophy; *(c)* A reopening of the door of interpretation of law and doctrine *(ijtihād)*, combined with a return to emphasis on the Koran, which could lead to a Protestant type of reform of Islam. Because of his concern for Islamic strength and unity, however, Afghānī opposed those who broke openly with the ulama or paraded their differences

---

[4] For a fuller discussion of these traditions, see Nikki R. Keddie, "Symbol and Sincerity in Islam," *Studia Islamica*, XIX (1963), 27–63.

with orthodoxy, and seems to have hoped that Islam would be reformed from above, without splitting the community. The negative "Muslim religion" of the "Answer to Renan" is Islam as it actually was; the positive "Islam" of other writings is his ideal.[5]

3. Afghānī's concern for unity, arising largely from the weakness of Muslim countries vis-à-vis the West, and the hope of rallying *all* Muslims against the West, involved political propaganda that would appeal differently to the different elements of society, according to their interests and understanding; hence the contradictions noted above. For all his scheming, Afghānī failed to achieve any of his important political goals, and many of his schemes on their face appear most impractical. It would seem he was caught in an unresolved contradiction between (*a*) the traditional ideas of the Muslim philosophers, who had little hope for the masses and concentrated on influencing the rulers and other elite of the Muslim community, and (*b*) more modern ideas of political opposition. The latter could have proved practicable only after a long prior organization and propaganda, which hardly suited Afghānī's impatient temperament. When he went in for revolutionary activities, they were generally of the nature of proposed assassinations or depositions rather than of an organized and gradually growing opposition movement. Assassinations are typical both of certain strains of the Islamic tradition and of immature modern revolutionary movements.

4. The fact that Afghānī spent most of his life in political activity, often with some of the most conservative figures of both the Islamic and Western worlds, and less time working for religious reform indicates that *the political unification and strengthening of the Islamic world and the ending of Western incursions there were his primary goals, while the reform of Islam was secondary.* This helps also to explain the third point. While Sultan Abdülhamid, the various conservatives with whom Afghānī made contact in the retinue of the Russian Tsar, and many others whom he tried to in-

---

[5] Al-Mujāhid, *op. cit.*, pp. 79–89, makes this terminological distinction a focal point in his argument that Afghānī was a true believer in Islam. He implies that Afghānī deliberately spoke of the "Muslim religion" in the "Answer to Renan," and not of true "Islam." This argument appears dubious, especially since Afghānī's "Answer" was published in French and used standard French terminology; there are no grounds for assuming that his Arabic original used a peculiar term for Islam.

volve in his schemes could not be expected to further the cause of Islamic reform, they might support his pan-Islamic and anti-British goals. The confusion of Afghānī's activities appears here as elsewhere. While he often recognized the importance of Islamic reform as a prerequisite to the acceptance of modern science and technology and the activism needed for self-strengthening, he was diverted by an illusory romantic hope of recreating, via a new caliph, the dynamism of the early caliphate. The rulers with whom Afghānī dealt could not share his vision, and their position was often based on support from the very forces of obscurantism that Afghānī opposed. It is only fair to add that at the very end of his life Afghānī may have seen the errors of his past activities. He apparently wrote a letter in which he recommends working against rulers, organizing to spread enlightenment, and opposing not individuals but the whole prevailing system of government.[6]

Afghānī's life and activity indicate that his main aims were what Westerners would consider political rather than religious; however, his political program, based partly on illusions of using vested religious and political influences for revolutionary ends, could have

---

[6] E. G. Browne, *The Persian Revolution of 1905–1909* (Cambridge, 1910), pp. 28–29, translates this letter from the Persian book in which it first appeared. I would have discussed this most interesting letter in the text, except that Sayyid Hasan Taqīzādeh has doubted its authenticity. It appears authentic, however, judging by its style and by its original publication in 1910 along with undoubtedly authentic documents. After noting the failure of his dreams for reform, Afghānī's letter says: "Would that I had sown all the seed of my ideas in the receptive ground of the people's thoughts! Well would it have been had I not wasted this fruitful and beneficent seed of mine in the salt and sterile soil of that effete Sovereignty! For what I sowed in that soil never grew, and what I planted in that brackish earth perished away. During all this time none of my well-intentioned counsels sank into the ears of the rulers of the East, whose selfishness and ignorance prevented them from accepting my words."

Addressing the Persians, he says: "Nature is your friend, and the Creator of Nature your ally. The stream of renovation flows quickly towards the East. The edifice of despotic government totters to its fall. Strive so far as you can to destroy the foundations of this despotism, not to pluck up and cast out its individual agents. Strive so far as in you lies to abolish those practices which stand between the Persians and their happiness, not to annihilate those who employ these practices. If you merely strive to oppose individuals, your time will only be lost. If you seek only to prevail against them, the evil practice will draw to itself others. Endeavor to remove those obstacles which prevent your friendship with other nations."

only infrequent and ephemeral success. Since Islam does not make the Western distinction between religion and politics, it might be more accurate to say that Afghānī stressed the practical, political side of Islam, rather than its speculative or theological side. When religious ideals conflicted with practical goals, it was the former that gave way. It is hard to escape the impression that what really appealed to him both in early Islam and in the modern West was political strength. His stress on holy war and his attempts to prove that the Koran enjoins the acquisition of the most modern and effective armaments support this idea. Even ideas that are usually called "religious," such as reopening the door of interpretation of religious law and doctrine, have as their main goal the introduction of innovations that would allow the Muslim world to progress militarily and politically. Also, there is a constant stress on the power of the state and community. This is not to say that Afghānī was not a reformer, or that he did not really hope for a diminution of absolutism and an increase in equality, justice, and consent of the governed; but when there was a potential conflict between these goals and Afghānī's primary goal of rebuilding a strong Islamic state capable of withstanding Western encroachments, he consistently opted for the latter.

Nor is this surprising, in view of the continual movement of Western Christian powers into Islamic territory, a trend that grew in Afghānī's own lifetime with the occupation of Tunisia, Egypt, and Central Asia and the reduction of Iran to a virtual Western protectorate. This constant advance was not being met by adequate measures within the Islamic states, where both rulers and ulama were often content with either stagnation, or halfhearted reform. Some young Muslim intellectuals, particularly in India, were being won over to a wholehearted endorsement of the West, accompanied by a sense of inferiority about their own community and its past.

To Afghānī, whose writings and speeches often indicate a broader knowledge and acceptance of modern Western ideas than he admitted to a mass Islamic public, the West thus appeared in a contradictory role. On the one hand it was an aggressive conqueror and oppressor, which was renewing its territorial conquests in the Muslim world. Afghānī also seemed to believe that Westerners were bent on undermining the Muslim sense of identity by turning their conquered subjects away from their own proud traditions. Afghānī had a profound dislike of Western rule in Muslim lands, probably based largely on his own experiences in India, and was apparently convinced that a people could be well-ruled only by men of their own community, traditions, and belief.[7] He was a strong anti-imperialist, and reserved his deepest hatred for those like Sayyid Ahmad Khān who advised Indian Muslims to cooperate with imperialist rule. Afghānī believed that the efforts of the Muslims should, on the contrary, be turned to ousting the Western conquerors and preventing them from making further conquests.

On the other hand, the West was the seat of the sciences, military technology, modern education, and political institutions that were needed for self-strengthening, so that the Muslims might oust their Western conquerors and once more enter the mainstream of progress. For Afghānī, however, it was important not to lay undue stress on the Western origin of what he was borrowing, as this might encourage the trend of admiration for the West and feelings of Islamic inferiority and helplessness. Thus for Afghānī, as for many other Asian modernists and anti-imperialists, there was good reason not to admit the Western origin of what he was borrowing, but instead to find origins within his own community. We find in Afghānī one of the increasingly popular idealized pictures of the early Islamic community, where there was equality of believers, consent of the governed, encouragement of science and of military strength. In conversations with his followers Afghānī apparently said that the Koran hinted at such things as railroads and the germ theory—an argument later worked out with appropriate, if farfetched, citations by the pan-Arabist Kawākibī.[8] Whether Afghānī really believed all he said about the early Islamic community seems doubtful, especially when one considers the more limited, evolutionist view of early Islam and the Koran he took in his "Answer to Renan" and elsewhere. There it is implied that early Islam represented an advance over the barbarism of the early Arabs, but would have to change and progress much further, as had Christianity since Luther. The initial period of Islam did have a genuine appeal for Afghānī because of its military strength and successes and the apparent cohesiveness and dynamism of the early Islamic community. Within the Islamic tradition there continued to be strains, notably in the philosophers and to a lesser extent the Sufis, in which he could find

---

[7] See the quotation from Afghānī in al-Mujāhid, *op. cit.*, p. 129.

[8] See 'Abd ar-Raḥmān al-Kawākibī, *Ṭabā'i' al-istibdād* (Cairo, n.d.), *passim.* Afghānī's words are in Makhzūmī, *Khāṭirāt* (2d. ed.; Damascus, 1965), pp. 100–104.

much genuinely to admire. Afghānī's appeal to the Islamic tradition
thus had genuine intellectual and emotional roots, and was strengthened by a desire to avoid identification with the Western oppressors
or feelings of inferiority toward them.

Although Afghānī's ideas were not necessarily the same as those of
his associates, many of his closest followers were not Muslims at all,
but Babis, Christians, Jews, and freethinkers. When they, at least,
made appeals to Islamic feeling it was done on political grounds,
with little or no basis in personal sentiment. As one of Afghānī's
associates, Malkam Khān, pointed out in a frank speech to an English
audience, a powerful reason for clothing Western ideas in Islamic
terms, and stating that Western institutions had originally been
borrowed from Islam, was that only in an Islamic form were new
ideas likely to reach the religious Muslim masses. Most Muslims had
long believed that Western Christians were enemies out to undermine Islam, enemies from whom nothing doctrinal should be borrowed.[9] It seems likely that such practical considerations also moti-
vated Afghānī, who was concerned to appeal not only to sophisticated
intellectuals who might be open to Western ideas in their original
state, but also to the traditionalist ulama and masses.

The conflict between a desire to Westernize and a need to avoid
identification with the West was one of the roots of the contradictions in Afghānī's ideas. In addition, there were latent contradictions within his program. For example, pan-Islam and the reform of
Islam could seem to him two sides of a program for strengthening
the Muslim world and defeating imperialism. But there were contradictions between them, even ignoring for the moment the developing nationalism that was ultimately to render pan-Islam abor-
tive. In Afghānī's time, there were many reasons to appeal to the
Islamic community as a whole; there was still a strong sense of
community among the Muslims of the world, and religious identification was usually stronger than national. Also, the Arabic-Persian
cultural tradition extended to much of the Muslim Middle East,
providing even modernists an identification with a supranational
community. Even such secularized intellectuals as Akhundov in the
Transcaucasus and Malkam Khān of Iran appealed to the whole
Islamic Middle Eastern community in their work for political and
script reform. Traditional hostilities between the Muslim and Chris-

---

[9] Malcom Khan, "Persian Civilization," *Contemporary Review*, LIX (Feb., 1891),
238-244.

tian worlds, and the modern domination of Muslims by Christians, might strengthen a sense of cultural identity vis-à-vis the West. In the face of Western attack, it was natural to call for a further drawing together of the Islamic community, and particularly an abandonment of sectarian differences in a common defensive effort. *But*, and here is the contradiction, the drawing together of all elements of the community meant that one set of enlightened people in that community could not struggle for a definite reform program that might alienate powerful traditionalist and conservative groups. Nor could Afghānī himself ever suggest a consistent and definitive theological reform program. He may have had the capacity to do so, but if he had done it and tried to fight for it, he would have split, not united, the Islamic community; and, as long as he was convinced that the Sultan or ulama might be enlisted to help his self-strengthening aims, he would try not to alienate them too far. It is significant that the religious reform aspect of his program found very little fulfillment, even in oppositional activity, in Afghānī's lifetime, but was forwarded by 'Abduh and other disciples only after they had dropped the pan-Islamic program.

The point is not that there is something *wrong* with Afghānī's concentration on the political and pragmatic aspects of Islam and his vagueness about anything we might regard as religious content in the revived Islam, but, rather, that it is a mistake for either Easterners or Westerners to look to him expecting to find a reconstruction of religious thought. If Afghānī's goals were mainly pragmatic or political, there is no reason to expect from him a well thought-out reconstruction of the Islamic religion.

Indeed, as suggested above, there were for Afghānī positive barriers to such a reconstruction. First of all, Afghānī wanted to reinforce pride in Islam and to use existing Islamic sentiment as an ideological weapon in fighting the Christian Western oppressors. In doing this he was unable to press too openly the point that Islam as the majority of Muslims knew and practiced it was very different from the ideal to which he referred. He clearly did stress this point to his personal followers, many of whom went on to work more successfully for modernization; but he did not press it in his writings, which had to appeal to the nonadept as well as the adept. Second, the desire to unite all branches of the Islamic community in a program of self-strengthening required that theological distinctions be played down and theological disputation rejected in favor of a rather vague belief in the superiority of Islam that could appeal to everyone. This is seen in his efforts to unite the Shi 'is and Sunnis; in his attacks on the sects in the "Refutation of the Materialists"; and in his refusal, probably prompted by fear of splitting the Islamic community, to imitate the open defiance of religious authorities pursued by his hero, Luther.

In none of his writings does Afghānī appear as a man moved by a truly original religious vision. It is hard to escape the conclusion, in reading Afghānī, that the "Islam" to which he appeals has almost exclusively secular virtues and little positive religious content.

The impression of pragmatic and worldly rather than religious concerns is strengthened by the fact that Afghānī was willing to appear in so many different religious guises to different audiences—to the Shi 'i ulama as a pious Shi 'i, interested in preserving the existing faith against an infidel Shah; to his followers as an excoriator of the backward clergy; to a mass Islamic audience as a defender of Islam against Western-inspired materialism; and to a Western audience as a defender of science and philosophy against religion. Islamic traditions and existing realities that encouraged expediency subordinated religious consistency to practical political goals. By assuming that Afghānī was most concerned about practical political goals, and that he hoped to harness many groups with different interests to his program, one can make sense out of the mass of contradictions between one and another of his works. The only apparent alternative is to postulate a hopeless confusion of thought, which seems unlikely in view of the intelligent men he impressed in both East and West. Those whom he impressed personally were mostly modernists, liberals, and even revolutionaries: hardly those who would be much moved by the pure defense of Islam that some later writers attribute to him.

Afghānī
and Islamic
Philosophy

In ADDITION to showing Afghānī's desire not to split the Islamic community, but rather to reinforce its ideological cohesion vis-à-vis the West, the "Refutation of the Materialists" reflects Afghānī's background in the Islamic philosophic tradition. Since this has not been stressed enough, it is necessary here to point to Afghānī's high evaluation of philosophy, whose teaching he tried to revive in the Islamic world, and also to some particularly relevant points in that philosophic tradition which are mirrored in Afghānī's writings.

There is no doubt that Afghānī was well trained in Islamic philosophy and that he valued it highly. The revival of philosophic studies and their understanding was one of the central points in his program of Islamic renewal. He wrote that philosophy was the way to bring man from darkness into light, the "integrating soul" of all branches of knowledge. In writings and talks directed to a Muslim audience he tried to prove that philosophical studies were not against Islam or the Koran, but that on the contrary, the spirit of the Koran favored them.[10]

Islamic philosophy with a Hellenistic base, or *falsafa*, despite all the variations among its practitioners, can be said to constitute a school with certain common features. The adherents of *falsafa* were heavily influenced by certain major figures and trends of Greek and Hellenistic philosophy, particularly by Aristotle and Neoplatonism. The logic and metaphysics of the Muslim philosophers were based on one or more of these Greek traditions. Like their Greek masters, the early Muslim philosophers generally believed in demonstrative, rational proof rather than revealed scriptural authority as the essential explanation of the workings of man and the universe. Living, unlike the Greeks, in a society whose laws and beliefs were based on a revealed scripture, the Muslim philosophers had to develop a means to reconcile their logic and metaphysics with the Prophet's revelations. The means adopted by the great philosophers from Fārābī and Avicenna down through the later Persian philosophers, who also influenced Afghānī, involved the belief that literalist revelation was necessary for the masses, but that the higher truth was to be uncovered by rationalist interpretation of scripture.

The political and ethical theories of the philosophers varied, but they generally involved a certain pessimism about the masses, who could only be kept in line by a revealed law sanctioned by vivid physical rewards and punishments in the afterlife. The philosophical

---

[10] See the translation of "The Benefits of Philosophy," in pt. 2 of the present work, pp. 113–114.

elite, who could pattern their political and ethical behavior on more rational bases, might dispense with belief in a physical afterlife as described by scripture, and might even be led by their rationalist arguments into disbelief in the immortality of the individual soul.[11]

Some of the post-Avicennan Persian philosophers whom Afghānī cites, such as the influential seventeenth-century philosopher Mullā Sadrā, seem to have believed that the same truths that are accessible through reason and through philosophical interpretation of revelation can also be reached by the mystic path of illumination.[12] And the Neoplatonism of even a philosopher like Avicenna had strongly religious elements involving an intellectualized version of the mystic path of the soul back to reunion with the First Cause. The mixture of rationalist elements, mystic tendencies, and citation of the Koran was not original to Afghānī, but is found frequently in Persian philosophy. Although the Persian philosophers were often considered heretical and were sometimes persecuted, some of their teachings, particularly the versions that stressed the reconciliation of rational philosophy and revelation, continued to be taught in the religious schools in Iran. This Persian tradition gave Afghānī a means unparalleled in the Sunni countries where philosophy was not so taught

---

[11] Regarding the aspects of Islamic philosophy discussed here, see in addition to the works cited in note 12: the article, "Falsafa," and those on individual philosophers in both editions of *Encyclopaedia of Islam (EI)*; Soheil M. Afnan, *Avicenna, His Life and Works* (London, 1958); *Averroes' Tahafut al-Tahafut*, trans. and ed. S. van den Bergh (London, 1954); Henry Corbin, *Avicenna and the Visionary Recital*, trans. Willard R. Trask (New York, 1960), and "Confessions extatiques de Mīr Dāmād," in *Mélanges Louis Massignon*, I (Damascus, 1956), 331–378; Louis Gardet, *La pensée religieuse d'Avicenne* (Paris, 1951), and "Le problème de la 'Philosophie Musulmane,'" in *Mélanges offerts à Étienne Gilson* (Paris, 1959); Nikki R. Keddie, "Symbol and Sincerity in Islam," *Studia Islamica*, XIX (1963), 27–63; Ralph Lerner and Muhsin Mahdi, eds., *Medieval Political Philosophy* (Toronto, 1963); E. I. J. Rosenthal, *Political Thought in Medieval Islam* (Cambridge, Eng., 1958); Leo Strauss, *Persecution and the Art of Writing* (Glencoe, Ill., 1952); Richard Walzer, *Greek into Arabic* (Oxford, 1962); and W. M. Watt, *Islamic Philosophy and Theology* (Edinburgh, 1962).

[12] On the later Persian philosophers see chaps. xlvii, xlviii, and lxxviii by Seyyed Hossein Nasr in M. M. Sharif, ed., *A History of Muslim Philosophy*, II (Wiesbaden, 1966); Seyyed Hossein Nasr, *Three Muslim Sages* (Cambridge, Mass., 1964); and the works referred to therein, particularly those by Henry Corbin.

for suggesting a reconciliation of science, religion, and even mysticism.

This brief summary necessarily skirts the many controversies that continue to exist regarding the exact nature of the beliefs of almost every one of the Muslim philosophers. Intellectuals who believed in apprehending the same truth in more than one way and in expressing themselves in different manners to different audiences have naturally invited a variety of interpretations, as has Afghānī himself. As far as Afghānī's relationship to the Muslim philosophical tradition is concerned, his writings indicate an emphasis on the rationalist and scientific side of Muslim philosophy, and on the means that philosophy provided for new interpretations of religions and for speaking differently to the masses and to the intellectual elite. Afghānī's statement that the Koran is an infinite source of wisdom whose meaning is never exhausted[13] may have been sincere, but its chief aim was not to glorify the Koran but to introduce Muslims to modern science and technology and to political struggle.

Traditional Islamic philosophy was understood as including science, or the knowledge of the world as it actually was through demonstrative proof; so Afghānī's injunctions to revive philosophy have broader implications than at first appear. In at least one talk Afghānī makes clear that *his* philosophy would include modern science.[14] In essence, Afghānī was reopening in the Sunni world the argument between the philosophers and the theologians and other orthodox as to the proper way to apprehend truth, by authority or by reason. The orthodox victory in this argument had been both a symptom and a cause of the decline of Islamic civilization. The notion that the Koran and Islam give positive injunctions to the use of reason and even to rationalist interpretations of scripture is not original in Afghānī's "Refutation," but is stressed particularly by the philosophers. The argument has some basis,[15] but the philosophers carried it further than did most other Muslims in an attempt to make a place for philosophy within the Islamic community. Much the same could be said of Afghānī: his insistence that Islam is

---

[13] See pt. 2, "The Benefits of Philosophy," p. 114.

[14] "Lecture on Teaching and Learning," *Maqālāt-i jamāliyyeh* (Tehran, 1312/ 1933–34), pp. 88–96; translated below.

[15] For a convincing argument on the rationalism of the Koran as compared with the Old and New Testaments, see the rich and brilliant book of Maxime Rodinson, *Islam et capitalisme* (Paris, 1966), chap. iv.

compatible with reason and modern science is not only defensive, but even more an attempt to make Islam conform to his rationalist ideal. This has not been clear, as Afghānī did not say explicitly in his widely publicized writings that he was holding up an ideal rather than describing Islam as it existed. The "Answer to Renan" and other evidence show that he had a much less exalted view of Islam than a superficial reading of the "Refutation" would suggest.

According to the philosophers, only the select few could be persuaded by scientific, demonstrative argument, while for the masses only emotional rhetoric would be persuasive. The common people should be told not to pay any attention to abstract intellectual matters. They should not be told the true interpretation (ta'wīl) of revelation, for expedient reasons. The Prophet Muhammad was assumed to have upheld law and revelation with the concrete images and material rewards and punishments that alone would be effective in keeping the masses believing and hence obedient. The Prophet was also supposed to have strewn the Koran with hints of the rational truth, which could only be appreciated by the philosophically minded. This procedure of scattering hints to the elite in texts directed to the masses was also followed by the philosophers themselves.

Avicenna, among several such references, says of the relation of a prophet to the masses:

> It is not necessary for him to trouble their minds with any part of the knowledge of God, save the knowledge that He is One, True, and has no like; as for going beyond this doctrine, so as to charge them to believe in God's existence as not to be defined spatially or verbally divisible, as being neither without the world nor within it, or anything of that sort—to do this would impose a great strain upon them and would confuse the religious system which they follow already, bringing them to a pass wherefrom only those rare souls can escape who enjoy especial favour, and they exceedingly uncommon. The generality of mankind cannot imagine these things as they really are except by hard toil; few indeed are they who can conceive the truth of Divine Unity and Sublimity. The rest are soon apt to disbelieve in this sort of Being, or they fall down upon the road and go off into discussions and speculations which prevent them from attending to their bodily acts, and often enough cause

them to fall into opinions contrary to the good of society and inconsistent with the requirements of truth. In such circumstances their doubts and difficulties would multiply, and it would be hard indeed by words to control them: not every man is ready to understand metaphysics, and in any case it would not be proper for any man to disclose that he is in possession of a truth which he conceals from the masses; indeed, he must not allow himself so much as to hint at any such thing. His duty is to teach men to know the Majesty and Might of God by means of symbols and parables drawn from things which they regard as mighty and majestic, imparting to them simply this much, that God has no equal, no like and no partner.

Similarly he must establish in them the belief in an after-life, in a manner that comes within the range of their imagination and will be satisfying to their souls; he will liken the happiness and misery there to be experienced in terms which they can understand and conceive. As for the truth of these matters, he will only adumbrate it to them very briefly, saying that it is something which "eye hath not seen nor ear heard." . . . There is therefore no harm in his discourse being interspersed with sundry hints and allusions, to attract those naturally qualified for speculation to undertake philosophical research. . . .[16]

Afghānī's "Refutation" shows a similar concern with the practical virtues of religion for the social order, an idea frequently mentioned by the philosophers. He also follows the philosophers' injunction to intersperse his text with brief hints for the benefit of the more philosophically minded. Avicenna, who made the statement quoted above, was the most influential philosopher in the Iranian tradition, and was one whose books Afghānī owned, annotated, and taught.

The Islamic philosophers were, like Afghānī, opposed to material-ism and naturalism, which they thought would corrupt man into following only his base appetites. They said also that any deviation from literalist revelation, even in the direction of philosophy, was dangerous for the masses, as it gave rise to sects and schisms that split the Muslim community. Thus Averroes, in his *Decisive Treatise* on the harmony of religion and philosophy, says:

---

[16] *Avicenna on Theology*, trans. A. J. Arberry (London, 1951), pp. 44–45.

The reason why we have received a Scripture with both an apparent and an inner meaning lies in the diversity of people's natural capacities and the difference of their innate dispositions with regard to assent. The reason we have received in Scripture texts whose apparent meanings contradict each other is in order to draw the attention of those who are well grounded in science to the interpretation which reconciles them.

... There are ... apparent texts which have to be interpreted allegorically by men of the demonstrative class; for such men to take them in their apparent meaning is unbelief, while for those who are not of the demonstrative class to interpret them allegorically and take them out of their apparent meaning is unbelief or heresy on their part. ...

It was due to allegorical interpretations—especially the false ones—and the supposition that such interpretations of Scripture ought to be expressed to everyone, that the sects of Islam arose, with the result that each one accused the others of unbelief or heresy. Thus the Mu'tazilites interpreted many verses and Traditions allegorically, and expressed their interpretations to the masses, and the Ash-'arites did the same, although they used such interpretations less frequently. In consequence they threw people into hatred, mutual detestation, and wars, tore the Scriptures to shreds, and completely divided people.[17]

Summarizing from this and other passages, George Hourani says that two reasons are given by Averroes for the prohibition of allegorical interpretation outside the elite:

One is that to teach allegorical interpretations to people who cannot understand them breaks down their religion, since it undermines their belief in the apparent meaning of scripture and sets nothing in its place. ... The second reason for the prohibition is that an interest in allegories by people who are unable to understand them properly gives rise to dissensions and strife in Islam through the growth of sects, each with a particular doctrine. ... In im-

---

[17] Averroes, *On the Harmony of Religion and Philosophy*, trans. and ed. George F. Hourani, (London, 1961), pp. 51, 59, 68.

posing these restrictions, ibn-Rushd is following a strong philosophic tradition. It is probable that by them he hoped to break the force of criticism of his defence of philosophy. . . .[18]

Afghānī's attacks in the "Refutation" on the sects and schisms that arise from weakening the masses' faith in their religion clearly echo those of the philosophers. Like the philosophers he was concerned to defend himself against charges of heresy and to gain for himself a recognized place with Muslim rulers and ulama. Even more than the philosophers he was concerned to foster the unity of the Islamic community and discourage schisms. At most, he could hint to the attentive and philosophically aware reader that he was not indulging in an absolute defense of Islam as it then was, as a surface reading might make it appear.

The methods of the philosophers were useful to Afghānī's position with rulers and ulama, and to encourage Muslim solidarity, but they were hardly appropriate for enlightening the masses and encouraging them to work for reform. True, the "Refutation" might strengthen the masses' confidence in their own culture, which was perhaps important after European cultural and material attacks. On the other hand, by providing a tool to attack reformers as unbelievers and by its ambiguity concerning the need for reform in the Islamic community, the treatise could discourage reform efforts and reinforce the hold of the conservative ulama and of tradition. The "Refutation" is one of many indications that Afghānī, when forced to choose between reform and Muslim solidarity against the West, opted for the latter.[19]

---

[18] George F. Hourani, "Ibn-Rushd's Defence of Philosophy," in *The World of Islam*, ed. James Kritzeck and R. Bayly Winder (London, 1960), pp. 155–156.

[19] This is clearly indicated in a rarely cited exchange that took place in 1883 between Afghānī and Khalīl Ghānim, a liberal Ottoman Arab whose newspaper criticized the Sultan. Afghānī wrote an open letter in Ghānim's paper taking him to task for criticizing Abdülhamid. In the face of Western encroachments, he said, unity of all Muslims in supporting the Sultan is the most important thing; the reforms Ghānim was seeking could come later, but attacks on the Sultan now could only weaken the primary goal of unity (*Al-Bāṣir*, no. 66, Feb. 8, 1883). The article is briefly summarized in Kedourie, *op. cit.* Thanks to Mrs. Homa Pakdaman of Paris for lending me photocopies of this exchange with Ghānim. The whole exchange is interesting in that it indicates two different approaches to the late nineteenth-century crisis of the Muslim world. It deserves to be translated from the Arabic and published.

In his pragmatic view of the function of revealed religion Afghānī also follows the philosophical tradition. This tradition saw the role of prophecy as chiefly legal and social. The philosophers had a pessimistic view of human nature, and thought that men could be brought to obey laws only if they thought them divinely sanctioned and backed by rewards and punishments in the next world. In some philosophical works, notably those of Ibn Khaldūn, the generally positive social role given religion is extended to include its ideological enforcement for group solidarity. Military conquests, social cohesion, and self-sacrifice are all results of such a firmly believed religion. All these notions are found, at times in somewhat modernized garb, in the works of Afghānī.

The
Indian
Background

IN ADDITION to its general background in Afghānī's life and in the Muslim philosophical tradition, the "Refutation of the Materialists" should be understood against its immediate background in the Muslim world, and especially India. The most direct and immediate aim of the book was to attack the ideas of Sir Sayyid Ahmad Khān, the most prominent Indian Muslim reformer of the period. To some who had known Afghānī before he wrote this book it caused surprise, because Afghānī until its appearance had been considered, as was Ahmad Khān, a supporter of unorthodox, heretical, and rationalist ideas.

The Government of India documents, Wilfrid Blunt's reports in *India under Ripon*, and Afghānī's writings from 1880 on all suggest that during his Indian stay of 1880–1882 Afghānī began to try to shake off his heretical reputation and present himself as a defender of orthodoxy. The "Refutation of the Materialists" is the *first* of Afghānī's writings in which he presents himself as a champion of Islamic orthodoxy against heretical and Western-oriented tendencies. From the scanty evidence concerning this Indian stay, what can be suggested about the reasons for this change?

First, Afghānī was following a trend already strong in the Muslim

world, as noted above. Various Western incursions had so strengthened anti-Western and pan-Islamic feelings throughout the Islamic
world that even many Muslim liberals were moved in a more pro-
Islamic direction.

Second, Afghānī, as he told Blunt, had noticed the rise in positive
feeling toward the Ottoman Sultan in India, which is also noted in
the Government of India documents as having occurred particularly
during the Russo-Turkish War of 1877–78. Blunt records in his
diary a conversation with Afghānī in 1883 about Blunt's projected
Indian trip:

> I asked him about the language I should most prudently
> hold regarding the Sultan, and he advised me to say nothing
> against the Sultan in India, or about an Arabian Caliphate;
> it had been spread about that the English were going to set
> up a sham Caliphate in Arabia, under a child, whom they
> would use to make themselves masters of the holy places;
> the Sultan's name was now venerated in India as it had not
> formerly been.[20]

Knowing the Sultan's position as a defender of Islam and the Indian
Muslims' positive attitude toward this, Afghānī may have tried to
increase his own popularity and influence by presenting himself also
as a great defender of Islam. In addition, the "Refutation of the
Materialists" may have had as one of its goals to ingratiate Afghānī
with the Sultan, particularly as it includes remarks calculated to
please him.[21]

Third, Afghānī saw in India that the most strongly Westernizing
group among the Indian Muslims, the followers of Sayyid Ahmad
Khān, were the partisans of his greatest enemies, the British. Sayyid
Ahmad Khān and his followers were at this time exerting a growing
influence upon the educated youth of India, but were opposed by
the religious conservatives. Ahmad Khān's enemies claimed he believed in nothing but nature, and dubbed his group the *Neicheriyya*,
the followers of nature. Afghānī's "Refutation" is specifically directed against this group, and its original Persian title is "The Truth
about the Neicheri Sect and an Explanation of the Neicheris." Only

---

[20] Wilfrid Blunt, *India under Ripon* (London, 1909), p. 13.
[21] See Niyazi Berkes, *The Development of Secularism in Turkey* (Montreal, 1964), pp. 266–267.

when it was translated into Arabic was the local reference, which was meaningless outside India, dropped from the title and the title "Refutation of the Materialists" given to the work (an abbreviation of the title used by 'Abduh, who did the Arabic version).

The "Refutation of the Materialists" can be better understood in the perspective of a series of articles and talks that Afghānī produced during this Indian stay and in which attacks on Ahmad Khān constitute one of a group of interrelated themes. While in India, Afghānī wrote a number of articles and gave lectures that were published. All were in the Persian language and they have received little publicity among non-Persian readers; yet these articles shed important light on Afghānī's mode of thought and discourse at this crucial transitional period of his life. Six of these articles were written for the first issues of a Hyderabad journal *Muʿallim-i Shafīq*, of which Afghānī may have been the inspirer and main writer. Five additional articles and lectures were published along with these original six in the first edition of the collected articles of Afghānī, *Maqālāt-i jamāliyyeh*, published in Calcutta in 1884.[22]

The contents of these articles may be discussed most conveniently according to their major themes. First of all, they are perhaps as interesting for what they omit as for what they contain. There is no mention of pan-Islam or of any scheme to unite the Muslims behind one leader, the ideas with which Afghānī was to become so intimately associated after he left India. On the contrary, there are local nationalist ideas that might seem at variance with pan-Islam. There is no mention of a particular Muslim leader or nation as a source of inspiration or emulation. There is also very little of the Islamic apologetics that were to be associated with Afghānī's style of argument; there is some, but much more defense of science and philosophy than of Islam. The defense of Islam usually comes in only as part of an attack on Sir Sayyid Ahmad Khān. These articles thus give a different picture of Afghānī than comes from reading only the "Refutation" and *al-ʿUrwa al-Wuthqā*. The articles show Afghānī's line of argument before he became primarily concerned to present himself as a defender of Islam and of pan-Islam.

Three striking themes of Afghānī's Indian articles are: (1) Advocacy of nationalism of a linguistic or territorial variety, meaning

[22] Iraj Afshār and Aṣghar Mahdavī, *Documents inédits concernant Seyyed Jamāl-al-Dīn Afghānī* (Tehran, 1963), pp. 26–27.

unity of Indian Hindus and Muslims, with little said about the unity of Indian Muslims with foreign Muslims. (2) Stress on the benefits of philosophy and modern science. (3) Attacks on Sir Sayyid Ahmad Khān as a tool of the foreigners.

On the first, nationalistic theme, there are two striking articles, both of which contradict the notion of Afghani as a consistent lifetime pan-Islamist. One is an article for *Mu'allim-i Shafīq* entitled, significantly, "The Philosophy of National Unity and the Truth about Unity of Language." This article starts with an Arabic heading: "There is no happiness except in nationality, and there is no nationality except in language, and a language cannot be called a language except if it embraces all affairs that those in manufacture and trade need for explanation and use in their work." Afghānī begins his article with an introduction that tries to show the significance of his subject in terms of man and the world in general, much in the manner of many of the medieval Islamic philosophers. In the course of this he notes that a common language is necessary to bring together scattered individuals, tribes, and groups into one nation that can work as a unit. He then goes on to express a preference for linguistic over religious ties as factors that are durable in the world:

> In the human world the bonds that have been extensive . . . have been two. One is this same unity of language of which nationality and national unity consist, and the other is religion. There is no doubt that the unity of language is more durable for survival and permanence in this world than unity of religion since it does not change in a short time in contrast to the latter. We see that a single people with one language in the course of a thousand years changes its religion two or three times without its nationality, which consists of unity of language, being destroyed. One may say that the ties and the unity that arise from the unity of language have more influence than religious ties in most affairs of the world.[23]

---

23 *Maqālāt-i jamāliyyeh*, pp. 75–87. This article has been partially translated into French by Mehdi Hendessi, "Pages peu connues de Djamal ad-Din al-Afghani," *Orient*, 6 (1958), 123–128. The translations here are from the Persian original.

After giving examples to show that linguistic ties are more important than religious ones, Afghānī goes on to say that a language can play its vital unifying function only if it has all the terms needed for the useful knowledge and arts of civilization. If these terms are lacking they should be invented, preferably from one's own linguistic stock. He states that teaching and learning should be done in the national language, which will encourage ties to the national past and make learning accessible to more people than if teaching is done in a foreign language. Encouragement of a national language is a requisite to national unity and patriotism; thus Indians should translate modern knowledge into their own languages, especially Urdu.

At the end of his article Afghānī attacks two main targets of his Indian writings—on the one hand the religious conservatives who oppose Western learning, and on the other, Sayyid Ahmad Khān and his followers, or the *Neicheriyya*. He says that anyone who refers to the principles of the *sharīʿa* (Islamic law) will know that the spread of science and learning is in no way against religion; on the contrary, useful knowledge strengthens religion, since its strength comes from that of its adherents, and their strength from wealth, position, and glory. On the other hand, if some "Indian ropedancer" *(neicheri)* claims that the English must be followed in everything, including their language, this will help lose India its nationhood and bring about complete conquest by the English. English arts and industries are necessary, but they should be spread through translation into one's own language.[24]

If one reads this article as a whole, it becomes clear that its purpose, like that of nearly all Afghānī's writings, is pragmatic rather than abstract. Within the Indian context of the time, it is quite clear why he stressed the importance of linguistic unity and the use of local languages, and deprecated the importance of religious unity. In the Indian phase of his activities Afghānī's primary anti-imperialist, and especially anti-British, purpose was best served by an emphasis on those factors that united Indians, and distinguished them from the British. Afghānī is not writing a theoretical tract on the relative weight of religion and language in human affairs, but rather an appeal to the Indians to utilize their own languages as the vehicle for the spread of modern knowledge. He is arguing on

---

[24] *Loc. cit.*

two fronts: against traditionalists who wished to maintain traditional learning in the old languages as it was, and against the modernizers who supported the British method of higher education and the spread of modern ideas through the medium of English. The remarks downgrading the importance of religious unity were probably based on a desire to see Indians of all religions united against the British. Nowhere in his writings does Afghānī appear as any kind of Muslim communalist or separatist in relation to India.

Afghānī's pragmatic approach to the problem of encouraging effective anti-imperialist activities frequently involved him in logical contradictions in his arguments. What he considered the best argument for a mixed Muslim-Hindu audience in India might be quite different from the arguments he used in his pan-Islamic writings from Paris, directed not especially at India but at the entire Muslim world. Thus we find in an article written in al-'Urwa al-Wuthqā in 1884 that Afghānī makes points almost directly opposed to those on nationality and religion in his Indian articles. Using the same word for nationality, jinsiyya, as he did in India, he now finds it something to blame rather than praise. He sees nationalism as a phase of tribalism that the Muslims have overcome. Muslims, he says, having passed this tribal stage, are bound by more universal ties, and are no longer concerned with racial and ethnic questions.[25]

Afghānī's appeal while in India to Indian unity rather than to pan-Islamic sentiment is even more clearly shown in a talk he gave while in Calcutta in 1882. The content of this lecture makes it clear that it was directed to a primarily Muslim audience, but its opening passages recall the assertions of the extreme Hindu nationalists. After saying he was happy at the presence of Indian youth at his lecture, Afghānī went on:

> Certainly I must be happy to see such offspring of India, since they are the offshoots of that India that was the cradle of humanity. Human values spread out from India to the whole world. These youths are from the very land where the meridian circle was first determined. They are from the

---

25 "Pages choisies de Djamal al-din al-Afghani: La Nationalité (djinsiya) et la religion musulmane," trans. M. Colombe (from al-'Urwa al-Wuthqā, no. 2, March 20, 1884), Orient, 22 (1962), 125–130.

same realm that first understood the zodiac. Everyone knows that the determination of these two circles is impossible until perfection in geometry is achieved. Thus we can say that the Indians were the inventors of arithmetic and geometry. Note how Indian numerals were transferred from here to the Arabs, and from there to Europe.

These youths are also the sons of a land that was the source of all the laws and rules of the world. If one observes closely, he will see that the "Code Romain," the mother of all western codes, was taken from the four *vedas* and the *shastras*. The Greeks were the pupils of the Indians in literary ideas, limpid poetry, and lofty thoughts. One of these pupils, Pythagoras, spread sciences and wisdom in Greece and reached such a height that his word was accepted without proof as an inspiration from heaven.

[The Indians] reached the highest level in philosophic thought. The soil of India is the same soil; the air of India is the same air; and these youths who are present here are fruits of the same earth and climate.[26]

The appeal to Indian Muslims to take pride in the Hindu past was, in the situation of the time, no stranger than Afghānī's earlier appeal to Egyptian Muslims to take pride in, and inspiration from, pre-Islamic Egyptian greatness. In both instances Afghānī was appealing to what appeared to be the most effective basis for solidarity against the foreigner. In Egypt, and even more in India, a stress on Muslim unity alone would have been more a divisive than a uniting factor in the antiforeign struggle.

It is within the context of pragmatic anti-imperialist and antiforeign goals that one can make sense of Afghānī's contradictory writings on national versus religious ties. The Indian writings are one of the major pieces of evidence indicating that Afghānī was a late convert to pan-Islam, not a lifetime devotee. Like other Persian sources on Afghānī, these writings have scarcely been utilized in arriving at an assessment of his life and ideas.

If the encouragement of nonreligious nationalism is the most unexpected feature of Afghānī's Indian writings, it is not the only ele-

---

[26] See pt. 2, "Lecture on Teaching and Learning," pp. 101–102.

ment that sheds light on his thought in addition to that which comes from his better-known Arabic writings. The second major feature mentioned above is Afghānī's stress on the benefits of modern science and philosophy. Here the picture of Afghānī that emerges is quite different from what a superficial reading of the "Refutation of the Materialists" and other "pro-Islamic" writings would indicate. Insofar as Afghānī speaks of Islam in these articles, unless it is as a source of anti-imperialist solidarity, it is in an effort to prove that true Islam is favorable to philosophy and science. The effort is clearly to convince nineteenth-century religious conservatives that they should favor modern science and philosophy; not, as in superficially similar articles written in a much more recent context, to convince modern Westernizers that Islam is in accord with their scientific values. Afghānī's arguments, however close to those of modern apologetics, have quite a different goal.[27]

In his 1882 lecture in Calcutta, "On Teaching and Learning," the opening of which is cited above, Afghānī's main stress was on the importance of modern science and philosophy. After praising the Indian past, Afghānī states: "If someone looks deeply into the question, he will see that science rules the world. There was, is, and will be no ruler in the world but science."[28] Afghānī goes on to state that all great empires have been supported by science, up to and including the European conquerors of the present. Ignorance is always subjugated by science, which is the basis of advanced technology in all fields. Afghānī then takes up the medieval philosophers' concept of philosophy as the organizing soul of the sciences:

> Thus a science is needed to be the comprehensive soul for all the sciences, so that it can preserve their existence, apply each of them in its proper place, and become the cause of the progress of each one of those sciences.
>
> The science that has the position of a comprehensive soul and the rank of a preserving force is the science of *falsafa* or philosophy, because its subject is universal. It is philosophy

---

27 The contrast between Afghānī's concern to arouse the Muslims to act in new ways and the apologists' desire to restore admiration for Islam is illuminated by the excellent characterization of contemporary Islamic apologetics in Wilfred C. Smith, *Islam in Modern History* (Princeton, 1957), pp. 85–89.

28 See p. 102.

that shows man human prerequisites. It shows the sciences what is necessary. It employs each of the sciences in its proper place.

If a community did not have philosophy, and all the individuals of that community were learned in the sciences with particular subjects, those sciences could not last in that community for a century, that is, a hundred years. That community without the spirit of philosophy could not deduce conclusions from these sciences.

. . . I may say that if the spirit of philosophy were found in a community, even if that community did not have one of those sciences whose subject is particular, undoubtedly their philosophic spirit would call for the acquisition of all the sciences.

The first Muslims had no science, but, thanks to the Islamic religion, a philosophic spirit arose among them, and owing to that philosophic spirit they began to discuss the general affairs of the world and human necessities. This was why they acquired in a short time all the sciences with particular subjects that they translated from the Syriac, Persian, and Greek into the Arabic language at the time of Manṣūr Davānaqī.

It is philosophy that makes man understandable to man, explains human nobility, and shows man the proper road. The first defect appearing in any nation that is headed toward decline is in the philosophic spirit. After that deficiencies spread into the other sciences, arts, and associations.[29]

The only thing for which Islam is praised here is that it prepared the way for science and philosophy, which are the real sources of knowledge. In another passage the modernized schools erected by the Ottomans and Egyptians are criticized, not for being irreligious, but on the contrary, for lacking a philosophical basis for the sciences they teach.

Afghānī goes on to a strong criticism of the Muslim ulama for its blindness and hostility toward modern science and technology:

---

[29] See pp. 104–105.

The strangest thing of all is that our ulama these days have divided science into two parts. One they call Muslim science, and one European science. Because of this they forbid others to teach some of the useful sciences. They have not understood that science is that noble thing that has no connection with any nation, and is not distinguished by anything but itself. Rather, everything that is known is known by science, and every nation that becomes renowned becomes renowned through science. Men must be related to science, not science to men.

How very strange it is that the Muslims study those sciences that are ascribed to Aristotle with the greatest delight, as if Aristotle were one of the pillars of the Muslims. However, if the discussion relates to Galileo, Newton, and Kepler, they consider them infidels. The father and mother of science is proof, and proof is neither Aristotle nor Galileo. The truth is where there is proof, and those who forbid science and knowledge in the belief that they are safeguarding the Islamic religion are really the enemies of that religion. The Islamic religion is the closest of religions to science and knowledge, and there is no incompatibility between science and knowledge and the foundation of the Islamic faith.[30]

To support his appeal to science, Afghānī cites the great theologian al-Ghazālī, although he does not mention Ghazālī's hostility to philosophy. Afghānī concludes his talk by saying that no reform is possible in Muslim countries until Muslim leaders and ulama have reformed their outlook, and notes that the decline of Muslim countries began with these leaders.

In an article in *Mu'allim-i Shafīq* entitled "The Benefits of Philosophy," Afghānī is even more forthright about his praise of philosophy above religion, and his view of the original Islamic revelation as a step on the road toward the higher truth of philosophy. In this article Afghānī begins with a series of questions about the meaning and aims of philosophy, ending with an interesting list of names that one may assume were included in his own philosophical knowledge: "Is complete satisfaction to be found in the works of Fārābī, Ibn Sīnā, Ibn Bājja, Shihāb ad-Dīn the Martyr, Mīr Bāqir, Mullā Sadrā, and the other treatises and notes concerned with philosophy,

---

[30] See p. 107.

or is it not?"[31] He goes on to state that the difficulties and special terminology of classic philosophic texts have rendered them unknown to most people. Therefore he renounces these traditional modes, and offers this explanation:

> Philosophy is the escape from the narrow sensations of animality into the wide arena of human feelings. It is the removal of the darkness of bestial superstitions with the light of natural intelligence; the transformation of blindness and lack of insight into clearsightedness and insight. It is salvation from savagery and barbarism, ignorance and foolishness, by entry into the virtuous city of knowledge and skillfulness.[32] In general, it is man's becoming man and living the life of sacred rationality. Its aim is human perfection in reason, mind, soul, and way of life. Perfection in one's way of life and welfare in livelihood are the chief preconditions for the perfection of mind and soul. [Philosophy] is the first cause of man's intellectual activity and his emergence from the sphere of animals, and it is the greatest reason for the transfer of tribes and peoples from a state of nomadism and savagery to culture and civilization. It is the foremost cause of the production of knowledge, the creation of sciences, the invention of industries, and the initiation of the crafts.[33]

In this article Afghānī comes close to a frank statement on the relations of Islam and philosophy; the revelation brought by Muhammad is seen as a necessary stage in bringing the Arabs from the ignorance and bestiality of their pre-Islamic savagery to a phase in which they were prepared to accept the higher truths of philosophy. Significant and striking is Afghānī's criticism of traditional Islamic

---

31 Al-Fārābī, died A.D. 950, and Ibn Sīnā (Avicenna), d. 1037, were two of the greatest masters, commentators, and developers of Greek and Hellenistic philosophy in Eastern Islam; as were Ibn Bājja (Avempace), d. 1138, and Ibn Rushd (Averroes), d. 1198, in Muslim Spain. Shihāb ad-Dīn Suhrawardī "the Executed," d. 1191, was the Persian founder of a more mystical "illuminationist" philosophy; while the seventeenth-century Persian philosophers Mīr Bāqir, better known as Mīr Dāmād, and his pupil, Mullā Ṣadrā, tried to reconcile mysticism, rationalism, and Shiʿi beliefs.

32 The phrase "the virtuous city" comes from a work of that name by Fārābī.

33 See pt. 2, "The Benefits of Philosophy," p. 110.

philosophy. Although his terminology and detailed arguments are often obscure, particularly to one without advanced training in Islamic philosophy, the main points are clear enough. The Muslim philosophers are criticized for accepting the arguments of the Greeks as absolute and final, which the Greeks themselves did not do. The Muslim thinkers thus accepted blind imitation, whereas, Afghānī states, philosophy and science are continually growing and developing subjects. Afghānī in an earlier passage bases this infinite growth of philosophy on the mystical idea of the infinity of meanings in the Koran.[34] Further, the Muslim philosophers are blamed for incorporating into their books some ideas that are not really philosophical, but come from the polytheistic cosmogony of the ancients, and they also incorporated some arguments that are imperfect and incomplete.

Afghānī is chiefly concerned in this article with an appeal to the ulama to apply rationalist methods to burning modern problems, instead of continuing their traditional scholastic discussions. Addressing the Indian ulama, he says:

> Why do you not raise your eyes from those defective books and why do you not cast your glance on this wide world? Why do you not employ your reflection and thought on events and their causes without the veils of those works? Why do you always utilize those exalted minds on trifling problems. . . .
>
> Yet you spend no thought on this question of great importance, incumbent on every intelligent man, which is: What is the cause of the poverty, indigence, helplessness, and distress of the Muslims, and is there a cure for this important phenomenon and great misfortune or not? . . .
>
> There is no doubt or question that if someone does not spend his whole life on this great problem, and does not make this grievous phenomenon the pivot of his thought, he has wasted and ruined his life, and it is improper to call him a sage, which means one who knows the essential conditions of beings. . . .
>
> Is it not a fault for a percipient sage not to learn the entire sphere of new sciences and inventions and fresh creations, when he has no information about their causes and reasons,

---

[34] See p. 114.

and when the world has changed from one state to another
and he does not raise his head from the sleep of neglect?
Is it worthy of an investigator that he speak in absolute
ignorance and not know what is definitely known? He splits
hairs over imaginary essences and lags behind in the knowledge of evident matters.[35]

This article is one of several indications that Afghānī had adopted
a progressive notion of the evolution of human knowledge. Islam is
incorporated into this notion by saying: first, that it raised the Arabs
from a state of barbarism and ignorance to one of civilization and rationality; second, that it encouraged the development of philosophy
among them; and third, that since the meanings of the Koran are
infinite and encompass all potential knowledge, no one stage of
philosophy can be taken as final and perfect. Afghānī criticizes his
contemporaries for assuming such finality and perfection for a state
of knowledge that may have been appropriate to the past, but is now
superseded.

In defending rationalism, reform, and science, while attacking on
nationalist grounds the main defenders of these modern virtues
among Indian Muslims—Sayyid Ahmad Khān and his school—Afghānī had to walk a thin and easily misinterpreted line. Like other
nationalists, and like the Islamic modernists who followed him, his
general argument for defending Islam, nationalism, and modernism
at the same time was to claim that modern virtues originated with
Islam, and that the Muslims who rejected them were acting against
the principles of their own religion. Like the early modernists of
many cultures, Afghānī apparently believed and hoped that the
rational attitudes and scientific innovations so necessary to self-
strengthening against the foreigner could be adopted without the
foreigners' cultural and linguistic baggage, the acquisition of which
he feared would disrupt national and religious unity and encourage
passive admiration for foreign conquerors.

In one of his Indian articles, "The True Causes of Man's Happiness and Distress," Afghānī includes both a call to nationalist zeal
and a warning against rejection of foreign science and innovation.
Afghānī begins by noting that all human qualities exist to benefit
man, but if men exaggerate in any of them this leads to evils. He

[35] See pp. 120–122.

then praises as good, though pointing out the dangers of their excess, such qualities as human appetites, love of life, striving for superior accomplishments, love of renown, the desire to serve humanity, the desire to know about other peoples and the history of the world, and the desire to know the causes of events and the properties and influences of things. Coming to the virtues of patriotic and religious zeal, and the dangers of their excess, Afghānī says:

> The desire to protect fatherland and nationality (*watan wa jins*) and the wish to defend religion and coreligionists, that is, patriotic zeal, national zeal, and religious zeal, arouse man to compete in the arena of virtues and accomplishments. They cause the adherents of religions and the members of nations, tribes, and peoples to strive to raise themselves. They make each of them employ his own effort and striving to attain the bases of greatness and glory and the means to power and majesty.

> It is this desire that leads nations and the followers of religions to climb the steps of nobility, and to acquire, through striving, all the distinctions of the human world. It is this desire that kindles the fire of zeal in souls. It is this desire that does not permit men to be satisfied with baseness. It is this desire that unites multifarious groups to erect the castle of glory and honor. It calls man to the preservation of public rights and arouses him to the protection of the fatherland and the defense of the honor of religion.

> But this sacred desire must not become the motive for the nullification of rights and the cause of oppression and injustice toward others. Nor should it become the cause of improper hatreds and useless enmities, since the heart was not created in order to be the house of hatred and the temple of enmity.

> Having reached this point, I wish to say with a thousand regrets that the Muslims of India have applied the desire to defend religion, or religious zeal, in a very bad way. For they have carried zeal, through misuse, to a point where it has become a cause of hatred for knowledge and the sciences, and a reason for aversion toward industries and innovation. They believed they must, out of religious zeal, hate and abominate what was connected with the opponents of faith, even though these things were sciences and arts.

Whereas, what was incumbent upon them from religious zeal was, whenever they saw a virtue, an accomplishment, a science, or a piece of knowledge, knowing themselves to be the first and rightest, to strive and make efforts to acquire it, and not to allow the opponents of the Islamic true religion to take precedence over them in any one among the virtues and accomplishments. A thousand regrets for this misuse of religious zeal, which finally will result in destruction and overthrow! I fear that the misuse of religious zeal by the Muslims of India has reached the point that the Muslims will, entirely washing their hands of life, abandon living because the opponents of the Islamic faith live in this world![36]

In addition to its recommendation of simultaneous attachment to one's own culture and willingness to borrow from others where this is useful, Afghānī's article is interesting for the explicit equivalence it expresses between patriotism and religious faith. Both are seen as leading to the same virtues. Indeed, after Afghānī's first sentence, which already implies equivalence between the "desire to protect fatherland and nationality and the wish to defend religion," both sentiments are treated as a single antecedent in Afghānī's subsequent references to "this desire." Here is one of many hints suggesting why it was so easy for Afghānī to pass back and forth among the defense of local nationalism, pan-Islam, and zeal for the defense of the Islamic religion.

It is within the context of Afghānī's anti-imperialist nationalism on the one hand, and his philosophic rationalism on the other, that the true import of his attack on Sir Sayyid Ahmad Khān—the third point stressed in his Indian articles—can be understood. The attack was not, as is sometimes thought, on Ahmad Khān's rationalism, reformism, and scant orthodoxy, all of which Afghānī shared. It was actually directed against Sayyid Ahmad Khān's belief in cooperation with the British rather than in nationalist opposition, and against his willingness to borrow as much as possible from the British and openly to abandon much of the Indian Muslim heritage, thus ridding the Indian Muslims of a source of nationalist, anti-imperialist pride.

The nationalist and anti-imperialist thrust of Afghānī's attacks on

---

[36] *Maqālāt-i jamāliyyeh*, pp. 130–131.

Sayyid Ahmad Khān is clearer from Afghānī's Persian and Arabic articles about him than it is from the "Refutation of the Materialists." Afghānī's longest Persian article about Ahmad Khān was called "A Description of the Aghūrīs." The Aghūrīs were a small, despised Indian sect, and Afghānī applied the name to the followers of Ahmad Khān as a piece of vituperation. According to one story, Afghānī inquired to find the name of the most despised sect in the Hyderabad area in order to apply it to the followers of Ahmad Khān.[37]

In this article, after an introduction saying that the blind, ignorant, and traitorous consider themselves clearsighted, wise, and courageous, Afghānī goes on to a specific attack on those who wish to harm their brothers in the interest of foreigners. "Why should someone who destroys the life-spirit of a people be called their well-wisher; why should a person who works for the decline of his faith be considered a sage? What ignorance is this?"[38] Afghānī queries.

In an oblique but clear attack on those who would follow the British path in education, Afghānī then asks whether one whose interests lie in the ignorance, corruption, and blindness of someone else would try to educate him to wisdom and cure his blindness.

Afghānī goes on to say that there are three types of education. First, a man can be educated to be part of a nation (qaum), and to serve its social order, which in turn will be his guardian. Second, education can be based on the interests of the individual, with no regard for the nation. And finally, education can be based on the interests of foreigners, of benefit to a group of which the pupil forms no part. With the third type, can one imagine that a man would learn to serve his nation and community? It would be a thousand times better to have no education at all than to have one that harms one's own nation. Only from the first kind of education can national unity be produced. In view of this it is impossible to imagine that foreigners [i.e., the British rulers of India] would support the first, national, type of education; they have certainly not come in order to strengthen the nationalism and community feeling (jinsiyya and qaumiyya) of others.

Returning to his attacks on the Ahmad Khān group, who are never named directly, Afghānī says that someone who embraces the killers

37 Qāzī Muḥammad 'Abd al-Ghaffār, Āsār-i Jamāl ad-Dīn Afghānī (Delhi, 1940), pp. 122–123, citing a man in Hyderabad who remembered Afghānī's stay there.
38 "Sharḥ-i ḥāl-i Aghūriyān bā shaukat wa sha'n," Maqālāt-i jamāliyyeh, p. 28.

of his brothers is the worst type of person. One sees such men putting out great efforts to strengthen the Christians by confirming the truth of the Torah and the Gospel.[39] These men teach slavery instead of freedom, and hence are obstacles to the progress of their people. They have no religion, and no interest other than to fill their own bellies. They use education only as a means to worldly goals. Here as elsewhere, Afghānī exaggerates the irreligion of Ahmad Khān's school, and vilifies them as "materialists" in the vulgar as well as philosophic sense.

In a passage that recalls Ibn Khaldūn and some of the other Muslim political philosophers, Afghānī goes on to say that when a community or nation is in a healthy state, it is under unified government, and all classes contribute their separate talents to the whole, like the various members of the human body. When that community's unity of thought is weakened, however, discord, division, vices, and corruption will ensue, and the society will become prey to foreign conquest and rule. Men who sow the seeds of disunity must thus be dealt with harshly.[40]

Afghānī then states that good habits can only be inculcated in a people through centuries of continuous education, and that interruption of this education with foreign ways can never produce the virtues found among foreigners, but can only be disruptive. The Aghūrīs in the schools are teaching the abandonment of virtues, disunity of the community (umma), and breaking the laws of humanity. They are opening the way of slavery to foreigners. They are like a dog who goes to a stranger rather than his own master just to get a bone. It is no cause for wonder that they act this way, but it is strange that others do not understand their acts and base aims. They try to call others to the road of perdition, claiming it is the road to salvation.[41]

In this article the nationalist basis of the attack on Sayyid Ahmad Khān and his school is clear. The group is attacked for undermining the unity of the community, and often it is even unclear whether the Indian community as a whole or the Indian Muslims are intended. The defense here is not, as it is in the "Refutation," of Islam as a religion, but of local customs as a shield against submission to

---

39 *Ibid.*, p. 33. The reference is to Ahmad Khān's unorthodox effort to show that the Bible was not, as Muslim doctrine stated, falsified.

40 *Ibid.*, pp. 38–40.

41 *Ibid.*, pp. 42–52.

foreign ways, which can only encourage slavery to foreigners. With almost no change of wording the entire article could apply to any group favoring wholesale introduction of the education and ways of foreign rulers in any colonial country—there is little reference to religion, much less to Islam specifically.

Afghānī's attack on the neicheris is thus essentially pragmatic, not doctrinal; Afghānī accuses them primarily of harming the Muslim community. It would in fact have been difficult for Afghānī to present a doctrinal argument, for his own ideas on religious reform, including greater rationalism, a return to the purer Islam of the early days, and a reopening of the door of interpretation, were very close to those of Ahmad Khān.[42] Blunt indicates that many of Afghānī's followers in India were associated with the Ahmad Khān school. The Government of India's Thagi and Dakaiti Department, which took some pains to gather information about Afghānī, reported regarding this period:

> He was in Hyderabad for about 20 months, and during his stay he associated chiefly with the rising generation of freethinkers, the followers of Sayad Ahmed of Aligarh. But in spite of all their kindness and hospitality towards him, he published a book in Persian against their doctrines.[43]

Indeed, Afghānī may have written the book partly because he was associated by others with the neicheris. Certainly it provided an ideal opportunity to try to cover up his own reputation for unorthodoxy.

The real basis for Afghānī's opposition to the Ahmad Khān school was political. Ahmad Khān worked for Muslim cooperation with

---

[42] For a detailed comparison showing the great similarity between the religious reform views of Afghānī and those of Sayyid Aḥmad Khān, see al-Mujāhid, *op. cit.*, chap. iv. For a comparison with different emphases see Aziz Ahmad, "Sayyid Aḥmad Khān, Jamāl al-dīn al-Afghānī and Muslim India," *Studia Islamica* XIII (1960), 55–78; a shorter version of this article appears in his *Studies in Islamic Culture in the Indian Environment* (Oxford, 1964), chap. iv.

[43] FO 60/594, memorandum by the Government of India, Thagi and Dakaiti Department, 1896. The accuracy of this report is doubted by Aziz Ahmad on the grounds that Aḥmad Khān had only a few followers in Hyderabad at this time, and they were not followers of Afghānī. Whatever the truth of this, the contemporary report from Sayyid Ḥusain Bilgrāmī, quoted in chap. i, n. 34, refers to Afghānī as a freethinker and radical westernizer.

the British, and implied that emulation of the British was necessary for reform. Such identification with the British lessened the possibility for an anti-British ideology, and tended to split the Muslim community. In fact, the neicheris were being listed as a separate sect on the Indian census. The political basis of Afghānī's attack is also shown in the article he wrote a few years later in *al-'Urwa al-Wuthqā*, "The Materialists in India," in which he specifies the objects of his attack much more directly than in the "Refutation." Here he says, in language very appropriate to the minds of the "people of rhetoric," as the philosophers called the masses:

> But Aḥmad Khān and his companions, just as they invited people to reject religion, [also] disparaged to them the interests of their fatherland and made people consider foreign domination over them a slight thing, and strove to erase the traces of religious and patriotic zeal. . . .
>
> These materialists became an army for the English government in India. They drew their swords to cut the throats of the Muslims, while weeping for them and crying: "We kill you only out of compassion and pity for you, and seeking to improve you and make your lives comfortable." The English saw that this was the most likely means to attain their goal: the weakness of Islam and the Muslims.[44]

The identification of religious and patriotic zeal was natural at a time when religious ideology was the main intellectual distinction between the Muslims and their foreign rulers, and in view of the long background of identification of the whole "Abode of Islam" as an entity against the "Abode of War." Afghānī was not the only Muslim of his period to combine nationalist and pan-Islamic ideals—both could be seen as part of the same coin of anti-imperialism.

In the same article Ahmad Khān is accused of *openly* casting doubt on Islamic dogma, which Afghānī did not do. Ahmad Khān was seen as weakening the Muslims' cohesion and resistance to the English.

The same point is made in another of Afghānī's articles directed against Ahmad Khān, this one written in the same period as the "Refutation" and the other Indian articles. It is called "Commen-

---

[44] See pt. 2, "The Materialists in India," pp. 178–179.

tary on the Commentator" (a reference to Ahmad Khān's commentary on the Koran), and is translated below. In this article Afghānī speaks of the need for a sage and renewer who will save the Muslims from their current condition of decline and corruption:

> There is no doubt that in the present age, distress, misfortune, and weakness besiege all classes of Muslims from every side. Therefore every Muslim keeps his eyes and ears open in expectation—to the East, West, North, and South— to see from what corner of the earth the sage and renewer will appear and will reform the minds and souls of the Muslims, repel the unforeseen corruption, and again educate them with a virtuous education. Perhaps through that good education they may return to their former joyful condition.[45]

Though Afghānī claims to have looked to Ahmad Khān (not named, but clearly indicated) as such a potential renewer, there seems little doubt that he actually pictured himself in this role. Afghānī is probably being frank when he goes on to object to Ahmad Khān's high evaluation of human nature; Afghānī here stands with the Muslim philosophical tradition. He does so also in his main point, that certain social benefits can only be assured by religious belief on the part of the masses:

> Even stranger is the fact that this commentator has lowered the divine, holy rank of prophecy and placed it on the level of the *reformer*. He has considered the prophets to be men like Washington, Napoleon, Palmerston, Garibaldi, Mister Gladstone, and Monsieur Gambetta. . . .
>
> Does he not understand that if the Muslims, in their current state of weakness and misery, did not believe in miracles and hell-fire, and considered the Prophet to be like Gladstone, they undoubtedly would soon abandon their own weak and conquered camp, and attach themselves to the powerful conqueror. For in that case there would no longer remain anything to prevent this, nor any fear or anxiety. And from another standpoint the prerequisites for changing religion now exist, since being like the conqueror, and having the same religion as he, is attractive to everyone.[46]

---

[45] See pt. 2, "Commentary on the Commentator," p. 125.
[46] *Ibid.*, p. 127.

Anything that undermines faith in Islam is thus seen as leading Indian Muslims to identification with their British conquerors, and it is this that Afghānī wants to avoid at all costs. Convinced of the political evils that would arise from the Muslims' following Ahmad Khān on his pro-British path, Afghānī could easily believe that all means, including the insincere rhetoric sanctioned by his tradition, were legitimate to discredit Ahmad Khān and his school.

The
"Refutation of
the Materialists"

With this background in mind, it is possible to take a fresh look at the "Refutation" itself. The main point to be noted throughout is its thoroughly pragmatic and this-worldly defense of religion. The virtues claimed for religion are purely social virtues. Like the philosophers, Afghānī repeatedly claims that religion is good for the people because it supports the social fabric, while the neicheris, like other sectarians, bring dissension and finally political ruin to the community.

Afghānī begins his work with a refutation of materialism as a theory of science. This section seems to be based partly on arguments traditional in the Muslim world and partly on often inaccurate things that Afghānī had heard about Darwin. Though his arguments against Darwin now seem foolish, it is worth remembering that at the time (1881) equally foolish arguments against Darwin were being made by educated people in the West.

Then Afghānī comes to his main argument. His first summary of his position is so close to the views and even the language of the philosophers on the utility of orthodoxy for the majority, and the harm brought by sects, that it is worth quoting at length:

> The materialists, or *neicheris*, have appeared in numerous forms and various guises among races and peoples, and under different names. Sometimes they have become manifest under the name of "sage," sometimes they have appeared adorned as those who remove oppression and repel injustice. Sometimes they have stepped into the arena dressed

as those who know the secrets and uncover the mysteries of truth, and as the possessors of esoteric knowledge. Sometimes they have claimed that their goal is the removal of superstitions and the enlightenment of peoples' minds. For a time they came forth as the lovers of the poor, protectors of the weak, and well-wishers of the unfortunate. Sometimes to fulfill their evil aims they have laid claim to prophethood like other false prophets. Sometimes they called themselves the educators, teachers, and benefactors of the community. But among whatever people they appeared, and whatever guise or name they bore, they became—because of their evil premises and false principles, their harmful teachings, deadly views, and fatal sayings—the cause of the decline and collapse of that people and the annihilation of that community. They destroyed the social order of those peoples and scattered their members.

For man is very cruel and ignorant. And to this treacherous, greedy, bloodthirsty creature there were supplied beliefs and qualities in the earliest period by means of religions. Tribes and peoples learned these beliefs and qualities as an inheritance from their fathers and grandfathers, and they adjusted their behavior accordingly, avoiding the evil and corruption that are the destroyers of the social order. As a result they enlightened their minds with that knowledge which is the cause of happiness and the foundation of civilization. Thus there was produced for them a kind of stability and continuity.

The sect of *neicheris*, among whatever people they appeared, tried to nullify those beliefs and corrupt those qualities. From them destruction penetrated the pillars of the social order of that people and headed them toward dissolution, until they were suddenly destroyed.[47]

The subsequent pages make clear that the heterodox sects are grouped with the materialists as being essentially the same and equally harmful to the community. The points of the above statement, which were shared by the Islamic philosophical tradition, are: (1) Those who spread religious doubts among the people, by claim-

---

[47] See pt. 2, "Refutation of the Materialists," pp. 140–141.

ing to be sages, saviors from oppression, repositories of hidden truths, or prophets, are the same in their effects because they undermine the social structure. (2) Most men are by nature evil and can be directed to virtue and social stability only by religion. Some of Afghānī's arguments might be put forth by the orthodox, but the emphasis throughout is purely pragmatic and not religious.

Afghānī goes on to discuss three important beliefs and three virtues imparted by religion, "each of which is a firm pillar for the existence of nations and the permanence of the social order." The first is the belief that man is the noblest of creatures. The second is each man's certainty "that his community is the noblest one, and that all outside his community are in error and deviation." Afghānī was surely not blind to the fact that not every community could be the noblest; again, it is the utility of this view, not its truth, that is important. Then, in a description of the afterlife that is more in line with Neoplatonic philosophy than orthodox ideas, Afghānī goes on:

> The third is the firm belief that man has come into the world in order to acquire accomplishments worthy of transferring him to a world more excellent, higher, vaster, and more perfect than this narrow and dark world that really deserves the name of the Abode of Sorrows.
>
> One should not neglect the important effect of each of these three beliefs on the social order, their great advantages for civilization, and their many contributions to order and the relations among peoples.[48]

None of the three beliefs has much connection with what is usually considered religion, and none of them concerns God: both their nature and utility are human and social.

Afghānī then discusses the virtues arising from each of the three beliefs. From the first belief, that man is the noblest creature, comes intellectual perfection for the chosen few, again described in terms recalling the philosophers. Man ascends the ladder of civilization and

> proceeds in proportion to his progress in the intellectual sphere, until he becomes one of those civilized, virtuous

---

48 *Ibid.*, p. 141.

men whose life with brothers who have reached this rung of civilization is based on love, wisdom, and justice. This is the ultimate goal of sages and the summit of human happiness in the world.[49]

The notion of a kind of mystic fraternity of the philosophical elite who have reached the highest human phase is found in Avicenna and in the more philosophical heretical sects, notably the Isma'ilis.

Just as the first belief, that man is the noblest of creatures, is seen to lead to an essentially philosophic conclusion, so too do the second and third beliefs. Afghānī may have had in mind an essentially evolutionary view of religion (an assumption supported by some of his other writings and talks that more openly express such a view), whereby revealed religion marked a stage in the progress of men from barbarism to civilization and gave them an important impetus to social cohesion and material progress. From the religiously based community there then could arise philosophic and scientific developments that went further in comprehending the true nature of the world than did literalist belief in revealed religion. Just as the "Islam" that is praised at the end of the "Refutation" is clearly not the Islam that had existed for many centuries, so it seems the "religion" praised in the earlier parts of the essay means something very special to Afghānī.

The second belief, the knowledge of every man that his own community is the noblest, is what pushes nations to achieve the extremes of civilization, science, and the arts. It stimulates peoples to compete with each other in knowledge, achievements, and progress. Again religion is seen as culminating in a philosophical virtue—the achievement of science and knowledge—by inculcating pride in one's own community and a desire to keep ahead of others. Here as elsewhere Afghānī may have had in mind his own idealized picture of the early Islamic community, and must have been well aware that the Muslim world of the nineteenth century presented no such picture.

The third belief, in rewards and a future life, is described, both the first time it is mentioned and in relation to the results flowing from it, entirely in the philosophical and intellectualist terms that had been rejected for centuries by Muslim orthodoxy. Even his terminology is of the Aristotelian and Neoplatonic type used by the philosophers:

---

[49] *Ibid.*, p. 142.

One of the inevitable consequences of the [third] belief, that man has come into the world in order to attain the perfections needed to transfer him to a higher and vaster world, is that when someone acquires this belief he will of necessity always strive to improve and enlighten his mind with true science and sound knowledge. He will not leave his intellect idle, but will bring out of concealment and into the light of the world what has been deposited in him of active power, lofty sentiments, and great virtues. In all stages of his life he will try to rid his soul of impure features and will not stint in the adjustment and improvement of its qualities. . . .

Thus this belief is the best impulse toward civilization, whose foundations are true knowledge and refined morals. It is the best requisite for the stability of the social order, which is founded on each individual's knowledge of his proper rights, and his following the straight path of justice. It is the strongest motive for international relations, which are based on truthful and honest observation of the bounds of human intercourse. It is the best basis for the peace and calm of the classes of humanity, because peace is the fruit of love and justice, and love and justice result from admirable qualities and habits. It is the only belief that restrains man from all evils, saves him from the vales of adversity and misfortune, and seats him in the virtuous city on the throne of happiness.[50]

The "virtuous city" is the terrain of al-Fārābī and later Muslim philosophers, as is the effort to rid the soul of impure qualities and to expand the sparks of virtue and knowledge that have been deposited in man. Afghānī's description, given before the above passage, of the superior world for which men are preparing themselves is entirely that of the philosophers—a world of the intellectually and spiritually perfect; and it is even ambiguous whether this world is not essentially the achievement of intellectual perfection on earth.

In discussing his three beliefs and the results that flow from them, Afghānī thus says that religion is good both because it leads to human and social virtues, and because it leads some men to philosophical and scientific conclusions. This is either, as suggested above, an

---

50 *Ibid.*, pp. 143–144.

evolutionary view of religion which really has the Islam of the earliest centuries in mind or it is something even less frank—the attribution to religion of virtues that his enlightened and attentive readers would see were really rather the virtues of philosophy.

After describing the three beliefs of religion and their results, Afghānī goes on to the three virtues he says are produced by religion: Shame, Trustworthiness, and Truthfulness. Again he shows not how these three arise from religion but how necessary they are to the proper functioning of the social order. His description of the good social state produced by their presence, and the ruin brought by their absence, seems more likely to point up the lack of these qualities in any existing state with Muslim rulers than to prove the superiority of such states.

Afghānī then specifies the social harm brought by the materialists. They undermine the belief that one's own religion is better than others, thus leading men to evil actions. They attack each of the three beliefs and three habits imparted by religion, teaching that all religions are false. This discourages men from practicing virtue, encourages the most bestial vices, and undermines the social order. They attack belief in the Day of Judgment and the habit of shame, which are the foundations of trustworthiness and truthfulness. They also spread a harmful equalitarianism, which will make the lower classes unwilling to perform menial jobs. Afghānī continues:

> In addition, this group has placed the foundation of their belief on license and communism, and has considered that all desirable things should be shared, and has regarded privileges and distinctions as usurpation, as shall be noted. There will no longer be a place for the attribution of treachery, since if a man chooses trickery to obtain his right to share things, that would not be treachery, and if he uses lying it would not be considered shameful. Therefore it is clear that the teachings of this group are the motive force of all treachery and lies, the cause of all evils, meanness, baseness, and wickedness.
>
> . . . The final goal and ultimate object of this group is that all men should share in all desires and delights; that privileges and distinctions should be abolished; that nobody should have superiority or a surplus of anything over another; and that all should be absolutely equal. If it be-

comes like that, naturally every person will refuse to perform hard and menial tasks and economic life will be disordered; the wheel of dealings and relationships will stop moving; and finally this weak species will be brought to the vale of perdition and will disappear completely. . . .

The real cause of the superiority of man is his love for privilege and distinction. When privilege and distinction are removed, souls are stopped from the movement toward eminence and minds neglect to penetrate the truth of things and to discover the subtleties of life. Men would live in this world like beasts of the desert, were it possible for them.[51]

This quite traditional belief in the necessity and utility of social distinctions, which must be bolstered by religious teachings, is consistent with Afghānī's intellectual elitism and his pessimism about human nature, both of which he shares with the philosophers.

When materialism spreads, egoism overcomes individuals and social solidarity is lost:

The quality of *egoism* consists of self-love to the point that if a personal profit requires a man having that quality to let the whole world be harmed, he would not renounce that profit but would consent to the harm of everyone in the world. This quality makes man put his personal interest above the general welfare, and makes him sell his nation for a paltry profit. Gradually, because of this base life, fear and cowardice overtook man, and he became content and happy with meanness, baseness, slavery, and abasement in his life.

When the state of individuals reached this point, the bond of fusion and interdependence was broken; the unity of the species was annihilated; the power of preservation and the means of survival were lost; and the throne of greatness, glory, and honor was overthrown.[52]

There is a striking resemblance between these ideas and those of Ibn Khaldūn, who also, as Muhsin Mahdi has shown, had his roots in the neo-Aristotelian philosophical tradition. Religion promotes

---

[51] *Ibid.*, pp. 149–150.
[52] *Ibid.*, pp. 151–152.

solidarity and its decline is accompanied by harmful individualism.[53]

There follows an account of the "materialist" sects in East and West which have caused the decline of nations, an account that includes the main Islamic sects. The Islamic sects attracted men into illegitimate allegorical interpretations and denial of the sacred law and religious duties. Their teachings drew men away from the general interests of the community toward their selfish desires and prepared the way for foreign invasions. Afghānī then criticizes Ottoman modernists as traitors in the recent Ottoman war against the Russians. In Europe materialism has culminated in the evil doctrines of socialism, nihilism, and communism.[54]

Afghānī reiterates his arguments in a discussion of Oriental materialists, and goes on to an interesting discussion of the possible ways of enforcing justice in the world. One of these is to count on the nobility of the human soul; but, he says, in passages again recalling the philosophers, each nation and class has its own standards of nobility, and the higher classes in particular consider themselves bound only by what they can get away with. Once again there is philosophic pessimism about ordinary human nature. After refuting the other means of securing justice, Afghānī says:

> Thus, no force remains for restraining men of passions from their transgressions and oppression other than the fourth way. That is the belief that the world has a Creator, wise and powerful; and the belief that for good and evil deeds there is a fixed recompense after this life. In truth, these two beliefs together are the firmest foundation for the suppression of passions and the removal of external and internal transgressions.
>
> . . . For the final cause of all acquired qualities and free acts, as was said above, is man himself; and when a person does not believe in recompense and requital, what else will bar blameworthy qualities to him and call him to good behavior? Especially when a man realizes that being characterized by bad qualities will not result in any loss for him in the world, nor will having good qualities bring him any benefit. . . .

---

[53] See Muhsin Mahdi, *Ibn Khaldūn's Philosophy of History* (London, 1957). Sylvia Haim, *Arab Nationalism*, p. 13 n. 14, points out the similarities of Afghānī's and Ibn Khaldūn's views on solidarity.

[54] See pt. 2, "Refutation of the Materialists," pp. 160–163.

Thus, from all we have expounded, it becomes clear in the most evident manner that religion, even if it be false and the basest of religions, because of those two firm pillars —belief in a Creator and faith in rewards and punishments— and because of the six principles that are enshrined in religions, is better than the way of the materialists, or *neicheris*. [It is better] in the realm of civilization, the social order, and the organization of relationships; indeed in all human societies and all progress of mankind in this world. . . . The nature of a great man, according to his God-given intelligence, which is an effect of the universal intelligence, will not accept these men [the *neicheris*].[55]

As in the article "Commentary on the Commentator," Afghānī is relatively indifferent to the truth of a religion—it is its social utility that concerns him.

The bulk of Afghānī's tract consists of a defense of religion as such, and only in the last few pages is he concerned to argue the superiority of Islam among religions. Islam is superior for several reasons: First, its insistence on the unity of the Creator, which excludes incarnation or any sharing of divine powers; second, its lack of inherent race or class distinctions; and third, its rejection of beliefs that do not rest on proofs.

In this section Afghānī, without saying so, is speaking of his ideal Islam, which may have existed in the past, but which he knew was far from the Islam of his own day. Under the second point, the lack of class distinctions, he speaks critically of the power of the priesthood in Christianity, probably with an eye to the power of the ulama in later Islamic history. On the third point, the necessity for proofs for religious beliefs, Afghānī's characterization of Islam is in the sharpest contrast with what he said about it elsewhere, notably in the "Answer to Renan." The presentation of Islam here surely represents a *desideratum* and not what Afghānī believed existed in his time. The whole passage is more an implied criticism than the encomium it appears to be on the surface:

[The third foundation of human virtues] is that the members of each community must found their beliefs, which are the first things written on the slates of their minds, on certain

---

55 *Ibid.*, pp. 166–168.

proofs and firm evidence. In their beliefs they must shun submission to conjectures and not be content with mere imitation (*taqlīd*) of their ancestors. For if man believes in things without proof or reason, makes a practice of following unproven opinions, and is satisfied to imitate and follow his ancestors, his mind inevitably desists from intellectual movement, and little by little stupidity and imbecility overcome him—until his mind becomes completely idle and he becomes unable to perceive his own good and evil; and adversity and misfortune overtake him from all sides.

It is no wonder that Guizot, the French minister, who wrote the history of . . . civilization of the European peoples, said as follows: One of the greatest causes for European civilization was that a group appeared, saying: "Although our religion is the Christian religion, we are seeking the proofs of the fundamentals of our beliefs." The corpus of priests did not give permission, and they said that religion was founded on imitation. When the group became strong their ideas spread; minds emerged from their state of stupidity and dullness into movement and progress; and men made efforts to achieve the perquisites of civilization.

The Islamic religion is the only religion that censures belief without proof, and the following of conjectures; reproves blind submission; seeks to show proof of things to its followers; everywhere addresses itself to reason; considers all happiness the result of wisdom and clearsightedness; attributes perdition to stupidity and lack of insight; and sets up proofs for each fundamental belief in such a way that it will be useful to all people. It even, when it mentions most of its rules, states their purposes and benefits. (Refer to the Holy Koran.)[56]

The argument that the Koran enjoins logical proofs and demonstrative reasoning is a favorite one of the Muslim philosophers. The favorable reference to the founders of Protestantism is one of several such references by Afghānī, who seems to have hoped to play the role of a Muslim Luther. He was convinced by Guizot's attribution of much of the West's progress to Protestantism, and his interest in

56 *Ibid.*, pp. 171–172.

Protestant reform was far more worldly and pragmatic than theological. The above passage, as other words by Afghānī indicate, is really an injunction to the Muslims to turn away from a stultifying imitation of their predecessors and toward a more rational and less restrictive faith that would allow room for progress and innovation. That Afghānī is talking not about the Islam he knew in his own day, but as he imagined it to have been in the past, is indicated at the end of his treatise:

> If someone says: If the Islamic religion is as you say, then why are the Muslims in such a sad condition? I will answer: When they were [truly] Muslims, they were what they were and the world bears witness to their excellence. As for the present, I will content myself with this holy text:
> "Verily, God does not change the state of a people until they change themselves inwardly."[57]

Afghānī was apparently the first to cite this Koranic passage as an admonition to modern change and progress. It has since become a favorite of the modernists.

The "Refutation" has not seemed to Western readers a particularly convincing argument for anything; yet it has had and continues to have considerable reputation among Muslims. It would seem that with it Afghānī accomplished several goals simultaneously: (1) He suggested to intellectuals the dangers of going too far in their open criticisms of Islam, since religion had the practical virtues of tying together the community and keeping men from vice. (2) To the same group he suggested a way of reform, through stressing certain passages of the Koran and certain parts of the Islamic tradition. (3) He combated the pro-British influence of Ahmad Khān and his followers by identifying them with the harmful materialists. (4) He suggested limits to politico-economic as well as religious reform. (5) To the less intellectual reader in particular he strengthened pride in Islam as the best religion, providing him with a useful counterweight to the British claims of cultural superiority. It would seem that Western disappointment in the book stems from an expectation of finding in it what we would call a "religious" document. It appears rather to be an expedient, political tract; not necessarily expressing

---

[57] *Ibid.*, p. 173.

the real opinions of the author, but written in order to accomplish certain goals.

In the ordinary sense of the word, I do not think the "Refutation" can even be classified under "Apologetics." Afghānī was concerned, as his whole activity shows, not with awakening passive admiration of Islam, but with harnessing Islamic sentiment to certain goals. In the course of time, however, as more and more people began to doubt Islam, the book began in fact to be read as an apologetic tract.[58] The "Refutation" is certainly not an attempt to "rethink" Islam, and, as has been suggested earlier, any consistent rethinking might in itself become sectarian, which was just what Afghānī wanted to avoid.

The

Exchange with

Ernest Renan

THAT the "Refutation" is a combination of philosophical doctrine on human nature, expedient rhetoric aimed at the "many," and hints for the "few" is suggested not only by internal evidence, but also by some of Afghānī's other writings. Most important is his "Answer to Renan," published in French in a French journal, and not intended to meet the eyes of the pious. The "Answer to Renan" was written the year *before* "The Materialists in India" and other similar articles, and so it cannot be explained by saying that live contact with Europe caused Afghānī to change his views on Islam.

The "Answer to Renan" was written in Paris in response to a lecture by Ernest Renan on "Islam and Science," first given at the Sorbonne and published March 29, 1883, in the *Journal des Débats*. Afghānī's answer was published in the same journal on May 18, 1883. Renan published a rejoinder the next day which spoke of the great

---

[58] When in Iran in 1959–60 I was told by several religious Iranians to read the "Refutation" as one of the best works proving the superiority of Islam. This indicates how in accord with certain Islamic traditions Afghānī was in considering pragmatic and political arguments a sufficient defense of Islam.

personal impression Afghānī had made on him, granted the justice of many of Afghānī's points, and praised him as a fellow rationalist thinker and infidel.[59]

In the Muslim world the discussion between Afghānī and Renan has been distorted by those who have not read Afghānī's response to Renan and assume that since Renan had called Islam hostile to science, Afghānī must have said that Islam was friendly to the scientific spirit. No part of Afghānī's actual argument can be construed in this sense, as a reading of the whole answer easily shows. Afghānī was just as categorical as Renan about the hostility of the Muslim religion to the scientific spirit; his quarrel with Renan rested on quite different points, points that were in large measure accepted by Renan in his rejoinder.

Renan in his lecture had stated that early Islam and the Arabs who professed it were hostile to the scientific and philosophic spirit, and that science and philosophy had only entered the Islamic world from non-Arab sources. The science and philosophy that are often called Arab are really Greek or Persian. Only one of the great Islamic philosophers was an Arab by birth, and to call their philosophy Arab, just because they wrote in Arabic, makes no more sense than to call medieval European philosophy Latin. Renan's argument, as Afghānī noted in his "Answer," has two major points. The first is a racist one: the Arabs by nature and temperament are hostile to science and philosophy, and these subjects were only advanced in the Islamic world by non-Arabs (in fact, though Renan does not here say this, mainly by people of Indo-European or "Aryan" origin). The second is that Islam is essentially hostile to science. This hostility was dominant when the Arabs ruled, and later under the Turks; it was temporarily and precariously overcome only during the short period when Greek and Persian influences were strong. Although it is true that Renan was hostile to all religious dogma and not only to Islamic dogma, it is not true, as has been claimed, that he was only saying of Islam what he would have said of any other religion. On this he is explicit. Islam, because it unites the spiritual and temporal realms and makes dogma rule in both, is "the heaviest chain that humanity has ever borne."[60]

Afghānī's "Answer to Renan" was apparently written first in

---

[59] See pp. 91–93.

[60] Ernest Renan, *l'Islamisme et la science* (Paris, 1883), p. 17.

Arabic and then translated into French.[61] We must assume the same of all his French articles, or at least that their style was corrected, since there are numerous witnesses to the fact that his written and spoken French was quite imperfect. There is no reason to think the French translation inaccurate, however, since Afghānī soon came to read French quite well, and never made any recorded complaint about the way the "Answer" was translated.

A remarkable point about Afghānī's answer is that in many ways it seems *more* in line with twentieth-century ideas than Renan's original argument. It rejects Renan's racism and puts in its place an evolutionary or developmental view of peoples. Renan, says Afghānī, states that the Muslim religion is opposed to science. But, Afghānī points out, no people in its earliest stages accepts science or philosophy. This "modern" view is then buttressed by arguments coming straight from the most skeptical of the philosophical thinkers of the Islamic world. All peoples in their first stages were incapable of being guided by pure reason, or of distinguishing good from evil so as to achieve their own welfare. There then arose prophets—here called "teachers" or "educators"— who, unable to make such primitive peoples follow the dictates of pure reason, found a means to civilize men and make them obedient to authority by attributing their own ideas to a supreme God:

> And, since humanity, at its origin, did not know the causes of events that passed under its eyes and the secret of things, it was perforce led to follow the advice of its teachers and the orders they gave. This obedience was imposed in the name of the supreme Being to whom the educators attributed all events, without permitting men to discuss its utility or its disadvantages. This is no doubt for men one of the heaviest and most humiliating yokes, as I recognize; but one cannot deny that it is by this religious education, whether it be Muslim, Christian, or pagan, that all nations have emerged from barbarism and marched toward a more advanced civilization.[62]

---

61 Kedourie, *op. cit.*, p. 41, citing the *Journal des Débats'* statement that it was presenting a translation of Afghānī's words.

62 "Réponse de Jamal ad-Din al-Afghani à Renan," in Jamāl ad-Dīn al-Afghānī, *Réfutation des matérialistes*, trans. A. M. Goichon (Paris, 1942), pp. 176–177.

Continuing the evolutionary argument, Afghānī goes on to recognize the great superiority of the modern Western intellectual climate, but attributes it to the fact that Christianity had an evolutionary head start on Islam:

> All religions are intolerant, each one in its way. The Christian religion, I mean the society that follows its inspirations and its teachings and is formed in its image, has emerged from the first period to which I have just alluded; thenceforth free and independent, it seems to advance rapidly on the road of progress and science, whereas Muslim society has not yet freed itself from the tutelage of religion. Realizing, however, that the Christian religion preceded the Muslim religion in the world by many centuries, I cannot keep from hoping that Muhammadan society will succeed someday in breaking its bonds and marching resolutely in the path of civilization after the manner of Western society. . . . I plead here with M. Renan not the cause of the Muslim religion, but that of several hundreds of millions of men, who would thus be condemned to live in barbarism and ignorance.
>
> In truth, the Muslim religion has tried to stifle science and stop its progress.

Christianity, Afghānī notes, has done the same, and the Catholic church still tries to do so. On the justness of Renan's view of the believing Muslim as a slave to dogma Afghānī has no quarrel—if anything he expresses himself in even stronger terms:

> A true believer must, in fact, turn from the path of studies that have for their object scientific truth. . . . Yoked, like an ox to the plow, to the dogma whose slave he is, he must walk eternally in the furrow that has been traced for him in advance by the interpreters of the law. Convinced, besides, that his religion contains in itself all morality and all sciences, he attaches himself resolutely to it and makes no effort to go beyond. . . . What would be the benefit of seeking truth when he believes he possesses it all? . . . Wherefore he despises science.[63]

---

63 *Ibid.*, pp. 177–178.

Afghānī then notes, very briefly, that Muslims, at one time, had had a taste for science and philosophy.

On Renan's second point, the innate hostility of the Arabs to science and philosophy, it would seem to most readers today that Afghānī gets the better of the argument. He notes, quite justly, that the Arabs assimilated with amazing rapidity the Greek and Persian sciences that had been developed over several centuries, and that under Arab rule science and philosophy continued to develop and were later passed to the Christian West. While granting that people who spoke and wrote another language, like the Persians, should not be called Arabs, Afghānī notes that to deny the name Arab to those whose first spoken and written language was Arabic, and to identify them instead with remote ancestors, would be contrary to all usual or sensible practice. Afghānī also notes that many of the Hellenized, philosophically minded peoples conquered by the Arabs were Semites and hence related to the Arabs even before they became Arabized.

If Afghānī rejects the racist side of Renan's argument, and brings in an evolutionary argument, he is, nonetheless, at least as severe as Renan on the hostility of the Islamic religion to science and reason. In conclusion, Afghānī states:

> It is permissible, however, to ask oneself why Arab civilization, after having thrown such a live light on the world, suddenly became extinguished; why this torch has not been relit since; and why the Arab world still remains buried in profound darkness.
>
> Here the responsibility of the Muslim religion appears complete. It is clear that wherever it became established, this religion tried to stifle the sciences and it was marvelously served in its designs by despotism.
>
> Al-Siuti tells that the Caliph al-Hadi put to death in Baghdad 5,000 philosophers in order to destroy sciences in the Muslim countries down to their roots. Admitting that this historian exaggerated the number of victims, it remains nonetheless established that this persecution took place, and it is a bloody stain for the history of a religion as it is for the history of a people. I could find in the past of the Christian religion analogous facts. Religions, by whatever names they are called, all resemble each other. No agreement and

no reconciliation are possible between these religions and philosophy. Religion imposes on man its faith and its belief, whereas philosophy frees him of it totally or in part. How could one therefore hope that they would agree with each other? . . . Whenever religion will have the upper hand, it will eliminate philosophy; and the contrary happens when it is philosophy that reigns as sovereign mistress. As long as humanity exists, the struggle will not cease between dogma and free investigation, between religion and philosophy; a desperate struggle in which, I fear, the triumph will not be for free thought, because the masses dislike reason, and its teachings are only understood by some intelligences of the elite, and because, also, science, however beautiful it is, does not completely satisfy humanity, which thirsts for the ideal and which likes to exist in dark and distant regions that the philosophers and scholars can neither perceive nor explore.[64]

This article is one of the most striking of the many proofs that Afghānī was far from being the orthodox believer he claimed to be before Muslim audiences. The "Answer" also contains within itself the explanation of why Afghānī chose to put on this orthodox religious guise. The masses are moved only by religious arguments, while the more truthful rational and scientific arguments can appeal only to a small elite (and hence not be politically efficacious). Reflecting the views of the traditional Islamic philosophers, Afghānī presents religion as useful to keep the masses moral and obedient.

Adumbrated in the "Answer" is Afghānī's knowledge of the fate of the medieval Islamic philosophers. Even though they were willing to grant the utility of orthodoxy for the masses, they were not permitted to pursue truth, but were attacked by rulers, theologians, and the orthodox. Afghānī, who even exaggerates the persecution suffered by Muslim philosophers, is pessimistic about the ultimate triumph of pure freedom of investigation. It is persecuted by those who place faith above reason and by their temporal allies; it is understood only by the elite, while the masses will always want to speak of otherworldly things that are inaccessible to reason. It can be hoped, however, that the Muslim religion may eventually be reformed as was Christianity to lessen the stifling power of anti-

---

64 *Ibid.*, pp. 183–185.

scientific dogma, while the masses presumably will be left with enough religious faith and injunctions to satisfy their cravings and keep them in line.

This is not to say that Afghānī was entirely consistent. Even within the "Answer" there is some variation between the optimism of the reformer or revolutionary in the early passages, and the pessimism at the end of the article, which voices the traditional philosophers' view of the very restricted circle who can understand truth and science. But contradictory tendencies within one complex individual, thrust from the medieval into the modern period and facing problems that were probably insoluble in his own time, are not to be wondered at, and can themselves be explained. If Afghānī was pessimistic about the possibility of appealing to the masses in the name of anything except religion, and, like the philosophers, thought that rational demonstrative argument could be understood only by the "few," this helps explain why he made what were essentially political appeals in the name of religion. The "Refutation" stresses the worldly achievements of Islam, while the "Answer" stresses another aspect—its stifling dogmatic rigidity. In a sense, it might be said, Afghānī is in each instance giving a one-sided presentation that is, however, accurate within limits. It seems quite true that the religious-ideological impetus given by early Islam was an important factor in the early flowering of its civilization, but that, on the other hand, the rigidification of dogma helped bring about decline and continuing stagnation.

Until very recently nearly all discussions of Afghānī have ignored, or treated as a temporary lapse, this "Answer to Renan," and have sought Afghānī's true beliefs in his writings aimed at a broad Muslim public or in 'Abduh's apologetic account. It is quite true that Afghānī's writings in defense of Islam have a much greater total bulk than have items like the "Answer to Renan." Yet, as seen in analyzing the "Refutation of the Materialists," even the writings defending Islam have very little content that can justly be called religious, and are designed rather to create political unity and solidarity. Besides this, it should have been proved sufficiently by now that for Afghānī, as for many philosophers and heretics in the Muslim world, it was quite proper to speak and write something other than one's true beliefs if this would lead to a desirable goal. It is in the spoken words to his closest followers and disciples and in writings directed to an elite audience that the true beliefs of such a man are to be sought. The "Answer to Renan" was directed to precisely such an elite Western audience, and it is significant that no translation appears to have been published in an Eastern language, and that it is nearly always misrepresented in Eastern languages as a defense of Islam. If the "Answer to Renan" does not represent Afghānī's true beliefs, it is almost impossible to imagine why he should have opened himself up in print to possible further attack from orthodox Muslims. Afghānī could quite easily have limited himself to noting the glory of Muslim Arab scientific achievement in the past and to maintaining that true Islam had been distorted in more recent centuries, but he chose rather to attack the Muslim religion in strong terms.

Aside from its explicit content, there are other circumstances surrounding Afghānī's "Answer to Renan" which indicate Afghānī's estrangement from Islamic orthodoxy. For instance, Renan's rejoinder to Afghānī, published in the *Journal des Débats* on May 19, 1883, indicates that Afghānī impressed this eminent rationalist and freethinker as a man of his own stripe. Renan granted the improvement that Afghānī had made on his argument by ridding it of the implication that Islam was somehow an even worse religion than Christianity. Muslim authors are accustomed to quoting from this rejoinder only a few sentences of general praise of Afghānī; but it is far more instructive to quote Renan's remarks almost in their entirety. (The first line is from the publication of Renan's *Islam and Science* in book form.)

> A remarkably intelligent Afghan Sheikh having presented observations on the above lecture, I answered the next day, in the same journal, as follows:
>
> We read yesterday with the interest they merited the very judicious reflections that my last lecture at the Sorbonne suggested to Sheikh Jemmal-Eddin. There is nothing more instructive than studying the ideas of an enlightened Asiatic in their original and sincere form. It is by listening to the most diverse voices, coming from the four corners of the globe, in favor of rationalism, that one becomes convinced that if religions divide men, Reason brings them together; and that there is only one Reason.

Renan says he met Afghānī about two months previously, which would have been in March, 1883, shortly after his arrival in Paris, through a collaborator (on the *Journal des Débats*), M. Ghanim. He goes on:

Few people have produced on me a more vivid impression. It is in large measure the conversation I had with him that decided me to choose as a subject for my lecture at the Sorbonne the relations between the scientific spirit and Islam. Sheikh Jemmal-Eddin is an Afghan *entirely divorced from the prejudices of Islam*; he belongs to those energetic races of Iran, near India, where the Aryan spirit lives still so energetically under the superficial layer of official Islam. He is the best proof of that great axiom we have often proclaimed, namely, that religions are worth the same as the races that profess them. The liberty of his thought, his noble and loyal character, made me believe while I was talking with him, that I had before me, restored to life, one of my old acquaintances—Avicenna, Averroes, or another of those great infidels who represented for five centuries the tradition of the human mind. For me there was an especially vivid contrast when I compared this striking apparition with the spectacle presented by the Muslim countries this side of Persia—countries in which scientific and philosophic curiosity is so rare. Sheikh Jemmal-Eddin is the best case of ethnic protest against religious conquest that one could cite. . . .

In the learned article of the Sheikh I see only one point on which we are really in disagreement. . . . Everything written in Latin is not the glory of Rome; everything written in Greek is not Hellenic; everything written in Arabic is not an Arab product; everything done in a Christian country is not the effect of Christianity; everything done in a Muslim country is not a fruit of Islam. . . . These sorts of distinctions are necessary if one does not wish history to be a tissue of approximations and misunderstandings. . . .

One point on which I may have appeared unjust to the Sheikh is that I did not develop enough the idea that all revealed religions manifest themselves as hostile to positive science, and that Christianity in this respect is not superior to Islam. This is beyond doubt. Galileo was no better treated by Catholicism than Averroes by Islam.

Renan then says his opinions on this point are well known, and that he has often stated that the human mind must be freed of all supernatural belief if it wishes to work on its essential work, which is the construction of positive science. This does not imply violent destruction nor brusque rupture. The Christian does not have to abandon Christianity nor the Muslim Islam. The enlightened parties of Christianity and Islam should arrive at that state of benevolent indifference where religious beliefs become inoffensive. This has happened in about half of the Christian countries, let us hope it will happen in Islam. Naturally on that day the Sheikh and I will agree in applauding. . . . There will be distinguished individuals (though there will be few as distinguished as Sheikh Jemmal-Eddin) who will separate themselves from Islam, as we separate ourselves from Catholicism. Certain countries, with time, will more or less break with the religion of the Koran; but I doubt that the movement of renaissance will be made with the support of official Islam.

Finally, Renan notes quite justly that Afghānī has provided additional arguments in favor of his own basic points:

Sheikh Jemmal-Eddin seems to me to have brought considerable arguments for my two fundamental theses: During the first half of its existence Islam did not stop the scientific movement from existing in Muslim lands; in the second half it stifled in its breast the scientific movement, and that to its grief.[65]

Equally significant in proving that Afghānī's "Answer to Renan" represented his esoteric doctrine, as voiced to elite audiences, is a letter from 'Abduh in Beirut to Afghānī, written a month after Afghānī's "Answer," on June 14, 1883. It is photographed in the Afshār-Mahdavī *Documents*, and has been summarized and partially translated by Elie Kedourie, who writes:

It is of some interest to follow the fortunes in the East of the exchange between Renan and Afghani. A letter from 'Abduh in Beirut to Afghani in Paris dated 8 Sha'ban 1300

---

[65] Ernest Renan, *Oeuvres complètes*, I (Paris, 1947), 960–965.

and reproduced in the *Documents* is of extreme importance in shedding light not only on this matter but on the nature of Afghani's esoteric teaching. The letter begins with those expressions of idolatry of which I have given . . . a characteristic specimen. Then 'Abduh goes on to say that news had reached him of Afghani's answer to Renan in the *Journal des Débats*; he had thought that a translation would serve to edify the believers and had asked a man of religion (*ba'd al-diniyyin*) to be ready to undertake it on receipt of the French text. But immediately afterwards, 'Abduh writes, he received two numbers of the *Journal* (presumably of 18 and 19 May 1883, containing Afghani's commentary and Renan's observations), together with a letter from Afghani. He goes on:

> "We then praised God Almighty that the numbers of the *Débats* had not been available before the receipt of your letter. We acquainted ourselves with these two numbers. . . . We then dissuaded our first friend from making the translation, alleging that [the] Arabic text was going to be sent, that it would be published then, and that therefore there was no need for a translation. Thus misfortune was averted *(fa'ndafa'a al-makruh)*, God be praised."

Since Afghani's commentary was a powerful attack on traditional Islam, it is not surprising that neither Afghani nor 'Abduh desired its dissemination in Islamic countries. But the sentences which immediately follow are even more significant:

> "We regulate our conduct," writes 'Abduh, "according to your sound rule: We do not cut the head of religion except with the sword of religion *(nahnu al-an 'ala sunnatika al-qawima la naqta'* * *ra's al-din illa bi-saif al-din)*. Therefore, if you were to see us now, you would see ascetics and worshippers [of God] kneeling and genuflecting, never disobeying what God commands and doing all that they are ordered to do. . . .[66]

It may be significant, as one more of the Middle Eastern attempts

---

[66] Kedourie, *op. cit.*, pp. 44–45. *An alternate reading is *la taqta'*.

to distort Afghānī's "Answer to Renan," of which Kedourie gives some examples, that the Persian summary of this letter in the *Documents* distorts and obfuscates its meaning.[67]

More important is what the letter shows 'Abduh knew of Afghānī. He nowhere indicates doubt that the French text correctly gives Afghānī's thought, or hope that the sending of Afghānī's original Arabic text would change the sense of the article. He also speaks explicitly of Afghānī's followers keeping to his "sound" external religious practices in order to "cut off the head of religion." In view of this rule, there is little wonder that 'Abduh was so upset by Salīm al-'Anḥūrī's biography of Afghānī, written shortly after this incident. The biography pointed to Afghānī's rationalist and evolutionary view of religion, which 'Anḥūrī had heard of in and from Egypt and which he describes in terms very similar to those used by Afghānī in the "Answer to Renan."[68] Just as 'Abduh hastened in 1883 to stop a translation that would have damaged Afghānī's religious reputation, so he hastened in 1885 to talk 'Anḥūrī into retracting his account, and to publish his own highly apologetic biography, which stressed Afghānī's devotion to the Muslim religion.[69]

It should not be forgotten, of course, that the "Answer" was directed toward, and calculated to impress, a European audience, and that this explains some of its emphases. It appears, however, to have been a document more sincerely expressive of Afghānī's beliefs than the "Refutation," not only because it is directed at some of the "elite" rather than at the "people of rhetoric," but because Afghānī might have taken various different lines of argument in Europe, and by putting this one in print was opening himself to possible further attack from orthodox Muslims.

---

[67] *Documents*, pp. 66–67, letter no. 220. The Arabic original is in *ibid.*, photos 138–140. Most of the other Arabic letters dealt with by the volume's Persian translator, and translated in their entirety, are without similar distortion.

[68] 'Anḥūrī's account is translated in chap. i, pp. 13–14.

[69] Kedourie, *op. cit.*, p. 17. 'Anḥūrī's account of the encounter with 'Abduh is in Rashīd Riḍā, *Tārīkh al-ustādh al-imām* (Cairo, 1931), I, 50. In his original biography, *ibid.*, p. 48, 'Anḥūrī noted the great change in Afghānī's religious image which occurred in the early 1880's, and to which I have called attention above. Regarding his first contact with Afghānī after Egypt, through *al-'Urwa al-Wuthqā*, 'Anḥūrī says he "realized from its tendencies that he [Afghānī] had come back to adherence to the straight faith and had taken a new course that would gain for him the favor and acceptance of the Muslim world."

Conclusion

IT IS striking that in Afghānī we find, in embryo at least, various ideological arguments that both in the Middle East and in the rest of Asia are usually associated with different points of view and stages of national development. There is aggressive cultural defensiveness: The traditional center of our culture, Islam, is better than the traditional Western center, Christianity, and the West became great only by borrowing from our culture. There is the nationalist pride (of the Arabs in the "Answer" but of Persians and Indians elsewhere): The *Arabs* developed science and philosophy, which the West had to borrow, while the religious dogmatism of Islam is here seen more as an excrescence of theologians and despots than an expression of the Arab essence. The "Answer" has an even more "modern" way of expressing the equivalence of East and West, namely, evolution: Christianity took *x* centuries to develop from dogma to free inquiry and science, and the Muslims could not be expected to do it in centuries less time. This final argument might impress Westerners but was hardly suitable for rallying the religious masses to combat the West. The conflict between a recognition of the urgent need to adopt Western techniques and the equal need to combat dumb admiration of the West and feelings of inferiority accounts for many of Afghānī's contradictions.

In none of the above am I trying to say that Afghānī had no religion. It appears likely that he was some kind of "Islamic deist," a believer in a Creator who set the world in motion and made it operate according to natural law. In this he would be following many of the Islamic philosophers, who believed in natural law and in God as the First Cause or Unmoved Mover. Afghānī may also have believed that a purified Islam would be a more rational religion than Christianity, since Islam was free of the irrational elements of Christianity. These irrational elements, named in Afghānī's "Commentary on the Commentator," include such dogmas as incarnation, the Trinity, and transubstantiation. Finally, he may have believed, as he said, that

the Koran's hidden meaning is infinite, and hence e
advances in human knowledge.

To the reconstruction and dissemination of a ratio
however, Afghānī devoted little time or effort. His m
rather to use Islam as an ideology—to strengthen its position as a
focus of identity and solidarity against the attacks of the Christian
West, and to use it as a rallying point for the repulsion of Western
conquerors. To young men with a traditional religious education
he also showed a way to adopt political and scientific ideas from the
West without abandoning their religious identification or pride in
their own traditions. Whatever later historians may conclude about
his exact influence, his position as a precursor and early teacher of
anti-imperialism, nationalism, solidarity against the West, and self-
strengthening reform—all of which causes have grown and flourished
since his lifetime—seems secure.

2

Translations of Texts
by Sayyid Jamāl ad-Dīn

Lecture*
on Teaching
and Learning

On Thursday, November 8 [1882], in Albert Hall, Calcutta, he said:

(I am very surprised at this *principal's** unexpectedly breaking his promise. He is a teacher of philosophy, and philosophy is a motive for truthfulness and the improvement of manners, and a cause of the civilization of the world. Thus, someone who is a teacher of philosophy must observe all the rules of the human sphere, and not commit acts that are contrary to the laws of humanity. Truly, this principal's breaking of his word is contrary to human honor and inconsistent with the dignity of science and philosophy.)

Allow me to express my pleasure that so many Indian youths are here, all adorned with virtue and attainments, and all making great efforts to acquire knowledge. Certainly I must be happy to see such offspring of India, since they are the offshoots of that India that was the cradle of humanity. Human values spread out from India to the whole world. These youths are from the very land where the meridian circle was first determined. They are from the same realm that first understood the zodiac. Everyone knows that the determination of these two circles is impossible until perfection in geometry is achieved. Thus we can say that the Indians were the inventors of arithmetic and geometry. Note how Indian numerals were transferred from here to the Arabs, and from there to Europe.

These youths are also the sons of a land that was the source of all the laws and rules of the world. If one observes closely, he will see that the "Code Romain," the mother of all Western codes, was taken from the four *vedas* and the *shastras*. The Greeks were the pupils of the Indians in literary ideas, limpid poetry, and lofty thoughts.

---

* In this article, words marked with an asterisk are in English in the original.

One of these pupils, Pythagoras, spread sciences and wisdom in Greece and reached such a height that his word was accepted without proof as an inspiration from heaven.

[The Indians] reached the highest level in philosophic thought. The soil of India is the same soil; the air of India is the same air; and these youths who are present here are fruits of the same earth and climate. So I am very happy that they, having awakened after a long sleep, are reclaiming their inheritance and gathering the fruits of their own tree.

Now I would like to speak of science, teaching, and learning.[1] How difficult it is to speak about science. There is no end or limit to science. The benefits of science are immeasurable; and these finite thoughts cannot encompass what is infinite. Besides, thousands of eloquent speakers and sages have already expressed their thoughts to explain science and its nobility. Despite this, nature does not permit me not to explain its virtues.

Thus I say: If someone looks deeply into the question, he will see that science rules the world. There was, is, and will be no ruler in the world but science. If we look at the Chaldean conquerors, like Semiramis, who reached the borders of Tatary and India, the true conquerors were not the Chaldeans but science and knowledge.

The Egyptians who increased their realm, and Ramses II, called Sosestris,[2] who reached Mesopotamia according to some and India according to others—it was not the Egyptians but Science that did it. The Phoenicians who, with their ships, gradually made colonies of the British Isles, Spain, Portugal, and Greece—in reality it was science, not the Phoenicians, which so expanded their power. Alexander never came to India or conquered the Indians; rather what conquered the Indians was science.

The Europeans have now put their hands on every part of the world. The English have reached Afghanistan; the French have seized Tunisia. In reality this usurpation, agression, and conquest has not come from the French or the English. Rather it is science that everywhere manifests its greatness and power. Ignorance had no

---

[1] Here, as elsewhere in the article, there is a play on several words with the common triliteral root '*lm*.

[2] Sosestris is the name of a pharaoh mentioned in Herodotus and other Greek sources who is supposed to have conquered the world, been a great lawgiver, and accomplished other important deeds. He has been considered by modern authors to be a compound of Seti I and Ramses II, in the nineteenth century B.C.

alternative to prostrating itself humbly before science and acknowledging its submission.

In reality, sovereignty has never left the abode of science. However, this true ruler, which is science, is continually changing capitals. Sometimes it has moved from East to West, and other times from West to East. More than this, if we study the riches of the world we learn that wealth is the result of commerce, industry, and agriculture. Agriculture is achieved only with agricultural science, botanical chemistry, and geometry. Industry is produced only with physics, chemistry, mechanics, geometry, and mathematics; and commerce is based on agriculture and industry.

Thus it is evident that all wealth and riches are the result of science. There are no riches in the world without science, and there is no wealth in the world other than science. In sum, the whole world of humanity is an industrial world, meaning that the world is a world of science. If science were removed from the human sphere, no man would continue to remain in the world.

Since it is thus, science makes one man have the strength of ten, one hundred, one thousand, and ten thousand persons. The acquisitions of men for themselves and their governments are proportional to their science. Thus, every government for its own benefit must strive to lay the foundation of the sciences and to disseminate knowledge. Just as an individual who has an orchard must, for his own profit, work to level the ground and improve its trees and plants according to the laws of agronomy, just so rulers, for their own benefit, must strive for the dissemination of the sciences. Just as, if the owner of an orchard neglects to tend it according to the laws of agronomy, the loss will revert to him, so, if a ruler neglects the dissemination of the sciences among his subjects, the harm will revert to that government. What advantage is there to a Zulu[3] king from ruling a society poor and barefoot, and how can one call such a government a government?

As the nobility of science has been somewhat clarified, we now wish to say some words about the relations between science, teaching, and learning. You must know that each science has a special subject and deals with nothing but the necessities and accidents of that special subject. For example, physics treats the special features

---

[3] The original reads *zuludburnu,* which does not appear in my dictionaries, and I have guessed at Afghānī's meaning.

of bodies that exist in the external world, and with its own special qualities, and does not enter into other matters that are necessary to the human world. *Kīmīyā*, or *chemistry** speaks of the special features of bodies with regard to analysis and composition. Plant science or *botany** fixes only plants as the subject of its discussion. Arithmetic deals with separate quantities and geometry with interconnected quantities, and similarly the other sciences. None of these sciences deals with matters outside its own subject.

If we observe well, we will learn that each one of these sciences whose subject is a special matter is like a limb of the body of science. Not one of them can maintain its existence individually and separately, or be the cause of benefit for the human world. For, the existence of each one of these sciences is related to another science, like the relation of arithmetic to geometry.

This need of one science for other sciences cannot be understood from the one science itself. Thus it is that if that science were isolated, progress would not be achieved in it, nor would it remain stable. Thus a science is needed to be the comprehensive soul for all the sciences, so that it can preserve their existence, apply each of them in its proper place, and become the cause of the progress of each one of those sciences.

The science that has the position of a comprehensive soul and the rank of a preserving force is the science of *falsafa* or philosophy,[4] because its subject is universal. It is philosophy that shows man human prerequisites. It shows the sciences what is necessary. It employs each of the sciences in its proper place.

If a community did not have philosophy, and all the individuals of that community were learned in the sciences with particular subjects, those sciences could not last in that community for a century, that is, a hundred years. That community without the spirit of philosophy could not deduce conclusions from these sciences.

The Ottoman Government and the Khedivate of Egypt have been opening schools for the teaching of the new sciences for a period of sixty years, and until now they have not received any benefit from those sciences. The reason is that teaching the philosophical sciences was impossible in those schools, and because of the nonexistence of philosophy, no fruit was obtained from those sciences

---

[4] The second word is *ḥikma*, philosophy or wisdom in a broader sense, which Afghānī uses almost synonymously with *falsafa*, (Greek-oriented) philosophy.

that are like limbs. Undoubtedly, if the spirit of philosophy had been in those schools, during this period of sixty years they themselves, independent of the European countries, would have striven to reform their kingdoms in accord with science. Also, they would not send their sons each year to European countries for education, and they would not invite teachers from there to their schools. I may say that if the spirit of philosophy were found in a community, even if that community did not have one of those sciences whose subject is particular, undoubtedly their philosophic spirit would call for the acquisition of all the sciences.

The first Muslims had no science, but, thanks to the Islamic religion, a philosophic spirit arose among them, and owing to that philosophic spirit they began to discuss the general affairs of the world and human necessities. This was why they acquired in a short time all the sciences with particular subjects that they translated from the Syriac, Persian, and Greek into the Arabic language at the time of Manṣūr Davānaqī.[5]

It is philosophy that makes man understandable to man, explains human nobility, and shows man the proper road. The first defect appearing in any nation that is headed toward decline is in the philosophic spirit. After that deficiencies spread into the other sciences, arts, and associations.

As the relationship between the preeminence of philosophy and the sciences has been explained, we now wish to say something about the quality of teaching and learning among the Muslims. Thus, I say that the Muslims these days do not see any benefit from their education. For example, they study grammar, and the purpose of grammar is that someone who has acquired the Arabic language be capable of speaking and writing. The Muslims now make grammar a goal in itself. For long years they expend philosophic thought on grammar to no avail, and after finishing they are unable to speak, write, or understand Arabic.

Rhetoric, which they call *literature*,* is the science that enables a man to become a writer, speaker, and poet. However, we see these days that after studying that science they are incapable of correcting their everyday speech.

Logic, which is the balance for ideas, should make everyone who

---

[5] A nickname for the first important Abbasid caliph, who ruled A.D. 754–775. In fact the main translations were done later under al-Ma'mūn (813–833).

acquires it capable of distinguishing every truth from falsehood and every right from wrong. However, we see that the minds of our Muslim logicians are full of every superstition and vanity, and no difference exists between their ideas and the ideas of the masses of the bazaar.

Philosophy[6] is the science that deals with the state of external beings, and their causes, reasons, needs, and requisites. It is strange that our ulama read Ṣadrā and Shams al-bāri'a[7] and vaingloriously call themselves sages, and despite this they cannot distinguish their left hand from their right hand, and they do not ask: Who are we and what is right and proper for us? They never ask the causes of electricity, the steamboat, and railroads.

Even stranger, from early evening until morning they study the Shams al-bāri'a with a lamp placed before them, and they do not once consider why if we remove its glass cover, much smoke comes out of it, and when we leave the glass, there is no smoke. Shame on such a philosopher, and shame on such philosophy! A philosopher is someone whose mind is stimulated by all the events and parts of the world, not one who travels along a road like a blind man who does not know where its beginning and end are.

Jurisprudence among the Muslims includes all domestic, municipal, and state laws. Thus a person who has studied jurisprudence profoundly is worthy of being prime minister of the realm or chief ambassador of the state, whereas we see our jurisconsults after studying this science unable to manage their own households, although they are proud of their own foolishness.

The science of principles consists of the philosophy of the shari'a,

---

6 Here ḥikma.

7 Of the Ṣadrā, Seyyed Hossein Nasr, in M. M. Sharif, ed., A History of Muslim Philosophy, II (Wiesbaden, 1966), says: "The works of Mulla Ṣadra have continued to be taught in the Islamic schools of the Indian sub-continent, especially his Sharḥ al-Hidāyah, which came to be known by the author's name as Ṣadra" (p. 960 n. 74). No source consulted lists a work entitled Shams al-bāri'a, which must be a typographical error for a book whose title is orthographically similar in Arabic, ash-Shams al-bāzigha. My research assistant, Miss Shannon Stack, found the latter work listed with Maḥmūd Jaunfūrī Farūqī as author. Of it Seyyed Hossein Nasr, Three Muslim Sages (Cambridge, Mass., 1964), p. 155 n. 51, says: "the extent of the influence of the doctrines of Suhrawardī and Mullā Ṣadrā can be guaged by . . . [several things including] their influence upon such later Indian works of philosophy as al-Shams al-bāzighah, which has always been a favorite text of philosophy in traditional schools of the subcontinent."

or *philosophy of law*.* In it are explained the truth regarding right and wrong, benefit and loss, and the causes for the promulgation of laws. Certainly, a person who studies this science should be capable of establishing laws and enforcing civilization. However, we see that those who study this science among the Muslims are deprived of understanding of the benefits of laws, the rules of civilization, and the reform of the world.

Since the state of these ulama has been demonstrated, we can say that our ulama at this time are like a very narrow wick on top of which is a very small flame that neither lights its surroundings nor gives light to others. A scholar is a true light if he is a scholar. Thus, if a scholar is a scholar he must shed light on the whole world, and if his light does not reach the whole world, at least it should light up his region, his city, his village, or his home. What kind of scholar is it who does not enlighten even his own home?

The strangest thing of all is that our ulama these days have divided science into two parts. One they call Muslim science, and one European science. Because of this they forbid others to teach some of the useful sciences. They have not understood that science is that noble thing that has no connection with any nation, and is not distinguished by anything but itself. Rather, everything that is known is known by science, and every nation that becomes renowned becomes renowned through science. Men must be related to science, not science to men.

How very strange it is that the Muslims study those sciences that are ascribed to Aristotle with the greatest delight, as if Aristotle were one of the pillars of the Muslims. However, if the discussion relates to Galileo, Newton, and Kepler, they consider them infidels. The father and mother of science is proof, and proof is neither Aristotle nor Galileo. The truth is where there is proof, and those who forbid science and knowledge in the belief that they are safeguarding the Islamic religion are really the enemies of that religion. The Islamic religion is the closest of religions to science and knowledge, and there is no incompatibility between science and knowledge and the foundation of the Islamic faith.

As for Ghazālī, who was called the Proof of Islam, in the book *Deliverance from Error* he says that someone who claims that the Islamic religion is incompatible with geometric proofs, philosophical demonstrations, and the laws of nature is an ignorant friend of Islam. The harm of this ignorant friend to Islam is greater than the harm of the heretics and enemies of Islam. For the laws of nature, geometric proofs, and philosophic demonstrations are self-evident truths. Thus, someone who says, "My religion is inconsistent with self-evident truths," has inevitably passed judgment on the falsity of his religion.

The first education obtained by man was religious education, since philosophical education can only be obtained by a society that has studied some science and is able to understand proofs and demonstrations. Hence we can say that reform will never be achieved by the Muslims except if the leaders of our religion first reform themselves and gather the fruits of their science and knowledge.

If one considers, he will understand this truth, that the ruin and corruption we have experienced first reached our ulama and religious leaders, and then penetrated the rest of the community.

I now wish to excuse myself, since, contrary to his promise, the *principal** caused this talk to be delivered only in an abbreviated form.

The
Benefits
of Philosophy

*Philosophy summons
scholars in its loudest voice
and demands her rights
from them before
the tribunal of reason.* *

W<small>HAT</small> is the meaning of philosophy, or *ḥikma*?[1]
What is its purpose and what are its benefits? What might be the true
cause of its appearance in the human sphere? What was the basic
reason for its spread among the Muslims? What is its general pre-
scription and venerated model, and where are its end and goal? Is
complete satisfaction to be found in the works of Fārābī, Ibn Sīnā,
Ibn Bājja, Shihāb ad-Dīn the Martyr, Mīr Bāqir, Mullā Sadrā,[2] and
the other treatises and notes concerned with philosophy, or is it not?

The ancients defined and described philosophy with pleasing and
close-fitting expressions. However, those definitions, because of
strange expressions, peculiar coinages, and difficulties in composition (as people find satisfaction in what is strange), caused their very
forms of expression to become the essential goal of teachers, the
fundamental object of scholars, the focus of the desires of the philosophers, and the field for the thoughts of the logicians. Their
meaning and significance were left behind and abandoned to such
an extent that it seemed the learned never had any aim or intention
with their definitions except to speak of Universality and Exclusion,
and to mention the Comprehensive Category and the Exclusive
Section.

Therefore, turning my eyes away from them, and abandoning the
bonds of tradition, although it is difficult, I say as follows:

---

* In Arabic.

[1] *Ḥikma* means "philosophy," or "wisdom," in a broader sense than *falsafa*,
which is limited to the Greek and Greek-inspired schools of philosophy. In Afghānī's articles the two words are used almost synonymously, however, and both
will be translated as "philosophy."

[2] On these philosophers, see p. 63 n. 31.

Philosophy is the escape from the narrow sensations of animality into the wide arena of human feelings. It is the removal of the darkness of bestial superstitions with the light of natural intelligence; the transformation of blindness and lack of insight into clearsightedness and insight. It is salvation from savagery and barbarism, ignorance and foolishness, by entry into the virtuous city of knowledge and skillfulness. In general, it is man's becoming man and living the life of sacred rationality. Its aim is human perfection in reason, mind, soul, and way of life. Perfection in one's way of life and welfare in livelihood are the chief preconditions for the perfection of mind and soul. [Philosophy] is the first cause of man's intellectual activity and his emergence from the sphere of animals, and it is the greatest reason for the transfer of tribes and peoples from a state of nomadism and savagery to culture and civilization. It is the foremost cause of the production of knowledge, the creation of sciences, the invention of industries, and the initiation of the crafts.

For man, in order to perfect his way of life, needs to cultivate, to plant trees, preserve fruits, procure animals, protect rivers, bring forth waters, dig canals, dikes, and dams, to spin and weave, in an agreeable and appropriate way. He must also know how to build buildings in such a way as befits human life, to preserve his health, and cure the unforeseen illnesses of his body. All of this is only produced through the use of digging, cutting, breaking, carving, boring, lifting, transporting, leveling, straightening, and weighing. And it is achieved only with knowledge of the times, seasons, and atmospheric phenomena; with a mastery of the nature of soils, climatic features, and atmospheric influences; and knowing the constitution of compound bodies and the action and reaction of the elements, the process of analysis and synthesis and its instruments.

Since the management by a single individual of all these manifold affairs is difficult, if not impossible, naturally, cooperation and exchange will be indispensable in the affairs that are designated as human relationships (mu'āmala). Hence human perfection in life requires innumerable details that have no end or limit. Therefore, it became incumbent upon man to group those details under general rules and universal laws. When he found that the general rules had become numerous, he classified them according to their relation and similarity, and occupied himself with the foundation of sciences and arts. Among these were the arts of husbandry and cultivation, and the sciences of animals, veterinary science, geometry, trigonometry, surveying, arithmetic, algebra, medicine, surgery, anatomy, physiology, the special features of drugs and the manner of their composition, astronomy, geography, astrolaby, navigation, mineralogy, geology, physics, mechanics, hydraulics, meteorology, and chemistry (which consists of the science of analysis of compounds and the composition of elements and their special properties). [Among them also] were domestic economy, the art of civil legislation, municipal regulations, and governmental policy. Since the basic aim of these arts was the performance of occupations, men made a great effort for conformity and adaptation between knowledge and practice, and to the degree that the numbers of men increased and their needs multiplied, progress was experienced in these arts and the problems relating to them increased and multiplied. It was for this reason that I said the primary cause of the majority of sciences, knowledge, and arts was the perfection of man's way of life.

Man, after achieving some comfort in his life, turns his attention toward his soul. He realizes that perfection of his livelihood and the sources of bodily comfort, when accompanied by the corruption of manners and evil internal habits, is pure deficiency. For what ease and tranquillity will exist, even though all the means of livelihood be present, for the coward upset by imaginary events and disasters, or the hydropic glutton who suffers from insatiable hunger, or the envious man pained by the wealth of others, or the choleric man inflamed over insignificant slips, or the miser barred from pleasures?

Therefore, it was through philosophy that virtuous characteristics were distinguished from vicious habits, so that spiritual perfection might be achieved through man's refinement and purification. Man invented the art of the rectification of morals (tahdhīb-i akhlāq) in order to control his soul and safeguard the holy virtues in it. Once reason had arranged for the welfare of the body and its livelihood, and for the rectification and straightening of manners, reason directed its thoughts toward itself, seeking its own anticipated perfection, true life, eternal happiness, and intellectual pleasures.

With the guidance of the philosophical spirit (ḥikma), reason began to deal with its own genesis and true nature, and to seek the causes of perceptions, the bases of mental faculties, and their relations with bodily sensations. It began to inquire into the consequences and effects of each of them, wanting to know the reasons for soundness and corruption in each one. It put forth great effort to understand the relation of minds and spirits to bodies. It investigated one by one the reasons for the differences of character among peoples and the cause for the acquisition of each character. It discussed the circumstances of the rise and fall of peoples in civilization, science, learning, and manufactures. It sought the causes of laws and the reasons for legislation. Making the universe the object of its thought and consideration, it reflected on and penetrated, in both a general and particular fashion, the universe's origin, source, and material, its accidents and incidents, and its causes and effects. It investigated the causes of attraction and repulsion, rapprochement and estrangement, and action and reaction, of the parts of the universe, and disclosed their movements and causes. It understood, to the extent that philosophy was able to help, the cause for the formation of the germs of plants and animals, the conditions of their transformation into organized bodies and firm and solid forms, and the aim of their existence.

[Man] reflected minutely on his immortality and felicity. Then, in order to collect the general laws and control the innumerable details that are connected with the above matters, he established several special fields: such as rational philosophy, ethical philosophy, the philosophy of history, the philosophy of law, metaphysical philosophy, and transcendental philosophy.

When the goal of philosophy became evident, it was clear and manifest that the first cause and true occasion for its genesis in the human sphere was, first of all, the necessity and difficulty in man's means of livelihood, and the arduousness of his life, like other animals; and, second, innate reason and natural intellect. For man's life and being depend on the perception of causes and reasons, and his delights and joys consist in the uncovering of unknown things and coming to know the secrets of the world of existence.

As for the reason for [philosophy's] spread among the Muslims, you must know that the higher ideas of every people (*qaum*), or even individual, are in proportion to the basic general capacities of that people or individual. Basic general capacities will be proportional to the particular items of knowledge, and the particular items of knowledge will be proportional to their necessities of existence and their way of life. This subject will become clear from a comparison of a rural child with an urban child. Consequently, a people immersed in nomadism and hardship, plunged in barbarism, and accustomed to hardness, roughness, harshness, and squalor in dress, food, dwelling, and shelter will have very few prerequisites for existence, necessities of life, and furnishings for living; and the life and existence of that people will be close to the life and existence of animals. When they are at this base degree and move and operate in this narrow sphere, naturally their individual capacities will be proportionally small. And when particular capacities, which are the source of derivation, are extremely small, never will the basic general capacities that spring from them reach the maximum level, nor will that people ever become the holders of lofty ideas. Rather in their intelligence they will also be close to the level of animals.

Whoever has a little acquaintance with the subject of history will know that in past centuries and ancient times no people could be found who were further from civilization, more immersed in nomadism, or more established in barbarism than the Arab people. Therefore, this people in ancient times had no learning besides some poems based on fancies. They were completely deprived of lofty intellectual stirrings, comprehensive rational conceptions, and great philosophical subjects until the time that the First Creator and Absolute Reality by means of His chosen Prophet sent his Precious Book. In that Precious Book, after summoning to Unity [tauḥīd—the absolute unity of God] and then demanding recognition for the prophets, who are the receptacles of divine decree, He in many places condemned as heinous, blameworthy acts, stupidity, blindness, following conjectures and superstitions, and pursuing imitation. On many occasions He eloquently praised knowledge, wisdom, learning, reflection, thought and insight. He explained with decisive phrases the harm of base morals, and revealed with firm examples the benefits of virtuous habits. He provided a description of former peoples, and in conjunction with that He noted the worldly reward to each of them for perseverance and moderation, and the immediate recompense for crookedness and deviation, in order that they should take heed. He explained the bases of the comprehensive laws of domestic and civil relationships so that they should become the cause of total happiness, and clarified the harm of oppression and injustice, which are the result of savagery and barbarism.

He said to man: That which is on earth was created for you; therefore, do not become monks, but take according to your just share of its pleasures and do not deprive yourselves of beauty, which is a divine gift. He promised those perfect in mind and soul, who constituted the virtuous, rule over the whole earth. In sum, in that

Precious Book, with solid verses, He planted the roots of philosophical sciences into purified souls, and opened the road for man to become man.

When the Arab people came to believe in that Precious Book they were transferred from the sphere of ignorance to knowledge, from blindness to vision, from savagery to civilization, and from nomadism to settlement. They understood their needs for intellectual and spiritual accomplishment, and for gaining a living. Those roots and foundations gradually grew up; ideas multiplied; and minds moved into vast spheres of the world in order to acquire perfection, until a group in the time of Manṣūr Davānaqī[3] noted that going through these stages and traversing these infinite degrees without seeking the aid of their fellow men would be fraught with hardship and difficulty. They realized that to be proud regarding learning is to be satisfied with ignorance.

Therefore, notwithstanding the glory, splendor, and greatness of Islam and the Muslims, in order to exalt and elevate knowledge, they lowered their heads and showed humility before the lowest of their subjects, who were the Christians, Jews, and Magians, until, with their help, they translated the philosophical sciences from Persian, Syriac, and Greek into Arabic.

Hence it becomes clear that that Precious Book was the first teacher of philosophy to the Muslims. It is the comprehensive exemplar of the macrocosm. Each individual is a letter, each species a word, each race a line, and each microcosm a page in it; and each movement and change an elucidation and annotation of it. No end exists for this great Book. Its letters, words, lines, and pages are incapable of being counted by man. In each word, and even in each letter, so many mysteries and secrets are hidden that if all the sages of the past and present had the lifetime of Noah, and each one solved a thousand mysteries and uncovered a thousand secrets each day, nonetheless they would remain incapable of fathoming it, and would confess their inablity.

Thus if someone claims that with two or three old sheets that he has in hand he has achieved a perfect comprehension of the world and has understood all its secrets, of course he is suffering from compound ignorance or madness,[4] and the latter is more likely.

---

[3] A nickname for the Abbasid caliph Manṣūr, who ruled A.D. 754–775.
[4] Arabic, from the Greek, malīkhūliyā.

Whatever anyone has written is in accord with the strength or weakness of his perception of unity and dissolution, and his insight into the book of the world. Since man's perfection in reason and life is in accord with the extent of his knowledge of the book of the world and his own state, it is clear that human perfection can have no limit or end. Therefore, it is incumbent on each individual separately and on each people collectively to set up for itself that universal exemplar in order to ascend the degrees of intellectual and existential perfection and, penetrating with the eye of insight, to obtain each day a fresh share and new portion of it.

When this became clear, then it was manifest and evident to everyone that philosophy has no limit or end, and that it has no measure. In each one of its degrees, considered in itself, there is perfection, but when one looks at a higher degree the former one would be considered imperfection. Stopping at any one of its degrees is a manifestation of neglect and shortcoming, or of blindness and compound ignorance, or of low endeavor and a base nature.

The works of the Islamic sages are in many respects defective and incomplete, not to mention their multiple insufficiencies in producing human perfection. *The First Respect* is that the subjects contained in those books, in fact and reality, are not clear to us as they were among the Greek philosophers. Rather, the Muslim philosophers showed them to us with the adornment of perfection and the garment of infallibility. They closed the doors of why and wherefore to pure minds. The reason for this was that they believed the Greek and Roman philosophers were all possessors of absolute reason, followers of pious habits, and endowed with celestial powers and true revelations, and that the scope of their senses and mental powers was above the scope of the senses of other men. Therefore, accepting their words like a celestial revelation, they followed them completely. They followed them in arguments and proofs just as the masses follow their leaders in objects and aims. Even Ibn Sīnā, despite the glory of his rank, when he wanted to contradict his teacher, Aristotle the Greek, on the problem of celestial souls, considered this a very great matter. Alarm and dread overcame him, and terror and fear enveloped him. Because of this he first, with great shame and regret, made a slight allusion to his innovation, and after that, in another place, he explained it with extreme helplessness and agitation. Mullā Sadrā had such strong faith in those people that he considered [suspicions of] unbelief, heresy, and irreligion impossible regarding them. He wished to defend Democritus, Thales, Empedocles, Epicurus, and the others, and taking every one of their sayings that clearly denied the Creator and interpreting them allegorically, he brought weak excuses in their behalf.

Shihāb ad-Dīn the Martyr,[5] widening the scope of imitation, accepted the sayings of Zoroaster too with complete confidence, without true proof or real arguments, and gave fresh luster to the doctrine of light and darkness. This confidence by the Muslim philosophers arose because of their belief that each one of those ancient philosophers had invented some branches of philosophy with extreme certitude and the utmost solidity, without the help of the ideas of others, notwithstanding the obscurity of their problems and the difficulty of their subjects. They disregarded the fact that the philosophic sciences, like the other sciences and arts, have achieved their aim through the succession of ideas and the progress of beliefs.

India was the first origin of the fundamentals of all these subjects, and from there they moved to Babylonia, and from Babylonia to Egypt. From Egypt they moved to the lands of the Greeks and Romans. In every move they acquired a new form, and in each migration they received fresh adornment. They were transferred from one state to another, just as the germs of plants and animals are transformed from a state of imperfection to perfection. The Greek and Roman philosophers contributed nothing new to those subjects except a few doctrines and some minor opinions; however, since they did not explicitly mention the names of their teachers, the Islamic philosophers believed they had brought these subjects from the concealment of non-existence into the world of existence, and had displayed them to view with no precedent. Some of the Islamic philosophers, operating in that same narrow sphere of imitation, inscribed on pages with great pleasure some types of artificial arguments and decorated discussions. In order to rhyme with Greek philosophy they named it Yamanite philosophy.[6]

---

[5] Suhrawardī "the Executed," who was killed in A.D. 1191 for his heretical views. He cited pre-Islamic Persian thinkers in support of his mystical "illuminationist" philosophy.

[6] The phrases rhyme in Persian. According to Seyyed Hossein Nasr, *Three Muslim Sages* (Cambridge, Mass., 1964), p. 151 n. 26: "Some writers like Mīr Dāmād, the influential Safavid sage, contrast ḥikmat-i yūnānī, or Greek philosophy—meaning rationalistic philosophy—with ḥikmat-i yamānī, or Yamanī wisdom—that is, a wisdom based on illumination."

The Second Aspect [of the imperfection of the Islamic philosophers] is the intrusion into the philosophic subjects in those books of, chiefly, the theological subjects of the Sabaeans.[7] The reason for that was that the Greeks and Romans were Sabaean in religion, having faith in celestial bodies and stars, and believing in numerous Gods. Therefore, they inserted their beliefs into the tablets of philosophy with artificial proofs, ornamented words, embellished statements, beautiful explanations, sweet speeches, and agreeable convictions, and imagined them to be the real problems of philosophy. Among these were: belief in the Platonic Idea and in the Gods of particular spheres who constituted their deities; their judgment concerning the impossibility of separation and fusion in the celestial spheres and their [the spheres'] belonging to the fifth element, and the proof of comprehensive minds and souls by way of them; and the glorification of problems connected with celestial bodies. The Muslim philosophers, not understanding this point, accepted all those problems out of trust in their authors and wrote them down in their own works.

If a fair person penetrates those matters somewhat with the light of insight it becomes clear to him that not even one proof is mentioned in order to substantiate them. Rather, as is the custom of the theologians of every religion, they have presented their own opinions for their audience, along with some adornments.

The Third Aspect is that the problems included in those books are in themselves incomplete and fragmentary. As for the problems of algebra and of astronomy, the authors themselves in their own books judged them to be incomplete. Take the *Khulāsa al-ḥisāb* and the *Tadhkira* of Tūsī.[8] Even Tūsī, after he added to his predecessors with the power of his thought, and in order to complete the questions of astronomy, gave the celestial universe several new celestial bodies out of the private world of his imagination, nevertheless several times confessed his own inadequacy.

As for the problems of nature, you must know that the whole problem of the composition of bodies from material substance and

---

[7] The Sabaeans, a pagan sect in northern Mesopotamia, especially Ḥarrān, followed a religion in which the Creator was to be reached through the intermediary of spirits who activated the stars, planets, and elements. They helped transmit science and philosophy to the early Muslims. Afghānī uses the word in a broad sense that includes Greek and Roman polytheism.

[8] Naṣīr ad-Dīn Ṭūsī, A.D. 1201–1274, was a prominent Persian philosopher and scientist of the Avicennan school.

form, and its appurtenances, depends on the fact that a necessary precondition of a body is the supposition of the extension of connected units of measure, and requires a quantity of measurements. As examples [take] the proof of total annihilation from the instance of separation; the coming into being of two things from nothingness; and the combining of union and separation in the same object. Here the authors have passed hastily, although in another place they have stipulated contrary to the bases of this problem, and said that only quantity is in itself capable of being separated. Afterward they became aware [of this] and arbitrarily decided on a division between quantitative separation and separation of dissolution, although the latter is a branch of the former.

They explained that there is no intermediary between potentiality and actuality, and that movement in the absolute sense has no existence. Rather, the existence of movement is in an intermediary sense, and it is instantaneous. After that they decided that movement is the emergence of a thing from potentiality to actuality by degrees, and this is the essence of the incompleteness of their words.

They stipulated that time exists and that it is a quantity of movement. Then they repeated that nothing else exists outside that current, and that is other than time. They said that nature is an extended quantitative thing, and that quantity is an accidental dimension, characterized by extension. They denied pure dimension, despite the fact that the supposed obstacle to the existence of pure dimension can be held true, with slight change, in respect to every corporeal image and quantity. Stranger than this is that, denying the existence of pure dimension, they then do not explain the existence of local movement.

They considered water, air, earth, and fire elements, and set down their inability to decompose them as proof. They noted the restriction of elements with a certain amout of doubt. It apparently was not possible that another doubt would increase that doubt. It was said that each one of them is either flammable or not, that each of them is either malleable or not, and so forth. There is no doubt that if this point had been understood, the number of elements would not have been limited to four from the time of Aristotle until now.

Regarding the transformation of elements, they were satisfied with mere conjectures. On some problems of meteorology, such as the rainbow, the just men among them confessed their helplessness, and the unjust ones expressed confused doctrines. In some other questions, like thunder, lightning, shooting stars, and winds, they generally followed their fancies, and had no proof at hand. Some questions, like tornadoes and hurricanes, they completely abandoned. Regarding minerals and earthquakes, they were satisfied with fantasies, and regarding plants and animals they spoke incompletely. They were not aware of the causes of growth and life, and the reasons for the differences of shapes and forms, and they did not speak decisive words that were based on proofs or true experiments regarding internal senses. Regarding vision, they mentioned their own imaginings without proof. They remained baffled with regard to colors, tastes, and odors. They were silent about the Milky Way, and the largeness or smallness of the fixed stars. They expressed bewilderment concerning the heat of the sun, the materials that are in the moon, and the various colors that are in the planets.

They judged that the forces inherent in a body embrace the particular meanings whose particularity consists of added incorporeal bodies, the individual lines that terminate at certain points, and the points of convergence of those lines.

After that, because of the perception of simple things consistent with reason which in minds are nothing but suggestive meanings and revealing forms, they accepted the separateness of the soul, and this is an occasion for surprise. They explained the relations of the soul to the body and the manner of its influence with ambiguous words. They considered it legitimate that matter be the place for the rational soul from all eternity. After connecting the soul and the body, and deriving a complete relationship, they [nonetheless] refused that the soul be subject to corruption, assuming that corruption, like accidental attributes, requires a place, despite the fact that corruption means annihilation and nonexistence.

As for the problems of divinity, let it be known that they believed first in the necessity of homogeneity and complete proportionality between the cause and effect (let reference be made to al-Muḥākamāt[9]). Afterward they said that God Almighty is the cause of all possibilities—some with no intermediary and some with meditation.

---

9 Al-Muḥākamāt (Trials), a fourteenth-century philosophical work by the Persian Quṭb ad-Dīn Rāzī, which discusses the merits of philosophic and theological commentaries on Avicenna's Ishārāt. (See Nasr, Three Muslim Sages, p. 47.)

They remained silent in explaining homogeneity and proportionality between the sublime necessary and the possibilities.

Regarding the happiness and unhappiness of the soul, they contented themselves with poetic doctrines. In sum, the majority of problems in those books are incomplete.

As for the books of the moderns, they are all full of discussions of "In the name of God," "Praise God," and "May the blessings and peace of God be upon Him;" and of disputes, quarrels, and a mixture of scientific topics. There is no doubt that the books of the ancients among the Muslim philosophers, with all their defects, from all points of view are better than the works of the moderns, just as the early Muslims were better than the Muslims of today in everything.

Since philosophy, its goal and writers, and the state of the books of the Muslim philosophers have become clear, now, addressing the scholars and learned men of India, I say: "O, possessors of pure talents, holders of good and clean instincts, masters of penetrating minds, and possessors of broad thoughts: Why do you not raise your eyes from those defective books and why do you not cast your glance on this wide world? Why do you not employ your reflection and thought on events and their causes without the veils of those works? Why do you always utilize those exalted minds on trifling problems, such as: Is science among the spontaneous things, not requiring definition? Does science belong to an active category or a passive category? Or, is it a category of addition or a category of condition? Is the subject of logic [one of] the secondary rational sciences or spontaneous concepts or beliefs, and if not, how was it possible that its totality be conceived in the mind and outside? [Since] the universal embraces the species, and the species embraces the universal, then what remedy should be chosen? And what difference is there between kind and matter? Is verification simple or compound? And what is the thing that depends on verification? Is creation simple or compound?

"Yet you spend no thought on this question of great importance, incumbent on every intelligent man, which is: What is the cause of the poverty, indigence, helplessness, and distress of the Muslims, and is there a cure for this important phenomenon and great misfortune or not? And has the First Principle and Absolute Reality established a cause, prerequisite, and motive force for their reform or not? And is the essence of reform of this community possible or impossible, and if it is possible, can it be realized or is it impracticable? If it is capable of realization, what would be the causes, conditions, and implements of that [realization] and what is its material and formal cause? What is its origin, and what is the name of the last component of its complete cause?"

There is no doubt or question that if someone does not spend his whole life on this great problem, and does not make this grievous phenomenon the pivot of his thought, he has wasted and ruined his life, and it is improper to call him a sage, which means one who knows the essential conditions of beings.

"If this eye was weeping from ardent love for someone other
    than Lailā,
Then those were wasted tears."[10]

Once more I call: O, ulama of India, O sources of exact views, mines of apposite opinions, and springs of deep thoughts; authors of many works and compositions, composers of beautiful treatises and commentaries: Is your pure nature and pious, divine character really satisfied and content that you expend your bright minds in these discussions of whether, at the time of consideration, verification of the unity of the diverse is necessary or not? And if Zaid says, "What I will say tomorrow will be a lie," and when tomorrow comes, he says, "What I said yesterday was a lie," will his lie involve a truth and his truthfulness involve a lie or not??!! And since what is externally impossible is impossible in the mind, then what will be the judgment regarding the impossibility of impossible things?

And you never once consider the telegraph lines that extend to all regions of India, nor ask about their causes. And you do not make electricity, which is the source of astonishing deeds and wonderful acts, the arena of your thought. Every day you repeat that vision is through the emission of rays. And photography, which has now spread throughout the entire land, does not stimulate your minds in any way, and you do not incline the reins of thought toward it. You do not ask about steam power, which transports loads and burdens from one country to another, moving with great speed on

---

[10] In Arabic, from one of the poems about the famous lovers Lailā and Majnūn.

iron rails. You do not take as a point and subject of investigation the phonograph,[11] the camera, the telescope, the microscope, and such things.

Is it permissible that you abandon investigation of these new things because they are not mentioned in the *Shifā* of Ibn Sīnā or the *Illuminist Philosophy* of Shihāb ad-Dīn?[12] Is it not incumbent upon you to serve those who will follow you with your highest thoughts, just as your revered predecessors served you? Is it not necessary for a philosopher, and even for every intelligent man who is dissatisfied with ignorance, not to be content with heedlessness. Is it not a defect for a person that his thought does not move so as to seek causes?

Is it not a fault for a percipient sage not to learn the entire sphere of new sciences and inventions and fresh creations, when he has no information about their causes and reasons; and when the world has changed from one state to another and he does not raise his hand from the sleep of neglect? Is it worthy of an investigator that he speak in absolute ignorance and not know what is definitely known? He splits hairs over imaginary essences and lags behind in the knowledge of evident matters.

This is a summary of what I wished to set forth in this regard, and, God willing, I will return again to this subject and speak in detail about it. I hope the learned ulama of India will look attentively at this article, and certainly after a true consideration my pure intention will become clear and manifest to them.

---

11 *Ḥāfiza aṣ-Ṣaut*, an Arabic coinage meaning "preserver of sound," which could refer either to the phonograph or, possibly, the telephone. Since both were invented in the United States in 1876–77, and Afghānī was writing in a princely state in South India in 1880–81, one sees the eagerness with which he followed modern Western inventions.

12 Reference is to two of the major works of the two philosophers. Afghānī uses the Persian title *Ḥikmat-i ishrāq* for Shihāb ad-Dīn Suhrawardī's work, although the Arabic form *Ḥikma al-ishrāq* is more correct.

*He who does not look
upon things with the eye
of insight is lost and
to be blamed.**

Commentary
on the
Commentator

Man is man because of education. None of the
peoples of mankind, not even the savage, is completely deprived of
education. If one considers man at the time of his birth, one sees
that his existence without education is impossible. Even if we assumed that his existence were possible without education, his
life would in that state be more repulsive and vile than the life of
animals. Education consists of a struggle with nature, and overcom-
ing her, whether the education be in plants, animals, or men.

Education, if it is good, produces perfection from imperfection,
and nobility from baseness. If it is not good it changes the basic
state of nature and becomes the cause of decline and decadence.
This appears clearly among agriculturalists, cattle raisers, teachers,
civil rulers, and religious leaders. In general, good education in these
three kingdoms [human, animal, and plant] is the cause of all perfections and virtues. Bad education is the source of all defects and
evils.

When this is understood, one must realize that if a people receives a good education, all of its classes and ranks, in accord with
the natural law of relationships, will flourish simultaneously and
will progress. Each class and group among that people, according to
its rank and degree, tries to acquire the perfections that are appropriate to it, and does obtain them. The classes of that people,
according to their rank, will always be in a state of balance and equi-
librium with each other. This means that just as great rulers will
appear among such a people because of their good education, so

---

* In Arabic.

there will also come into existence excellent philosophers, erudite scholars, skilled craftsmen, able agriculturalists, wealthy merchants, and other professions. If that people because of its good education reaches such a level that its rulers are distinguished beyond the rulers of other peoples, one can be certain that all its classes will be distinguished above the classes of other countries. This is because perfect progress in each class depends on the progress of the other classes. This is the general rule, the law of nature, and the divine practice.

When, however, corruption finds its way into that people's education, weakness will occur in all its classes in proportion to their rank and to the extent of the corruption. That is, if weakness appears in the ruling circles, this weakness will surely overtake the class of philosophers, scholars, craftsmen, agriculturalists, merchants, and the other professions. For their perfection is the effect of a good education. When weakness, disorder, and corruption are introduced into a good education, which is the causative factor, inevitably the same weakness, disorder, and corruption will enter into the effects of that education. When corruption enters a nation's education it sometimes happens that, because of the increase of corruption in education and the ruin of manners and customs, the various classes, which are the cause of stability, and especially the noble classes, are gradually destroyed. The individuals of that nation, after removing their former clothes and changing their name, become part of another nation and appear with new adornments. This happened to the Chaldeans, the Phoenicians, the Copts, and similar people.

Sometimes Eternal Grace aids that people, and some men of high intelligence and pure souls appear among them and bring about a new life. They remove that corruption which was the cause of decline and destruction, and rescue souls and minds from the terrible malady of bad education. And through their own basic luster and brightness they return the good education and give back life once more to their people. They restore to them greatness, honor, and the progress of classes.

This is why every people who enter into decline, and whose classes are overtaken by weakness, are always, because of their expectation of Eternal Grace, waiting to see if perhaps there is to be found among them a wise renewer, experienced in policy, who can enlighten their minds and purify their souls through his wise management and fine efforts, and do away with the corrupt education. By the policies of that sage they could return to their former condition.

There is no doubt that in the present age, distress, misfortune, and weakness besiege all classes of Muslims from every side. Therefore every Muslim keeps his eyes and ears open in expectation—to the East, West, North, and South—to see from what corner of the earth the sage and renewer will appear and will reform the minds and souls of the Muslims, repel the unforeseen corruption, and again educate them with a virtuous education. Perhaps through that good education they may return to their former joyful condition.

Since I am certain that the Absolute Truth *(haqq-i muṭlaq)* will not destroy this true religion and right *shari'a,* I more than others expect that the minds and souls of the Muslims will very soon be enlightened and rectified by the wisdom of a sage. For this reason I always want to keep abreast of the articles and treatises that are now appearing from the pens of Muslims, and be thoroughly acquainted with the views of their authors. I hope that in these readings I may discover the elevated ideas of a sage who could be the cause of good education, virtue, and prosperity for the Muslims. I would then hope, to the extent of my ability, to assist him in his elevated ideas and become a helper and associate in the reform of my people.

In the course of discussions and investigations about the ideas of the Muslims, I heard of one of them who, mature in years and rich in experience, took a trip to European countries. After much labor and effort he wrote a Commentary on the Koran in order to improve the Muslims. I said to myself, "Here is just what you wanted."

And as is customary with those who hear new things, I let my imagination wander, and formed various conceptions of that commentator and that commentary. I believed that this commentator, after all the commentaries written by Traditionists, jurists, orators, philosophers, Sufis, authors, grammarians, and heretics like Ibn Rāwandī and others, would have done justice to that subject, unveiled the truth, and achieved the precise goal. For he had followed the ideas of both Easterners and Westerners. I thought that this commentator would have explained in the introduction to his commentary, as wisdom requires, the truth and essence of religion for the improvement of his people. That he would have demonstrated the necessity of religion in the human world by rational proofs, and that he would have set up a general rule, satisfying the intellect, to distinguish between true and false religions. I imagined that this commentator had undoubtedly explained the influence of each of the prior, untrue religions on civilization and the social order and on men's souls and minds. I thought he would have explained in a philosophical way the reason for the divergence of religions on some matters, along with their agreement on many precepts, and the reason for the special relation of each age to a particular religion and prophet.

Since he claims to have written this commentary for the improvement of the community, I was certain he had in the introduction of his book described and explained in a new manner, with the light of wisdom, those divine policies and Koranic ethics that were the cause of the superiority and expansion of the Arabs in every human excellence. I was sure he had included in his introduction those precepts that were the cause of the unity of the Arabs, the transformation of their ideas, the enlightenment of their minds, and the purification of their souls; and all that when they were in the extremity of discord, savagery, and hardship.

When I read the commentary I saw that this commentator in no way raised a word about these matters or about divine policy. In no manner are Koranic ethics explained. He has not mentioned any of those great precepts that were the cause of the enlightenment of the minds and purification of the souls of the Arabs. He has left without commentary those verses that relate to divine policy, support the promulgation of virtuous ethics and good habits, rectify domestic and civil intercourse, and cause the enlightenment of minds. Only at the beginning of his commentary does he pronounce a few words on the meaning of "sura," "verse," and the separate letters at the beginning of the suras. After that all his effort is devoted to taking every verse in which there is mention of angels, or *jinns*, or the faithful spirit [Gabriel], revelation, paradise, hell, or the miracles of the prophets, and, lifting these verses from their external meaning, interpreting them according to the specious allegorical interpretations of the heretics of past Muslim centuries.

The difference is that the heretics of past Muslim centuries were scholars, whereas this unfortunate commentator is very ignorant. Therefore he cannot grasp their words correctly. Taking the subject of man's *nature* as a subject of discourse, he pronounces some vague and meaningless words, without rational demonstrations or natural proofs. He apparently does not know that man is man through education, and all his virtues and habits are acquired. The man who is nearest to his nature is the one who is the farthest from civilization and from acquired virtues and habits. If men abandoned the legal and intellectual virtues they have acquired with the greatest difficulty and effort, and gave over control to the hands of nature, undoubtedly they would become lower than animals.

Even stranger is the fact that this commentator has lowered the divine, holy rank of prophecy and placed it on the level of the *reformer*.* He has considered the prophets to be men like Washington, Napoleon, Palmerston, Garibaldi, Mister Gladstone, and Monsieur Gambetta.

When I saw the commentary to be of this kind, amazement overtook me, and I began to ask myself what was the purpose of this commentator in writing such a commentary. If the goal of this commentator is, as he says, the improvement of his community, then why does he try to end the belief of Muslims in the Islamic religion, especially in these times when other religions have opened their mouths to swallow this religion?

Does he not understand that if the Muslims, in their current state of weakness and misery, did not believe in miracles and hell-fire, and considered the Prophet to be like Gladstone, they undoubtedly would soon abandon their own weak and conquered camp, and attach themselves to a powerful conqueror? For in that event there would no longer remain anything to prevent this, nor any fear or anxiety. And from another standpoint the prerequisities for changing religion now exist, since being like the conqueror, and having the same religion as he, is attractive to everyone.

After these ideas and reflections, it first occurred to me that this commentator certainly believes that the cause of the decline of the Muslims and of their distressed condition is their religion itself, and that if they abandoned their beliefs they would restore their former greatness and honor. Therefore, he is trying to remove these beliefs, and because of his motivation he could be forgiven.

Having reflected further, however, I said to myself that the Jews, thanks to these same beliefs, rescued themselves from the humiliation of slavery to the pharoahs and rubbed in the dust the pride of the tyrants of Palestine. Has not the commentator heard of this?

And the Arabs, thanks to these same beliefs, came up from the desert lands of the Arabian peninsula, and became masters of the whole world in power, civilization, knowledge, manufacture, agri-

---

* In English.

culture, and trade. The Europeans in their speeches referred aloud to those believing Arabs as their masters. Has not this fact reached the ears of this commentator? Of course it has.

After considering the great effects of these true beliefs and their followers, I looked at the followers of false beliefs. I saw that the Hindus at the same time that they made progress in the laws of civilization, and in science, knowledge, and the various crafts, believed in thousands of gods and idols. This commentator is not ignorant of this. The Egyptians at the times when they laid the foundations of cilivization, science, and manufactures, and were the masters of the Greeks, believed in idols, cows, dogs, and cats. This commentator undoubtedly knows this. The Chaldeans, at the time that they founded observatories, manufactured astronomical instruments, built high castles, and composed books on agricultural science, were worshippers of the stars. This is not hidden from the commentator. The Phoenicians, in the age that they made manufacture and commerce on land and sea flourish, and colonized the lands of Britain, Spain, and Greece, presented their own children as sacrifices to idols. This is clear to the commentator.

The Greeks, in that century that they were rulers of the world, and at the time that great sages and revered philosophers appeared among them, believed in hundreds of gods and thousands of superstitions. This is known to the commentator. The Persians, at the time when they ruled from the regions of Kashgar to the frontiers of Istanbul, and were considered incomparable in civilization, had hundreds of absurdities engraved in their hearts. Of course the commentator remembers this. The modern Christians, at the same time as they acknowledged the Trinity, the cross, resurrection, baptism, purgatory, confession, and transubstantiation, assured their domination; progressed in the spheres of science, knowledge, and industry; and reached the summit of civilization. Most of them still, with all their science and knowledge, follow the same beliefs. The commentator knows this well.

When I considered these matters I realized that the commentator never was of the opinion that faith in these true beliefs caused the decline of the Muslims. For religious beliefs, whether true or false, are in no way incompatible with civilization and worldly progress unless they forbid the acquisition of science, the earning of a livelihood, and progress in sound civilization. I do not believe that there is a religion in the world that forbids these things, as appears clearly from what has been said above. Rather I can say that the lack of faith results only in disorder and corruption in civil life, and in insecurity. Reflect—this is *Nihilism!**

If the lack of faith brought about the progress of peoples, then the Arabs of the Age of Ignorance would have had to have precedence in civilization. For they were mostly followers of the materialist path, and for this reason they used to say aloud: "Wombs push us forth, the earth swallows us up, and only time destroys us." They also always used to say: "Who can revive bones after they have decomposed?"[1] This despite the fact that they lived in the utmost ignorance, like wild animals.

After all these various thoughts and considerations, I understood well that this commentator is not a reformer, nor was his commentary written for the improvement and education of the Muslims. Rather this commentator and this commentary are for the Islamic community at the present time like those terrible and dangerous illnesses that strike man when he is weak and decrepit. The aim of his modifications has been demonstrated above.

The goal of this commentator from this effort to remove the beliefs of the Muslims is to serve others and to prepare the way for conversion to their religion.

These few lines have been written hastily. Later, by the power of God, I will write in detail about this commentary and the aims of the commentator.

---

* In English.

[1] Koran 36:77.

The Truth
about the
Neicheri Sect
and an Explanation
of the Neicheris

by

JAMĀL AD-DĪN
AL-HUSAINĪ,[1]
1298 h. [1880-81]

*"Announce the good news
to my servants—those
who listen to the word
and heed the best of it.
"It is they whom God
has guided and they
who are endowed
with understanding."*
(Koran 39: 17–18)

[*The book opens with the following letter to Jamāl ad-Dīn.*]

In the name of God, the merciful, the compassionate.
To our Teacher, Jamāl ad-Dīn al-Husainī.

These days the sound, "neicher, neicher," reaches us from all over India—the Western and Northern states, Oudh, the Punjab, Bengal, Sind, and Hyderabad in the Deccan. Some men called "neicheris" are to be found in every city and town. It seems that this group is constantly growing, especially among the Muslims. I have asked many of this group: What is the truth about *neicher*, and when did this school appear? Is this *neicheriyya* group trying to reform civilization by its new policy, or do they have a different aim? Is this school incompatible with religion or does it accord with religion? How might one compare its total effects on civilization and the social order with those of religion? Also, if this is an ancient sect, then why has it not begun to spread in the world until now? If it is recent, then what effects will result from its existence? But not one of these people gave a decisive and adequate answer to my questions.

Therefore I pray that Your Honor explain for me in detail the truth about *neicher* and the *neicheriyya*.

[SIGNED] MUHAMMAD VĀSIL Instructor in Mathematics at the Madrasa-i A'azza—Hyderabad, Deccan.
—19 Muharram, 1298 hijrī [December 22, 1880]

---

[1] *Husainī* was one of the appellations used by Afghānī, indicating descent from the Imām Husain, a grandson of Muhammad.

[*To this question Jamāl ad-Dīn answered.*]

My dear friend:

Neicher means nature and the *neicheriyya* school is the same as the materialist school that appeared in Greece in the fourth and third centuries B.C. The basic aim of this *neicheriyya* sect is to abolish religions and lay the foundations of license and communism[2] among all peoples. To fulfill this aim they have made great efforts and have appeared in various guises. In every nation where they have existed they have corrupted morals and brought about decline. If one examines the aims and principles of this group, it will become clear to him that the only results of their views are the ruin of civilization and the corruption of the social order. For without doubt religion is the basic link of the social order, and without religion the foundations of civilization could never be firm.

The first doctrine of this sect is the overthrow of religions.

The reason the group has not spread, although it first appeared centuries ago, is as follows: the ordering of human society, which is a product of far-reaching divine wisdom, has always moved men to work to remove this sect. For this reason it has never enjoyed stability and permanence.

To explain these points I have written a little treatise, hoping it will be accepted by the honored intellect of my learned friend, and that those of clear intelligence will look on this treatise with confidence. Here is the treatise.

---

2 *Ishtirāk* today means "socialism," but is translated "communism" throughout this work because Afghānī later explicitly translates the French "socialistes" and "communistes" as *ijtimāʿiyīn* and *ishtirākīyīn* respectively. (The use of the genitive for the nominative plural is Afghānī's.) See p. 160 of the text.

**Religion is the Mainstay of Nations and the Source of their Welfare.
In it is their Happiness and around it is their Pivot.
Neicheriyya is the Root of Corruption and the Source of Foulness.
From it comes the ruin of the Land and the Perdition of Man.**[3]

THE word *neicher* has spread to all corners of India
in recent times. This word is mentioned at every gathering. The elite
and the masses, each according to the degree of its knowledge, explain
and interpret this word. Most of them, however, are unaware of its
true meaning, origin, and current use.

I therefore considered it my duty to set forth the true meaning and
basic purport of this word; to elucidate from the beginning the state
of the *neicheris*; to explain in detail, through history, the harm and
corruption that have occurred in the sphere of civilization and the
social order from this group; and to demonstrate by rational proofs
that this sect, in whatever nation it appears, inevitably causes the
decline and disappearance of that nation.

[The Greek
Materialists]

THE accurate histories show that in the fourth and
third centuries B.C. the Greek philosophers were divided into two
groups. One group believed that behind sensate beings and beyond
material creations there are beings devoid of matter and duration.
Those beings are free from the inseparable attributes and the acci-

---

[3] In the original this is written in Arabic in bold script as a heading to the work.

dental attributes of bodies, and pure of the defects of corporeal objects. They said that the hierarchy of these material and incorporeal beings culminated in an incorporeal being that is devoid of all attributes. This being cannot in any sense be conceived of as composite or compounded. Its existence is identical with its essence and reality, and its essence and reality are identical with its existence. It is the first cause and prime mover, the creator of all beings, whether material or immaterial. This group became known as the theists *(muta'allihūn)*, meaning those who worshipped God. Among the theists were Pythagoras, Socrates, Plato, Aristotle, and others like them.

The other group believed that nothing exists except *matière,** meaning matter and material objects that are perceived by one of the five senses. This group was called materialists. When they were asked the cause of the various effects and properties of different materials, the most ancient representatives of that group answered that they all arise from the nature of matter. Nature in the French language is "nātūr," and in English it is "neicher." Therefore this group also became known as naturalists; naturalist *(ṭabī'ī)* in French is "naturalisme," and materialist *(mādī)* is "matérialisme." *[sic]*[4]

The earliest members of this group, i.e., the materialists, then diverged regarding the formation of the stars and the genesis of plants and animals. Some believed that the genesis of the higher and lower heavenly bodies and the formation of these stable and perfected creations occurred through chance. Because of the weakness of their reason they apparently preferred to accept this view as probable so long as none more likely existed.

This belief originated with Democritus. He said that the whole terrestrial and celestial universe is composed of small hard particles that are naturally mobile, and that they appear in their present form by chance.

Some others believed that the heavens and earth have existed in their present form from eternity, and that they will always be so, and

---

* In this translation an asterisk indicates a word used in French in the original.
4 The Arabic in each case is an adjective, and the French a noun. Afghānī fairly consistently confuses his "iste" and "isme" endings. Afghānī's argument comes, in part, from the great theologian al-Ghazālī (d. 1111). In al-Ghazālī's *Confessions*, trans. C. Field (London, 1909), he classifies philosophers into three schools—the materialists and naturalists, who are accused of bestial sensuality, and the theists, including Socrates, Plato, and Aristotle (pp. 25–26). (The Arabic title of this work is *Munqidh min al-ḍalāl*, or "Deliverance from Error.")

that the chain of species of plants and animals has no beginning. In every seed a plant is enclosed, and in every one of these enclosed plants seeds are hidden, and so forth. Similarly in each animal germ an animal is concealed, in a perfectly created state, and in each of these concealed animals are hidden germs, and so on, ad infinitum. They ignored the fact that this belief necessitates the existence of infinite quantities in a finite quantity.

Another group believed that the hierarchy of plant and animal species is uncreated, as are the heavenly and earthly systems and bodies, but that the germs of plants and animals are not eternal. Rather each individual one of them is like a frame for the creation of germs that take on their form and likeness. They forgot that there are many malformed animals that give birth to perfectly formed animals.

And a small group has expressed its beliefs in summary fashion, saying that the species of plants and animals with the passage of time changed from one form to another until they reached their present form.

This supposition appeared with Epicurus, one of the followers of Diogenes the Cynic. He said that men at first were like hairy wild boars and gradually emerged into their present pleasing form. But he adduced no proof to show why the passage of time should cause this change in forms. The moderns of this group, the *neicheris,* when they saw that the science of *géologie,** or geology, nullified the belief in the infinity of the chain of species, abandoned this belief. After that they diverged in their views.

[The Modern
Materialists,
Especially Darwin]

REGARDING the creation of the germs of the various species of plants and animals [one group said] that all the germs of the species came into existence when the burning earth began to cool, and that now no more germs are being created. Another group said that there are still germs being created, especially on the equator, because of its great heat. Both groups were incapable of explaining the origin of life in these germs, whether plant or animal—especially when they observed that life is active in the elements of these germs, is the cause of their coalescence, and is the agent that takes the lifeless parts and nourishes them to life. Whenever there is a deficiency in life, there results weakness and debility in the cohesion and mutual attraction of these elements.

One group believed that these germs were on the earth at the time it separated from the sun. This is very strange because they say that the earth was then a ball of fire. How could these germs and seeds burn without their components decomposing?

The modern *neicheris* or materialists disagreed about the transformation of those germs from a defective state to perfection—from the realm of imperfection to their present perfected and durable forms. Some believed that each species has special germs, and that these germs move according to the demands of their nature, and make lifeless particles part of themselves by feeding them [*sic*], so that they take on the appearance of their species. They neglected the fact that chemical analysis has shown no difference between human sperm and the sperm of the bull or donkey. In none is there any excess or deficiency in the basic elements. Therefore, from where do special characteristics and distinctions come?

One group decided that the germs of all species, especially animals, are identical, that there is no difference between them, and that the species also have no essential distinctions. Therefore, they said, those germs transferred from one species to another and changed from one form to another through the demands of time and place, according to need and moved by external forces.

The leader of this school is Darwin. He wrote a book stating that man descends from the monkey, and that in the course of successive centuries as a result of external impulses he changed until he reached the stage of the orangutan. From that form he rose to the earliest human degree, which was the race of cannibals[5] and other Negroes. Then some men rose and reached a position on a higher plane than that of the Negroes, the plane of Caucasian man.

---

[5] *Yamyam* is a word that appears in some Turkish dictionaries and means "cannibal." We have not found it in Arabic, Persian, or Hindi dictionaries.

According to the views of this individual [Darwin], it would be possible that after the passage of centuries a mosquito could become an elephant and an elephant, by degrees, a mosquito.

If one should ask him about the species of trees and plants that have been in the forests of India from the oldest times, and were shaped in one corner of the globe by one climate, and their roots formed in the mud of one soil—why do they vary in structure, length, leaves, flowers, fruit, nourishment, and age; and what external causes have affected them despite their unity of climate and place?—he would certainly be unable to answer. If one asked him why the fish of Lake Aral and the Caspian Sea, although they share the same food and drink, and compete in the same arena, have developed different forms—what answer could he give except to bite his tongue?

Similarly, were he asked [to explain the variation among] the animals of different forms that live in one zone and whose existence in other zones would be difficult; or the insects of different kinds which do not have the power to traverse great distances—what explanation could he give except to stammer? Moreover, if one asked him: What guided those defective, unintelligent germs to the production of perfect and sound external and internal members and limbs, whose perfection and soundness the wisest men are unable to fathom, and whose benefits the masters of physiology are unable to enumerate; and how could blind necessity be the wise guide of the germs toward all these perfections of form and reason—naturally he could never raise his head from the sea of perplexity.

Only the imperfect resemblance between man and monkey has cast this unfortunate man into the desert of fantasies, and in order to control his heart, he has clung to a few vain fancies.

The horses of Siberia and the land of Russia have more hair than the horses that are born in the Arab land. The reason for this is given as need or lack of need; whereas the cause is exactly the same as the cause of the abundance or scarcity of plants in a single soil in different years because of the abundance or scarcity of rainfall and water. The same reason accounts for the leanness of the inhabitants of hot lands and the obesity of the dwellers of cold lands, because of the abundance or scarcity of decomposition.

He reports that one society used to cut off the tails of their dogs, and after they had persevered for several centuries their dogs began to be born by nature without tails. He apparently is saying that since there was no longer need for a tail, nature refrained from giving it. Is this wretch deaf to the fact that the Arabs and Jews for several thousand years have practiced circumcision, and despite this until now not one of them has been born circumcised?

Some others among the modern materialists, or *neicheris*, when they became aware of the evils of the opinions of their predecessors, turned aside from these views. They took a new path and said: "It is not possible that insensate matter can be the cause and origin of these perfected orders, stable forms, elegant shapes, and attractive figures." Therefore they took the view that the cause of these heavenly and earthly combinations and the determinant of all these forms is compounded of three things: *matière,** *force,** *intelligence,** meaning matter, force, and intelligence.

They believed that matter, because of the force in it and with the help of its intelligence and perception, has manifested and still manifests itself in these stable forms and shapes. Whenever it takes on the form of living bodies, whether living plant bodies or animal bodies, it considers the members and limbs needed for the preservation of the species and the individual, and takes account of time, place, and season. Since their line of thought is false and rotten, they neglect the fact that the belief of this group and of other modern materialists in the composition of bodies out of the Democritan particles confounds and renders useless the principle they have created with a thousand efforts and with which they have satisfied their hearts; because every Democritan atom has in this case a special force and a special intelligence, since it is impossible to posit that a single essence with individual unity can be in two places.

Since it cannot be so, I ask them: How did these separate, scattered particles become aware of each other's aims and by what instrument of explanation did they explain their affairs? In what parliament and senate did they confer in order to form these elegant and wonderful beings? And how did these separate particles know that if they were in a sparrow's egg they must there take on the form of a grain-eating bird, and that its beak and maw should be so formed as to make its life possible? And if they were in the egg of a royal falcon or an eagle they must make the beak and claw so that they can be used for hunting prey. Whence did they know before the event that this bird is going to be carnivorous?

When they are in the placenta of a dog, forming a small female dog, how do they know before the fact that this small dog will in the future be pregnant and will bring forth numerous offspring at one time, and therefore they must create for her numerous teats? And how do these scattered atoms reason that animals in their lives need a heart, lungs, a liver, brain, bone marrow, and the rest of the members and limbs?

Naturally when [the members of] this group hear these questions, their heads will sink into a sea of perplexity, and they will not be able to answer, unless they blind the eye of reason and say: "Each one of these Democritan atoms knows everything that has been and will be, and each atom in the celestial and terrestrial world coordinates its movements with those of the other atoms, so that nothing results that is contrary to order. Thus the world exists and persists according to a single order and system." In this event I would say:

First: According to this theory it would be necessary that in the small dimension of a Democritan atom, which is not visible even with a microscope, there should exist infinite dimensions. For every knowable form that is drawn on a material inevitably takes on a part of the dimension of that material; and the knowable forms of those particles, according to this false view, are infinite. Therefore infinite dimensions must exist in those finite particles, which contradicts common sense.

Also, if the atoms are so perceptive and intelligent, then why do they not cause the beings composed of them to attain their own perfection? Why do they create pain, distress, and grief? And why is the perception of man and other animals, which according to this theory is none other than the atoms, unable to fathom their own condition or to preserve their own lives?

The strange thing is that the modern materialists, despite all their inventions, have remained baffled by some questions. They cannot apply any one of their false bases or principles, whether it be nature or absolute intelligence. For they saw that the basic elements of a group of variegated beings turned out to be identical when they were analyzed. Thus, after all their idle talk they said, guessing in the dark: The atoms have different forms, and according to different circumstances of the different particles various effects are forthcoming from them.

In sum, these ten doctrines are the doctrines of that group that denies divinity and does not believe in the existence of an exalted Creator. This group both in its own usage and the usage of those who believe in God are called materialists and naturalists and *dahrīs*,[6] or if you wish *neicheris* and *naturalismes* and *matérialismes* [*sic*]. Later we will write a treatise giving details of their doctrine, and will expose the corrupt principles of this group with rational proofs.

Let it not be thought that our object will be to cavil against these Indian *payāchūs*,[7] meaning these clowns who make empty boasts. Far from it! Because they have no part or share in intelligence, wisdom, and knowledge. They have not even a share in humanity. Naturally such people are not worthy of either question, answer, or of being addressed. If they were worthy of something it would be that if someone wished to produce a *théâtre** (the *katputlī*[8] show of civilized peoples) he should use them. My basic aim will be rather the exposition of the facts, the disclosure of reality, and the expression of the truth.

Now I wish only to expose the corruption that has come into the

---

6 *Dahrī* is one of the two common Arabic words for "materialist," and the one chosen by 'Abduh in his Arabic title for the treatise on the *neicheris*. Afghānī himself usually employs the Arabic term more common in Persian, *mādī* (literally "materialist"). A full discussion of *dahriyya* by I. Goldziher, revised by A. M. Goichon, is in *EI*[2]. This defines *dahriyya* as "holders of materialistic opinions of various kinds, often only vaguely defined." *Dahr* (whose most common later meaning is "time") is a Koranic word meaning a long period of time. Its philosophic development is said to originate in the Koran 45:24, where the ungodly are cited as saying that nothing exists outside life in the world, and only *dahr* makes men perish. As a result of philosophic and literary development, traced in the *EI* article, *dahrī* came to have two philosophic connotations. "It denotes, firstly, the man who believes in the eternity of the world whether in the past or in the future, denying, as a result of this opinion, resurrection and a future life in another world; secondly, the *mulḥid*, the man who deviates from the true faith." The common Western confusion of "materialist" in its philosophic and its popular, hedonistic, sense is also found in the Arabic. The *EI* article cites al-Jāḥiẓ' *Book of the Animals*, in which "*dahrī* denotes the man who 'denies the Lord,' creation, reward and punishment, all religion and all law, listens only to his own desires and sees evil only in what conflicts with them; he recognizes no difference between man, the domestic animal and the wild beast. For him it is a question only of pleasure or pain; good is merely what serves his interests, even though it may cost the lives of a thousand men." Afghānī's description of the materialists perpetuates this confusion.

7 From the Italian *pagliaccio*, which passed into Turkish and is found in some Turkish dictionaries (with the "l" that Afghānī omits). Afghānī defines this exotic word with another exotic word for clown, *khalbūṣ*, which is Egyptian Arabic.

8 *Kaṭhputlī* is Hindustani for "puppet," but with the addition of "tamāshā," as here, it can mean a theatrical show.

sphere of civilization from the materialist or *neicheri* sect, and the harm that has resulted in the social order from their teachings, and to explain and elucidate the virtues, advantages, and benefits of religions, especially the Islamic religion.

[The Social Virtues
of Religion and
the Social Harm
of the Materialists]

THUS I say: The materialists, or *neicheris*, have appeared in numerous forms and various guises among the races and peoples, and under different names. Sometimes they have become manifest under the name of "sage," sometimes they have appeared adorned as those who remove oppression and repel injustice. Sometimes they have stepped into the arena dressed as those who know the secrets and uncover the mysteries of truth, and as the possessors of esoteric knowledge. Sometimes they have claimed that their goal is the removal of superstitions and the enlightenment of peoples' minds. For a time they came forth as the lovers of the poor, protectors of the weak, and well-wishers of the unfortunate. Sometimes to fulfill their evil aims they have laid claim to prophethood like other false prophets. Sometimes they called themselves the educators, teachers, and benefactors of the community. But among whatever people they appeared, and whatever guise or name they bore, they became—because of their evil premises and false principles, their harmful teachings, deadly views, and fatal sayings—the cause of the decline and collapse of that people and the annihilation of that community. They destroyed the social order of those peoples and scattered their members.

For man is very cruel and ignorant. And to this treacherous, greedy, bloodthirsty creature there were supplied beliefs and qualities in the earliest period by means of religions. Tribes and peoples learned these beliefs and qualities as an inheritance from the fathers and grandfathers, and they adjusted their behavior accordingly, avoiding the evil and corruption that are the destroyers of the social order. As a result they enlightened their minds with that knowledge which is the cause of happiness and the foundation of civilization. Thus there was produced for them a kind of stability and continuity.

The sect of *neicheris*, among whatever people they appeared, tried to nullify those beliefs and corrupt those qualities. From them destruction penetrated the pillars of the social order of that people and headed them toward dissolution, until they were suddenly destroyed. They [the materialists] are even now following the same evil path. The plain explanation of this is as follows:

Mankind from ancient times has attained from religions three beliefs and three qualities, each of which is a firm pillar for the existence of nations and the permanence of the social order; a stable foundation for the civilization and progress of peoples and tribes; and an active agent for the repulsion of the evil and corruption that are the cause of the dissipation of peoples.

[Religions'
Three Beliefs]

THE FIRST of these great beliefs is that there is a terrestrial angel (man), and that he is the noblest of creatures.

[Second] is the certainty that his community is the noblest one, and that all outside his community are in error and deviation.

The third is the firm belief that man has come into the world in order to acquire accomplishments worthy of transferring him to a world more excellent, higher, vaster, and more perfect than this narrow and dark world that really deserves the name of the Abode of Sorrows.

One should not neglect the important effect of each of these three beliefs on the social order, their great advantages for civilization, and their many contributions to order and the relations among peoples. Each has excellent fruits in preserving the human race and in the coexistence of its individuals in a peaceful and amical way, and each has good results in the progress of nations in intellectual and spiritual accomplishments. Each belief has, intrinsically, special virtues and concomitants that are inseparable from it.

One of the concomitants of man's belief that his species is the noblest is that he inevitably feels disdain for bestial qualities, and an aversion to animal characteristics. There is no doubt that the firmer this belief becomes, the more evident will this aversion be; and the more this aversion takes hold, the greater will be the progress of man in the intellectual sphere. His ascent on the ladder of civilization proceeds in proportion to his progress in the intellectual sphere, until he becomes one of those civilized, virtuous men whose life with brothers who have reached this rung of civilization is based on love, wisdom, and justice. This is the ultimate goal of sages and the summit of human happiness in the world.

Thus this belief is the greatest obstacle keeping man from living in the world like wild asses, cows, or beasts of the desert. It prevents him from being satisfied with the life of cattle and quadrupeds who are unable to repel harm, pain, and illness; do not know how to preserve their own lives; and pass their entire lives in a state of terror and fear. It is the greatest deterrent to men's rending each other to pieces like tearing lions, raging wolves, and biting dogs. It is the greatest obstacle keeping men from having the low and base qualities of animals. It is the best incentive for intellectual activity and the use of man's mental faculties. It is the most influential factor in purifying souls of impure vices.

Just consider: if a people or tribe did not have this belief, but rather believed that man is like other animals, or even lower than they, how many evils and vices would appear among them; what iniquities would come forth from them; how low and base their souls would be; and how their minds would be deterred from intellectual activity.

One of the consequences of the certainty that one's own community is the best one and that all others are in error is that the man who believes this will inevitably enter into rivalry and competition with the other communities; will compete against them in the arena of virtues; and will seek to be superior to and above all other communities in all the human virtues, whether intellectual, spiritual, or material. Such a man will never be satisfied with decline, baseness, or ignobility for himself and his community. He will be unable to see in another people any nobility, greatness, felicity, or prosperity without wanting it in higher measure for his own people. Because of this belief he knows himself and his own people to be the most worthy of all things that are considered in the eyes of humanity to have excellence, virtue, and nobility. If his people, owing to external forces, declines in any human virtue or excellence, his heart will never be at rest, but as long as he lives he will strive to remedy it. This belief is the best motive for peoples to compete in civilization; the greatest cause for man to seek knowledge, wisdom, and the arts; and the firmest reason for peoples to strive to obtain titles to prestige and the prerequisites of nobility.

Consider: if a community were not certain of its superiority, how much apathy there would be in the striving of its members toward the virtues; how much weakness there would be in their zeal; how much baseness and misery would envelop that people; and how it would remain in slavery, humiliation, and abasement, especially if it considered itself lower than other peoples, as do the materialist and Manichean peoples.

One of the inevitable consequences of the [third] belief, that man has come into this world in order to attain the perfections needed to transfer him to a higher and vaster world, is that when someone acquires this belief he will of necessity always strive to improve and enlighten his mind with true science and sound knowledge. He will not leave his intellect idle, but will bring out of concealment and into the light of the world what has been deposited in him of active power, lofty sentiments, and great virtues. In all stages of his life he will try to rid his soul of impure features and will not stint in the adjustment and improvement of its qualities. He will continually strive to earn property in a worthy and proper fashion, and not by use of dishonesty, deceit, treachery, swindling, bribery, and cynical flattery. He will spend it in ways that are worthy and fitting, and not in false ways.

Thus this belief is the best impulse toward civilization, whose foundations are true knowledge and refined morals. It is the best requisite for the stability of the social order, which is founded on each individual's knowledge of his proper rights, and his following the straight path of justice. It is the strongest motive for international relations, which are based on the truthful and honest observation of the bounds of human intercourse.[9] It is the best basis for the peace and calm of the classes of humanity, because peace is the fruit of

---

[9] The word here translated as "human intercourse" is *mu'āmalāt*, which has no short satisfactory English translation. It is a large category in Islamic law, concerned with all dealings between human beings and their behavior. Elsewhere in this text it is translated as "dealings" or "relationships," whichever seems the most appropriate.

love and justice, and love and justice result from admirable qualities and habits. It is the only belief that restrains man from all evils, saves him from the vales of adversity and misfortune, and seats him in the virtuous city on the throne of happiness.

Imagine: if a community did not have this belief, how widespread would be discord, hypocrisy, lying, trickery, and venality; how notorious would be greed, covetousness, treachery, murder, the denial of rights, disputes, and fighting; and what neglect would occur in the acquisition of knowledge.

[The
Three Qualities
Produced by Religion]

[As for] those three qualities that have been produced in peoples and nations from the most ancient times because of religion: [One of them] is the quality of *shame* (*ḥayā'*). That is, the shame of the soul at committing acts that would cause foulness and disgrace, and its reluctance to take on qualities that are considered to violate the world of humanity. One must realize that the influence of this quality on the regulation of the social order and in dissuading men from committing obscene acts and shameful deeds is greater than hundreds of laws or thousands of inspectors and police. For if there is no shame, what punishment except execution can detain a man who moves into the arena of vices and baseness from committing deeds that will bring on the corruption of the social order? And it is not proper that, as with Solon, the punishment for every shameful act be execution.

This quality is attached to nobility of soul, and the two cannot be separated. And nobility of soul is the basis of good order in human relations, the foundation of truthfulness in promises and firmness in treaties, and the cause of man's trustworthiness in words and deeds. This characteristic is the source of the quality of pride or zeal, which is called by two names according to its different aspects. Pride and zeal are the cause of the progress of nations, peoples, and tribes in the sciences, knowledge, honor, glory, greatness, riches, and wealth. If a people did not have pride and zeal it would never progress but would forever remain in a state of lowliness, baseness, humiliation, poverty, and subjection.

This quality, i.e., shame, is the bond of human alliances, associations, and societies, since an alliance within a group takes place only when rules are maintained, and the maintenance of rules is never achieved except with this noble trait.

It is this quality that adorns man with good manners, separates him from the obscene acts of animals, and calls him to straightforwardness and righteousness in what he does or refrains from doing. With this quality man is distinguished from other animals and removed from the sphere of bestiality. It is this unique trait that encourages rivalry for the sake of virtues, bans shortcomings, and does not allow men to be content with ignorance, stupidity, vileness, and baseness. This is the guiding wheel without which the realization and perpetuation of truth, trust, and faith would not be possible. It is the prime quality aiding teachers, educators, and counselors to exhort men to generous deeds, material and moral virtues, and external and internal nobility.

Do you not observe that wherever a teacher wants to summon his pupil to excellence he addresses him and says: "Are you not ashamed that your companion has surpassed you in excellence?" If this quality did not exist, reprimand could have no influence, disgrace would have no fruit, nor exhortation any benefit.

It thus becomes clear that this quality has been and is the basis of all virtues and excellence, the motive force of all progress. Think: if this quality were not to be found in a people what treachery and lying would be manifested among individuals, and how many vicious, obscene acts and ugly, shameful deeds would openly be committed among them! What evil, meanness, and baseness of manners would encompass them, and what animality and bestiality would overtake them.

The second quality is *trustworthiness*. It is clear to everyone that the survival of the human race and its life in this world is dependent on dealings and reciprocal relations, and the life and soul of all dealings and reciprocal relations is trustworthiness. If trustworthiness did not exist, dealings would be broken off, and the thread of reciprocal relations would be cut. If the order of dealings is torn to pieces, life and survival will never be possible for man in this world.

Also, the prosperity and peace of peoples and nations, and the regularity of their livelihood, can only be realized under a form of government, whether republican, constitutional, or absolute. Government in all its forms is created and takes on shape and reality only through a group endowed with the qualities of guardians, who prevent the encroachments of foreigners on the borders of the country, and try to uproot and suppress murderers, rapists, highwaymen, and thieves within the country. Government also requires a group that knows the revealed law and the civil laws and arrangements of governments and peoples, and sits on the chair of decision and judgment in order to decide legal and criminal disputes and settle enmities. And it needs persons who collect taxes and tribute from the people according to the laws of government, and keep them in the government treasury, which is really the treasury of all the subjects. It requires people who spend that accumulated money in an economic manner for the benefit of the entire people, as in building schools and libraries; constructing bridges and roads; founding hospitals; and paying the appointed salaries of civil servants, including the guardians, judges, and others.

The performance of their duties in a manner that keeps corruption from entering the government by this fourfold group, who are the four pillars of governments, is based on the quality of trustworthiness. If they are not trustworthy the entire nation will be deprived of tranquillity and security; rights will be nullified; killing and plunder will become flagrant; the roads of trade will close; and the doors of poverty and indigence will open before the people. The state treasury will bcome empty and the road to salvation will be closed.

Any people administered by such a treacherous and dishonest government will either suffer total decline or fall prisoner in the hands of foreigners and taste the bitterness of slavery, which is worse than the bitterness of decline and downfall. Moreover it is manifest that the domination and command of one people over others will only take place when the individuals among that dominating people become so united and consolidated that they can be considered a single individual. This type of unity is impossible without the quality of trustworthiness. Thus it becomes evident that the quality of trustworthiness is the support of human survival and the basic foundation of government, and that peace and security cannot occur without it. Dominance, greatness, and command are not created without it, and the spirit and body of justice consists of the very same quality.

Take note: if a people did not have this quality, what calamities, misfortunes, and disasters would overtake its members; how poverty and misery would envelop them; and finally how they would be overthrown and annihilated.

[The third] of those qualities is *truthfulness* and honesty. Know that man's needs are many and the necessities of his life are innumerable. The things whereby he meets his needs are each hidden under a curtain. Each one is secluded somewhere under a concealing veil, and hidden without a name or sign. Know that thousands of calamities, misfortunes, and disasters lurk in every corner of the world. A deadly arrow aiming at man's destruction is hidden in the bow of ages and in the turns of fortune. Man, aided only by his five weak senses, will never be capable of being aware of all his interests or of meeting his needs. Although he may have come to realize the calamities that wait in ambush for him, he is unable to preserve his life.

Therefore each man, to secure his interests and repel evils, needs to appeal for the help of his fellow men and must seek their guidance so that, because of their direction, he may be saved as far as possible from injuries and attain some of his needs in life. This help is only useful from those who have the quality of truthfulness, since a liar would make what is near far and what is far near, and would present a benefit as an injury and an injury as a benefit.

The quality of truthfulness is the firmest pillar of the survival of the human race, and the strong bond of the social order of nations. No society can come into being without it—neither the society of a home nor that of a civilization.

Look: if a group did not possess truthfulness, how much adversity and misfortune would come upon it; how the chain of order would be broken; and how it would be overtaken by affliction.

[How the *Neicheris* Undermine the Six Beliefs and Qualities]

THESE deniers of divinity, the *neicheris*, in whatever age they showed themselves and among whatever people they appeared had this basic aim and goal: Through corrupt principles and false foundations to extirpate that six-sided castle of human happiness that is built of those three noble beliefs and three great qualities. They aimed to open the gates of misfortune and calamity before unfortunate man, to bring him down from the throne of civilization and seat him in the dirt of the baseness of savagery and animality. For the foundation of their teachings rests first of all on this: that all religions are false, and are among human vanities and forgeries. Therefore, a people should not affirm its nobility and righteousness above all other peoples by means of religion.

After this corrupt teaching, which causes the weakening of ambition and the slowing of progress, they said that man is like other animals, and has no distinction over the beasts. Rather, his nature and temperament are baser and lower than those of most animals. With this belief, they [the *neicheris*] opened the gates of bestiality before man. They facilitated for man the perpetration of shameful deeds and offensive acts, and removed the stigma from savagery and ferocity.

Then they explained that there is no life aside from this life, and that man is like a plant that grows in the spring and dries up in the summer, returning to the soil. The happy man is he who attains in this world animal appetites and pleasures. Because of this false opinion they gave currency to the misfortunes of perfidy, treachery, deception, and embezzlement; they exhorted men to mean and vicious acts; and prevented men from discovering truths and traveling toward perfection.

These pestilences and plagues of the human world, the *neicheris*, saw that these corrupt teachings would not affect the souls of men of modesty, and that those having shame would never enter the sphere of animality nor consent to license and the sharing of food and women. Therefore they began to strive for the removal of shame. They said that shame came from the weakness and deficiency of the soul, and that if a person were strong and perfect he would never feel shame or modesty regarding any act. Thus the first duty of man is to strive for the removal of this quality, until he attains perfection of the soul.

With this intrigue the *neicheris* remove the obstacles in the path of animality, and facilitate for the soul the way of bestiality, which consists of communism and license.

Let it be clear that there are two motive forces for trustworthiness and truthfulness: [One], belief in the Day of Judgment [and the other], the habit of shame.

And it has become clear that among the basic teachings of this group of *neicheris* is the removal of that belief and the ending of that quality. Hence, the influence of their teachings in spreading treachery and falsehood is greater than the influence of someone who exhorts to treachery and falsehood directly. For if the above noble belief and honorable quality, which are the cause of trustworthiness and truthfulness, were in a man, he would resist the words of someone calling to treachery and falsehood, even if his resistance were mixed with weakness, and the effectiveness of his beliefs were weakened. Often the holder of that belief and the bearer of that quality will abstain from treachery and falsehood.

The contrary [will occur] if the basic motive is erased from the slate of the soul, since in this case no motive or exhorting force will remain to cause abstention.

In addition, this group has placed the foundation of their belief on license and communism, and has considered that all desirable things should be shared, and has regarded privileges and distinctions as usurpation, as shall be noted. There will no longer be a place for the attribution of treachery, since if a man chooses trickery to obtain his right to share things, that would not be treachery, and if he uses lying it would not be considered shameful. Therefore it is clear that the teachings of this group are the motive force of all treachery and lies, the cause of all evils, meanness, baseness, and wickedness.

Inevitably, if this type of thing is disseminated in a people, they will decline and be annihilated. From what we have said it can be clearly seen how this group becomes the cause of the annihilation and perdition of peoples, tribes, and nations.

Now I wish to say that this group was and is the greatest enemy of man, and they desired and still wish, under the pretext of the reform that has been traced out in their sick[10] imaginations, that the fire of corruption be kindled and that the opponents of their wretched species be burned and their name effaced from the slate of existence.

It is clear to everyone that the survival of humanity in this world, because of its needs, is dependent on some arts and trades that differ in nobility and baseness, and in ease and difficulty. The final goal and ultimate object of this group is that all men should share in all desires and delights; that privileges and distinctions should be

---

[10] The Arabic word used, *mālikhūlīyā*, is from the Greek. In Arabic it means, approximately, sick-mindedness.

abolished; that nobody should have superiority or a surplus of anything over another; and that all should be absolutely equal. If it
becomes like that, naturally every person will refuse to perform hard
and menial tasks and economic life will be disordered; the wheel of
dealings and relationships will stop moving; and finally this weak
species will be brought to the vale of perdition and will disappear
completely.

The results of the reforms proposed by those sick-minded men will
be only this. Even if we grant an impossibility, that the life of man
would be possible in this abominable state, you must know that
undoubtedly all his good qualities, beauties, and luxuries would disappear in the winds of annihilation. All external and internal perfections, all material and moral progress, and science, knowledge,
and the arts would be destroyed. Man's throne of glory and nobility
would be overturned and he would dwell in the desert of savagery
like the other animals, with a thousand pains and illnesses, in the
extremity of fear and dread.

The real cause of the superiority of man is his love for privilege
and distinction. When privilege and distinction are removed, souls
are stopped from the movement toward eminence and minds neglect
to penetrate the truth of things and to discover the subtleties of life.
Men would live in this world like the beasts of the desert, were it
possible for them. Alas, alas!

Let it be known that the *neicheris* have chosen several paths for
the spread of their corrupt teachings. In times of safety and security
they exposed all their principles and goals to the world with the
greatest clarity, but in times of fear and insecurity, considering
gradualness necessary, they trod the path of hints, allusions, and
symbols with the foot of deceit.

Sometimes they have tried to demolish all at once the six pillars
of that castle of man's happiness. Sometimes, according to the exi-
gencies of the situation, they decided to take some of those pillars as
a focus for their false teachings, and tried their best to undermine
them. Sometimes, in accordance with necessity, they undertook the
negation of those necessary results and causes whose negation entails
the negation of the pillars also. Sometimes they contented themselves
with the denial of the Creator and the ending of belief in rewards
and punishments, since they knew that the end of these two beliefs
would inevitably lead to all their harmful goals. Sometimes they
were silent about principles and were concerned with the embellish-

ment and beautification of their fundamental goal, which is license
and the sharing of all in all. Sometimes, in order to repel the opponents of their corrupt principles, they engaged in assassination
and spilt the blood of thousands of innocents with intrigues and
ruses.

[In sum], when their teachings appeared in a community, they
pleased all those with wicked souls whose final object is the attain-
ment of bestial desires, whether by means of truth or falsity. Having
no regard for results and consequences, these men were happy and
content with such corrupt opinions, and strove for their propagation
and diffusion.

Another group, although they did not believe in or adhere to these
opinions, nonetheless have not been preserved and immune from
their injury and corruption. Damage, corruption, and destruction
penetrated the foundations of their salutary beliefs and the bases of
their useful qualities. Since most men in their beliefs and habits are
followers of custom and imitation, and since the smallest doubt or
uncertainty suffices to upset the pillars of imitation and custom,
therefore corruption will then overtake the manners of all members
of such a nation. Lying, deceit, trickery, and treachery will spread
among them; the veil of shame will be removed; and deeds unworthy
of the human status will appear openly among them.

And since, because of those corrupt opinions, each of them believed that there is no life but this one, the quality of *egoism*[11] overcame them. The quality of *egoism* consists of self-love to the point
that if a personal profit requires a man having that quality to let
the whole world be harmed, he would not renounce that profit but
would consent to the harm of everyone in the world. This quality
made a man put his personal interest above the general welfare, and
made him sell his nation for a paltry profit. Gradually, because of
this base life, fear and cowardice overtook man, and he became
content and happy with meanness, baseness, slavery, and abasement
in his life.

When the state of individuals reached this point, the bond of
fusion and interdependence was broken; the unity of the species
was annihilated; the power of preservation and the means of survival

---

[11] In French, *égoiste*. Probably Afghānī is here again confusing his "isme" and
"iste" endings, as he often does elsewhere; but it would be possible to translate
this phrase as "the quality of an egoist."

were lost; and the throne of greatness, glory, and honor was over-thrown.

These are the particulars about those nations that, after greatness and nobility, were overtaken by humiliation and poverty, because of the teachings of the *neicheris*, i.e., materialists. And this is a description of the ways of the teachings of the materialists, or *neicheris*.

[How the Materialists
Undermined the
Great Nations of the Past]

THE Greeks were a nation small in number, but they possessed the three above-mentioned great beliefs, especially the belief that their nation was the noblest of all the nations of the world; and those three noble qualities, particularly the quality of modesty, which is either the source of shame or its first result. After the diffusion among them of science and knowledge, they stood for long years facing the Persian Empire, which extended from the regions of Kashgar to the borders of Istanbul. Fearing humiliation and slavery, which are incompatible with nobility, and which are rejected by the possessor of shame and modesty, they pressed forward with the step of manliness, so that in the end they overturned that great Persian Empire and extended their sway to India. The quality of trustworthiness had reached such a height in them that they preferred death to treachery.

Thus Themistocles, when Artaxerxes ordered him to lead a Persian force to conquer Greece, took poison and killed himself. He would not consent to betray his people and nation, despite the fact that the Greeks, after his outstanding services and his victory over the Persians, had banished him and he was compelled to find refuge among the Persians. Refer to the History of the Greeks.[12]

But when Epicurus the naturalist and the Epicureans appeared in Greece and called themselves sages, they first denied divinity, [a denial] which is the basis of all corruption and the source of all evils

---

[12] The Persian phrase sounds as if a particular work entitled [*The*] *History of the Greeks* is being referred to, which is why "History" is capitalized here.

and ruin, as will be demonstrated below. They said as follows: Man, because of conceit, arrogance, and vanity believes that the world was created entirely for his defective existence, and that he is the noblest of creatures and the final cause of all beings. Because of the greed, covetousness, selfishness, and even madness that overcomes him, man thinks he has a luminous sphere and an eternal world, to which sacred world he will move after his departure from this earth, and that he will there attain perfect happiness, without a stain of fault or defect. Therefore he has bound himself in opposition to *neicher*, or nature, with many bonds and chains; has charged himself with innumerable harsh labors; and has barred the doors to the delights of natural pleasures and inborn joys.

[And they said:] In fact, man has no superiority and distinction in anything over any animal, but rather is the most defective and lowest of the animals according to nature and temperament. Those arts that have become available to him, and which he prides himself on, have all been taken over as an imitation of other animals: for example, weaving from the spider; building and construction from the bee; the erection of castles and monasteries from the white ant; the storing of daily food from the black ant; and music from the nightingale. Therefore this conceited man should know that his life is like the life of the plants, and that there is no other world beyond this world, and no life apart from this life.

Thus, man should not throw himself vainly into toil and trouble; and should not place on his back, to no purpose, the heavy burden of duty; nor deny himself, contrary to nature, the various kinds of delights and pleasures. Rather, in whatever way is possible to him, and in whatever manner is feasible, he should gain his share in the delights of this world, and should not lend his ear or bind his heart to the fables of the lawful, the forbidden, the worthy, the suitable and unsuitable, and the other fictions with which men have bound themselves.

When this group saw that their teachings would be useless as long as the quality of shame was firmly rooted in souls, they started to remove that noble quality. They said that shame and modesty come from weakness of the soul and that every man should strive to remove them and to break the bonds of habit, until he becomes able to perpetuate all the deeds that men consider shameful without his soul being touched or ashamed by the open performance of those acts.

Finally these Epicureans rent the veil of shame and exposed man to ignominy. Wherever they saw a table of food they got to it, until often the owners of tables addressed these latter-day sages as "dogs," and drove them away by hitting them with bones. Despite this, these dogs in human form were not deterred, and they proclaimed the community of property, and continued to attack from every side. This is one of the reasons they became known as Cynics.[13]

The corrupt teachings of these Greek *neicheris*, the Cynics, in the course of time influenced the souls and minds of the Greeks. They brought intellects to the point of stupidity; the bazaar of knowledge and wisdom became sluggish, and manners became corrupt. That people's nobility of soul changed to baseness; their trustworthiness to treachery; their modesty and shame to impudence and vice; their courage to cowardice; and their love of race and homeland to self-love.

In sum, all six pillars of their castle of happiness and all the foundations of their humanity were overturned. Therefore their greatness and glory disappeared, and they fell prisoner in the hands of Rome, that is the Latin race. Because of the misfortune of these corrupt teachings they passed long years in the bonds of subjection, after they had at one time been considered the unopposed rulers of this world.

The Persians were a nation that had reached the highest degree in these six foundations of happiness. They considered themselves so noble that they believed the only foreign peoples who were happy were those under their protection or those who had the honor of being located near them. Trustworthiness and truthfulness were the first religious teachings of that people. Even when they were in need they would not try to obtain a loan, fearing lest they be unable to avoid a lie.

Because of these beliefs and qualities the greatness, dignity, and extent of their kingdom rose to such a height that in order to present it a *Shāhnāma* would be needed. François Lenormant, the historian, says that the Persian Empire in the time of Darius the Great comprised twenty-one provinces. One of these provinces included Egypt, the shores of the Red Sea, Baluchistan, and Sind. If for a time some weakness affected their power, in a short time those true principles

---

[13] Arabic *kalbī*, "like a dog." The Arabs translated "Cynic" literally from the Greek. (The Greek word "Cynic" is an attributive adjective or noun from the word for "dog" [*kyōn*, stem *kyn*].) Afghānī's etymology is fictitious.

prepared them to return to their former condition and supreme power.

Then, in the time of Qubad, Mazdak the *neicheri*, or naturalist, appeared in the guise of a remover of oppression and suppressor of tyranny. With one of his teachings he uprooted all those foundations of the fortune of the Persian people and flung them to the winds of annihilation. For he said as follows: The laws, norms, and customs established by men are all causes of oppression and tyranny, and they are all baseless. But the sacred law of *neicher*, or nature, has still not been abrogated, but has remained preserved and inviolable among the animals and beasts. What knowledge or reason can attain the rank of nature? Nature has established the right of sharing all food, drink, and women among all who eat, drink, and take women. Therefore why should men, because of the forgeries of fancy which they call laws and customs, be barred from their mothers, daughters, and sisters while others enjoy them? What sense has it that an individual should bring under possession common properties, and claim ownership; or that when he takes a woman in marriage he should bar others from her? What justice is there in laws that consider the usurpers of the common property to be the rightful owners, while the unfortunate man who artfully obtains enjoyment of his rights is called a usurper and a traitor? Therefore it is incumbent on every person to remove the oppressive yoke of the laws and customs of defective human reason from his neck; to obtain his rights in property and women in whatever way he can, in accord with the sacred law of nature; and to detain the usurpers, by force and compulsion, from improper deeds of usurpation and tyranny.

When these false teachings spread among the Persians, shame disappeared, perfidy and treachery became widespread, baseness and meanness spread, bestial qualities became dominant, and their natures became completely corrupted. Although Anushirwan killed Mazdak and some of his followers, he was unable to eradicate these corrupt teachings. Therefore this people was unable to sustain one attack of the Arabs, whereas their peer and contemporary, Byzantium, struggled and fought against the Arabs for many centuries.

The Muslims were a community who, because of their true divine religion and right heavenly law, saw produced among their members such noble beliefs and excellent qualities, and in whom the bases of those six pillars were so firm, that in one century, as a result of those beliefs and praiseworthy qualities, they occupied lands from the Alps to the wall of China. They rubbed the pride of Caesars and Khusraus in the dust of humiliation, even though they were only a small band. Their virtuous habits reached such a point that through the magnetism of their manners, they attracted in a short time nearly 100 million non-Muslims to their religion, despite the fact that they had left them free choice between a modest tribute tax and Islam.

The superiority and greatness of this noble community remained thus until in the fourth century [h.] the *neicheris*, or naturalists, appeared in Egypt under the name of the *bāṭiniyya* and the knowers of the hidden.[14] They spread their program to all sides and corners of the Muslim world, and especially to Iran. Since these *neicheris*, the followers of the esoteric, saw that the light of the law of Muhammad had enlightened all the Muslims, and that the ulama of the chosen religion, with perfect knowledge, ample virtue, and extreme vigilance, were striving to protect this firm religion and to preserve the beliefs and manners of the Muslims, therefore in order to spread their own corrupt beliefs they took the path of hypocrisy and gradualness. They laid the foundations of their teachings on the following: First create doubt in the Muslims about their beliefs; and after the establishment of doubt in their hearts take an oath and promise from them, and present this oath and promise to the eyes of the Perfect Guide. They said it was necessary for the teacher of their teachings always to act in a dissimulating way with the heads of the Muslim religion, and to be capable of establishing his argument.

When someone was caught in the net of the Perfect Guide the first thing he taught him was as follows: External observances are only for those people who have not arrived at the truth. The truth consists of the Perfect Guide, and since you have reached the truth you must repudiate these external corporeal observances. Some time later he would say to him: All external and internal duties, and all beliefs and ties, are for the imperfect who may be likened to the sick. When you become perfect you shed all these external and internal bonds and enter the vast sphere of free action, whether lawful or prohibited, whether loyalty or treachery, whether truth or lying, and whether virtue or vice.

---

14 *Bāṭiniyya*, or esoterics, here refers to the Isma'ili sect of the Shi'i branch of Islam. Among their tenets was that the truest interpretation of Islamic law and scripture was an esoteric, or *bāṭinī*, interpretation, rather than a literal one. See M. G. S. Hodgson, "Bāṭiniyya," *EI²*.

After establishing license in the souls of his followers, he brought into play other ruses for the denial of divinity and the demonstration of the *neicheri* belief. He said: If God existed he would be like existing things, and if he did not exist he would be like the nonexistent. But God is free of all resemblance, therefore he is neither existent nor nonexistent. This means you acknowledge a name and deny the thing named.

For a period of time this group of *bāṭinīs* strove in a hidden way to corrupt the manners of the Muslims by means of these teachings, until the ulama of the faith and the other leaders of the Muslims became informed of it and planned an opposition. When the *bāṭinīs* saw how numerous were their opponents, they assaulted and spilled the blood of thousands of ulama, worthy men, and princes of the Muhammadan community in order to spread their false beliefs.

One of them found an opportunity to declare publicly to the world these corrupt, harmful beliefs in the *minbar* at Alamut.[15] He said: "At the time of the Resurrection there will be no duties incumbent upon mankind, neither external nor internal ones. The Resurrection consists of the rising of the True Redeemer, and I am the True Redeemer. After this let everyone do whatever he wants, since obligations have been removed." This meant that the doors of humanity were closed and the gates of bestiality opened.

In sum, these *neicheris*, the people of the *bāṭin* and the adherents of allegorical interpretation, or the *naturalistes** of the past Muslim centuries, with perfect trickery called people to every fault and vice that overthrows peoples and nations, and through the ruse of their counterfeit holiness, they obliterated belief in divinity, which is the foundation of all human happiness in this world. With the passage of time they corrupted the manners of the Muhammadan community, East and West, and shook the pillars of the admirable beliefs and qualities of that noble community. Finally their courage and bravery were changed to fear and cowardice; their trustworthiness and truthfulness to treachery and lying; and their love of Islam to bestial self-love. For this reason a band of Frankish beggars in the fifth century attacked the Syrian lands, destroyed hundreds of cities and villages, and gratuitously spilled the blood of thousands.

---

15 Alamut—the center of the "Assassin" branch of the Isma'ilis in Iran. The incident described occurred in A.D. 1164. See M. G. S. Hodgson, *The Order of the Assassins* ('s-Gravenhage, 1955).

For almost two hundred years the Muslims remained unable to repel those beggars, despite the fact that previous to that corruption of manners and destruction of belief the Franks had not been safe from the advances of the Muslims in their own countries.

Similarly, a group of Tatar, Turkish, and Mongol ruffians came with Chinghiz Khan and ruined most of the cities of the Muhammadans, and spilled the blood of millions. The Muslims did not have enough power to repel this calamity, although in the early days of Islam, for all their small numbers, the arena of their horses extended to the wall of China. This humiliation, degradation, ruin, and desolation was all brought on the Muslims by the treachery, lying, cowardice, sluggishness, and weakness that resulted from corrupt teachings.

Since their former manners, habits, and Muhammadan religion had not been altogether removed from the souls of the majority of Muslims, therefore with a thousand efforts and after long years they took away the lands of Syria from the Franks and ennobled the followers of Chinghiz with the honor of Islam. They could not, however, completely remove their weakness or restore their domination and strength; for that domination was a result of those true beliefs and admirable qualities, and after the entry of corruption its restoration became difficult.

This is why historians have taken the wars of the Crusades as the beginning of the decline of Muslim power. It would be more correct to date the beginning of Muslim weakness and division from the appearance of those corrupt teachings and false opinions.

Let it be noted that the *Bābīs*, who recently appeared in Iran and iniquitously spilled the blood of thousands of God's servants, were the apprentices of those same *neicheris* of Alamut and the slaves, or bearers of begging bowls,[16] of those men of the mountain, and their teachings are an example of *bāṭinī* teachings. We must anticipate what further effects their beliefs will have among the Iranian people in the future.

The French were the only nation that by means of that sixfold foundation of felicity, elevated the banner of science and skill in the

---

16 *Chīlahā ya'ni kajgūl bardārhā. Chīla* comes from Hindi, and Steingass' *Persian-English Dictionary* gives its Persian meaning as "slave." *Kajgūl* is apparently either a variant or misprint for *kachkūl* or *kashkūl*, the dictionary forms.

continent of Europe after the Romans. They became the civilizers
of all the European peoples. Because of those glorious foundations
they were influential in most periods in most Western countries.
Until, in the eighteenth century A.D., Voltaire and Rousseau appeared claiming to remove superstitions and enlighten minds.

These two men exhumed the grave of Epicurus, the Cynic, and
revived the old bones of *naturalisme*.* They overthrew duty, and
sowed the seeds of license and communism. They considered manners and customs superstitions, and religions the inventions of men
of deficient reason. They openly engaged in denying divinity and
slandering the prophets. Voltaire even wrote books charging the
prophets with error, and deriding, slandering, and vilifying them.
These false beliefs influenced the souls of the French, who totally
abandoned the Christian religion.

They opened the doors of the sacred law of *neicher*, meaning
license, one day even bringing a girl and placing her on the altar of
a church. The spokesman of that group cried: O people, after this
do not fear thunder and lightning, and do not believe that they were
sent by the Lord of heaven to terrorize you. Rather know that they
are all the effects of nature, and aside from nature nothing exists
in the world. Therefore no longer worship fancies, and do not invent
a God for yourselves in accord with fantasies. And if you wish to
worship something, then here is the *mademoiselle** in the altar,
standing like a statue.

The corrupt *neicheri* teachings of these two persons first caused
the famous French Revolution. Second, they caused corruption of
manners, hatred, and division in beliefs to take hold of the individuals of that nation, until gradually each group of followers of
different beliefs and divergent sects was occupied with itself; and
they tried to achieve their own goals and pleasures, and turned
their backs on the general welfare. For that reason their influence
abroad began to diminish, both in the West and in the East.

Although Napoleon I restored the Christian religion, nonetheless
the influence of the above teachings did not disappear, and differences of belief were not removed; and it finally all culminated in
defeat at the hands of Germany. The French were hit by losses that
they could not make up for many long years. Those harmful teachings were the reason that the group of *socialistes,** i.e., socialists,
appeared among them, and the harm and losses brought on France

by this group are no less than the harm and losses brought by Germany. Refer to the History of the French War.[17]

If the holders of good beliefs and praiseworthy qualities had not been prepared, these people, in order to carry out their hidden aims, would have turned France upside down, and would have pulled it to the ground.

It is no secret that the Ottoman nation, because of the appearance of these corrupt opinions of the *neicheris* among some of their amirs and great men, has fallen into its present sad state. Those military officers who committed treason in the recent war and were the cause of ruin and destruction were the same ones who marched in the *neicheri* road, and considered themselves holders of new ideas.[18]

Because of *neicheri* teaching they thought that man is like other animals, and these manners and qualities that he has considered virtues for himself are all contrary to *nature*,* and result from the meddling of the mind. And each man, to whatever extent and by whatever means he can, should obtain animal pleasures for himself, and not foolishly forbid himself pleasures because of the superstitious rules and artificial chimeras of ignorant men. And since man is mortal, what are honor, shame, trustworthiness, or truthfulness? Therefore they accepted a great degree of baseness and threw to the winds the ancient noble house of the Ottomans for a paltry price.

The *socialistes,* communistes,* and *nihilistes** (i.e., the *ijtimā'īyīn, ishtirākīyīn,* and *'adamīyīn*) are all three followers of this path. They present themselves as lovers of the poor, the weak, and the unfortunate. Each of these three groups, although it outwardly expresses its aims in a particular way, has the final goal of removing all distinctions between men, and, as with Mazdak, that all should share in all.

---

17 As with "History of the Greeks," above, it appears that a specific book is intended.

18 Of this passage Niyazi Berkes, *The Development of Secularism in Turkey* (Montreal, 1964), p. 267, says: "Abdül-Hamid must have been delighted to see that the book confirmed the wisdom of his persecution of the constitutionalists, and to learn that the same *nacharis* and *dehris* who destroyed law and order in the world at large were also responsible for the calamities of Turkey. He must have rejoiced to see the author refer, as usual anonymously, to Midhat Paşa and Süleyman Paşa as men who, like all *nacharis*, had sold their country to its enemies for petty gains. He had just court-martialled both, and had sentenced one to death and the other to permanent exile; but even he had not gone to the extent of accusing them of treason."

How much bloodshed they have caused in order to achieve this corrupt aim, and what disorders and revolts they have raised, and how many buildings and villages they have burned.

They say that all appetites and pleasures on this earth are among the bounties of *nature*,* or nature. Therefore it is wrong that someone should have a private right to one of these pleasures without having others share it with him. Rather all pleasures and desires should by right be shared among all mankind.

They say that the greatest barrier and firmest obstacle to the spread of the holy law of nature, which is license and communism, are religions and monarchies. Therefore these two must be uprooted from their foundations, and kings and the leaders of religion must be destroyed. If someone reserves for himself a pleasure or is distinguished by a talent or distinction, and acts against the holy law of nature, he must be killed so that others will not deviate from the rule of that law, and will not be refractory.

This threefold group found no ruse or trick better, in order to spread their corrupt ideas, than to found schools or to be teachers in the elementary and higher schools of others, and gradually to place their thoughts in the pure ears of children. Some of them therefore set about founding schools, and some others divided up, each one going to one of the higher schools of Europe to teach. They strove to publish and spread their false opinions, and their parties became numerous and spread in all lands and countries of Europe, especially in the Russian Empire.

Undoubtedly, if these three groups become strong, it will cause the decline and downfall of the human race, as was previously related. May God protect us from the evils of their words and deeds!

Mormon, that latter-day prophet of nature, who was first in England and then migrated to America, through the inspiration of nature saw fit to bestow the great gift of license and communism only on those who believed in nature. Therefore he formed two companies, one of male believers and the other of female believers, and he said: Every male believer has absolute possession of every female believer. Thus, if one of the female believers is asked, "Whose wife are you?" she answers, "The wife of the company." Similarly if one of their children is asked, "Whose child are you?" he will answer, "The child of the community."

Up to now the flame and evil of their corruption has not spread beyond the abyss of their community. God the highest knows whether that flame will spread to the world, and the house and home of humanity will be burned and ruined.

As to all those deniers of divinity, or *neicheris*, who have come disguised in the clothing of reformers and friends of the community, and well-wishers of the people: they have made themselves both the accomplices of the thieves and the companions of the caravan, and have lifted the banner of their knowledge and skill before the foolish and stupid. They have a new plan for treachery, having waxed proud with two or three stolen and incomplete phrases, and they are swollen up with haughtiness and disdain. They named themselves leaders and guides, and for all their ignorance and studipity, their base manners and blameworthy qualities, they have presented themselves as reformers. They found intelligence and wisdom only in perfidy, embezzlement, and dissimulation. I am deeply ashamed to mention them and to write of their ways and deeds, for their aims are exceedingly vile.

They wish for their own appetites to uproot the foundations of their community, and to tear up the bonds of its solidarity. The scope of their thoughts is very narrow, and they have not yet made a step beyond their stomach. The pen cannot move freely in that confined and filthy atmosphere. I can say this much: they are *payāchū*,[19] meaning noisy braggarts over others. Let the reader know the rest.

From all that has been said it becomes clear to all that this group of *neicheris,* or materialists, in whatever community they appear, through a thousand disguises and hypocrisies corrupt the manners of the individuals of that community with their corrupt teachings. They undermine the foundations of the castle of their happiness and give currency to treachery, lying, sluggishness, and lust, until they gradually erase the name of that people from the slate of existence or entagle them in humiliation, poverty, and subjection.

Despite this, some of this group have hypocritically hidden their basic aims, which are license and communism, and externally content themselves with denying divinity and the Day of Judgment. Therefore, I wish to explain that this teaching alone suffices to corrupt the social order and shake the pillars of civilization. No cause more effective than this teaching can be found to corrupt

---

[19] From the Italian *pagliaccio* (see p. 139 n. 7).

manners. It is impossible for someone to be a *neicheri* and despite this be refined in manners, trustworthy, truthful, manly, and generous.

[Why the *Neicheris*
Undermine the
Restraint of Passion]

T<small>HUS</small> I say that every individual, according to his temperament and nature, has desires and lusts, to meet which certain pacifiers of passions are placed in the outside world. Those lusts in themselves make man try to acquire what he desires and to cure his appetites thereby, and to break the power of desire, whether these appetites are acquired in a right manner or a wrong one; whether their acquisition be a cause of sedition, corruption, bloodshed, and usurpation of rights; or whether they would be obtainable without these evils.

Four things can be imagined which might prevent these strong needs and effective motives from having an immoderate influence; make the possessor of these powerful appetites be satisfied with his rights; and bar transgressions and oppressions.

[These four are]: Either each possessor of a right must take sword in hand, put a shield on his back, put one foot in front and one in back, and night and day strive for the preservation of his right; or else nobility of soul, as is claimed by men of passion; or government; or the belief that the world has a wise creator, and that after this life there is a clear retribution for good and evil deeds—in other words, religion.

The first way would mean that in order to protect rights and repel transgressions torrents of blood would flow. Hills and valleys would be dyed with the blood of men, and every strong man would crush and grind the weak, until finally this race would be overthrown and its name erased from the slate of existence.

As to the second way: You must know that nobility of soul is the quality that restrains its possessor from blameworthy deeds and shameful acts before his tribe and nation. And baseness of soul is that whose possessor does not abstain from mean acts. Disgrace and disapproval do not touch him.

It is clear that this quality, nobility of soul, does not have a fixed value or defined reality among people such as would enable it to place a moderate limit on desire; make everyone satisfied with his own rights; and make firm the foundation of order. Do you not observe how many affairs there are whose perpetration among one people is considered baseness and meanness, while the same affairs among another people are marks of nobility and perfection of soul, and occasions for praise and glory, despite the fact that really they are none other than tyranny, oppression, and treachery. For example, plunder, pillage, theft, highway robbery, and killing among the tribes and peoples of the mountains and deserts are considered the limit of perfection and the extreme of nobility. But the people of cities consider them all signs of baseness and meanness. Similarly with ruses, tricks, and hypocrisy: among one people they are considered vileness, while among other people these things are considered intelligent, skillful, and perfect.

Also, if you think deeply in this affair, you will see that every created thing has a cause, and the final cause of the acts of human will is man himself. You will easily perceive that man's seeking to be endowed with nobility of soul, and the effort to attain it, and the fear of baseness and meanness arise from man's desire and his longing to expand his means of livelihood and to avoid strictures in life. For he knows that the one endowed with nobility of soul will be worthy of trust and become known for trustworthiness and truthfulness. He will have many helpers and companions, and with many friends his ways and means of livelihood will be abundant. On the other hand, a reputation for meanness and baseness of soul, which causes the aversion of hearts and a paucity of friends, will close the gates to a livelihood.

The degree that a man seeks nobility of soul; the strength and weakness of that quality; its permanence and impermanence; its degrees and stages; and its influence in deterring the lustful from transgressions are in accord with ways of life of the different classes of men. That is to say, the classes of men will strive to acquire that quality to the extent that their lives are benefited and they are preserved from loss and injury. Every class considers nobility of soul that quality with which its rank and livelihood can be preserved.

And as to that which is superfluous for this, its lack will never be considered a defect or fault, although in other classes it is considered to be base and a defect, and [the first class] will make no effort to achieve it.

Look at most rulers and princes, how they are unconcerned over breaking treaties, especially with those lower than they in pomp and majesty, for all their belief in nobility. They do not shun injustice, tyranny, and vile deeds, nor do they consider any such deeds to be mean and base. Despite this, if one of these deeds originated with one of their subjects he would be considered a vile person, base of soul, and on this account his livelihood would be injured. The other classes themselves do not consider these matters among their rulers and princes as base and vile, but rather interpret them in other ways.

Similar is the state of each of the higher classes with regard to the classes lower than they, class after class. This is because the higher classes know themselves to be immune and protected from the damage of their heinous acts. Thus, if the pivot of the world order were nobility of soul, every higher class would place the hand of oppression on the lower class and would open the gates of evil and corruption before these unfortunate men.

Also, since the motive for acquiring this quality is to expand the means of livelihood and take precautions against strictures on life's way, as has become clear, therefore this quality can never bar men from internal transgressions, hidden treachery, and bribery in the corners of courtrooms. For man, seeking an easy life, knows that by means of these hidden evils he will reach his fundamental goal, without becoming known for baseness. You can observe what sort of acts appear in the corners of courtrooms from those who call for nobility of soul. Thus, someone who has set up nobility of soul as the criterion of justice should not believe that with this quality one can make everybody satisfied with his rights or create a bar to all open and secret oppression and transgressions.

If someone says that one cause for seeking nobility of soul is love of praise, and that everybody in order to receive praise should endow himself with the utmost nobility of soul and remove himself from all baseness, transgression, and oppressions—I would answer: First, few people can be found who prefer praise and eulogy to the pleasures of their bodily appetites. If you study the classes of mankind this will be manifest and evident. [Second], the first cause for the praise and eulogy of these animal-like men, and the first grounds for the praise of deceitful historians and lying poets, is riches, wealth, position, glory, and power, even when these are achieved by unworthy means and a thousand oppressions and transgressions intrude in their acquisition. Therefore the majority of men in this matter would try to make themselves the owners of wealth and riches, and the lords of position and glory, even though it be by means of perfidy, oppression, and treachery. Thus they both procure bodily pleasures and have themselves praised by falsifiers. Few people are found who would seek rightful praise by means of righteousness, virtue, and nobility of soul.

From what has been said it appears that the quality of nobility of soul is in no way sufficient for the moderation of passions, the prevention of oppression, and the order of the world. But if it is supported by a religion, and in that religion its essence is specified and delineated, then because of that it will become the source and basis of the means of ordering the chain of relationships, [but] not by itself, as we pointed out in explaining shame.

As to the third means, it should be clear that the power of government is limited to the suppression of external oppression and transgressions. How can it prevent secret misappropriations, impostures, calumnies, corruptions, and transgressions by men of passion? How can it be informed of hidden tricks, deceits, and injustices, in order to strive to suppress them? Besides, the ruler and his helpers all have passions. What will bar these holders of power from the demands of active passions? What will deliver the weak, unfortunate masses from the hands of their evil and greed, since there is nothing to prevent or prohibit the latter? Of course that ruler is secretly the leading thief, and has publicly become the head of the highway robbers. His followers and helpers would all be tools of oppression, tyranny, and treachery; instruments of evil and corruption; and tools of misappropriation. They would strive for the denial of the rights of God's servants, outraging their honor and plundering their property. They would satisfy their sensual thirst with the blood of the unfortunate, and would paint and adorn their castles with the blood of the helpless. In sum, they would work toward the destruction of men and the ruin of the land.

Thus, no force remains for restraining men of passions from their transgressions and oppression other than the fourth way. That is, the belief that the world has a Creator, wise and powerful; and the belief that for good and evil deeds there is a fixed recompense after this life. In truth, these two beliefs together are the firmest foundation for the suppression of passions and the removal of external and internal transgressions. They are the strongest pillar for overthrowing tricks, impostures, and hypocrisy, and the best motive for the determination of truth. They are the cause of complete security and tranquillity. Without these two beliefs the social order would never come into actuality, civilization would never come into existence, the foundation of human dealings would not be firm, and society and association could not be free of guile and fraud.

If someone does not possess these two beliefs, he will have no possible motive for virtue and nothing to prevent vice. Nothing would keep him from treachery, lying, hypocrisy, and deceit. For the final cause of all acquired qualities and free acts, as was said above, is man himself; and when a person does not believe in recompense and requital, what else will bar blameworthy qualities to him and call him to good behavior? Especially when a man realizes that being characterized by bad qualities will not result in any loss for him in the world, nor will having good qualities bring him any benefit. What will force him into cooperativeness, mutual assistance, mercy, manliness, courage, and the other qualities on which the social order depends?

[The Evils
of the *Neicheris*
and Virtues of Religion]

I⊤ ʜᴀs become plain to the reader that the first teaching of the naturalists, or *neicheris,* is the rejection of those two beliefs that are the foundation of all religions; and their last teaching is license and communism. Thus these are the people who are throwing the social order to the winds. They are the destroyers of civilization and the corrupters of morals; the destroyers of the pillars of knowledge and wisdom. They are the annihilators of peoples; the obliterators of pride, zeal, and honor; the roots of baseness and treachery; and the plants of vices and vileness. They are the bases of sordidness and depravity; the standards of lying and falsehood; and the callers to animality. Their love is deceit, their companionship a trick, and their gentleness perfidy. Their kindness is a ruse, their truthfulness a deceit, their claim to humanity imaginary, and their call to science and knowledge a snare and a forgery. They make trustworthiness into treachery; will not keep a secret; and will sell their closest friend for a copper coin. They are slaves to the belly and bound by lust.

They do not refuse to perpetrate any kind of base and low act in order to fulfill their passions. They in no way recognize honor, pride, or shame, and they know nothing of nobility of soul. Sons in this group are not safe from their fathers, nor can either of them be barred from daughters according to the ways of nature.

If someone is deceived by their snakelike smoothness to touch and becomes contaminated by their viperous spots and stripes; if the allurements of their speech attract him, and their tricks find a place in his heart, he then comes to believe that these people are the motive force of civilization and the cause of the order of the land and of the spread of knowledge and wisdom. Or else he believes that they are friends and supporters and keepers of secrets in time of need. One must both laugh and cry at his intelligence because it is an occasion for both laughter and tears.

Thus, from all we have expounded, it becomes clear in the most evident manner that religion, even if it be false and the basest of religions, because of those two firm pillars—belief in a Creator and faith in rewards and punishments—and because of the six principles that are enshrined in religions, is better than the way of the materialists, or *neicheris*. [It is better] in the realm of civilization, the social order, and the organization of relationships; indeed in all human societies and all progress of mankind in this world.

Since the order of the world has been laid according to the ways of wisdom, and the order of human affairs is a part of the total order, whenever these disrupters of the social order, the *neicheris*, have appeared, human souls have striven to eradicate them, and the lords of the true order of civilization, which is religion, have expended great efforts to remove them. The nature of a great man, according to his God-given intelligence, which is an effect of the universal intelligence, will not accept these men [the *neicheris*]. He rejects them like waste matter.

Therefore this sect has never become firm and durable, although they appeared in this world long ago and some treacherous souls from among the powerful, because of their own aims, have strengthened them in every age. In whatever age they have appeared they have soon dispersed and disappeared like summer clouds, and the true order of the human realm, that is, religion, remained firm and well established, while these sources of disorder passed away and disappeared.

Since it is known that religion is unquestionably the source of man's welfare, therefore, if it is placed on firm foundations and sound bases, that religion will naturally become the complete source of total happiness and perfect tranquillity. Above all it will be the cause of material and moral progress. It will elevate the banner of civilization among its followers. It will cause those who are religious to attain all intellectual and spiritual perfections and to achieve good fortune in this world and the next.

If we think deeply about religions we will find no religion resting on such firm and sure foundations as the religion of Islam.

For, the rise of nations on the ranks of perfection; the climbing of peoples on the steps of knowledge; the ascent of groups on the stairs of virtue; the awareness of the nations of humanity of the details of truth; and their acquisition of true and complete happiness in this world and the hereafter—all these depend on several things:

[First] That the slate of the minds of tribes and nations be clear of the muddiness of superstition, and the rust of vain and groundless beliefs. For superstitious belief is a dirty curtain that intervenes between the holder of such a belief and truth and reality. It prevents the discovery of the reality of a matter. When someone accepts a superstition his reason comes to a stop and he refrains from intellectual movement. Then he will take up many similar beliefs, and will accept all superstitions and fancies. This will cause him to fall far short of true perfection, and the truths of existent beings will be hidden from him. It will even cause him to spend all his life in fantasies, loneliness, fear, terror, and dread. He will fall into shuddering from the movements of birds and the stirrings of beasts. He will be upset by the blowing of winds, the sound of thunder, and the gleam of lightning. He will be kept from most of the occasions of his happiness through belief in evil omens, and he will submit to every trick, ruse, and impostor. What misfortune, ill luck, or bad life could be worse than such a life?

The first pillar of the Islamic religion is that by the luster of unity [*tauḥid*—the absolute unity of God] it purifies and cleans off the rust of superstition, the turbidity of fantasies, and the contamination of imaginings. Its first teaching is that man should not consider another man or an inanimate object, high or low, to be the Creator, the Possessor, the Omnipotent, the Giver, the Preventer, the Strengthener, the Debaser, the Healer, and the Destroyer. Nor should he believe that the First Cause has appeared, or will appear, in human guise to improve or worsen things. Nor that Pure Being in order [to secure] some benefits bore, in human guise, pains and illnesses; nor other such superstitions, any one of which alone suffices to blind reason. Most existing religions are not free of these fancies and superstitions. Look at the Christian, Brahman, and Zoroastrian religions.

[Second] Their souls must be characterized by the greatest nobility. This means that every member of that community considers himself worthy and suited for any human rank and stage, except for the rank of prophecy, which is a divine rank. He does not imagine in himself deficiencies, decadence, and lack of ability. When the souls of men are endowed with this quality, each one competes with others in the wide arena of virtues, and enters into contest and competition; and they spare nothing to attain greatness and honor, and to acquire a high rank in the world.

If some men believe that their nature and character has less nobility than others, and that their rank is lower than others, naturally there will be defects in their zeal, languor in their movements, and weakness in their perception. They will remain deprived of many perfections, of high degree and worldly happiness, and will remain within the boundaries of a narrow arena.

The Islamic religion opens the doors of nobility before souls; strengthens the right of each soul to every excellence and perfection; and removes the distinction of nobility of race and occupation, basing distinctions among human beings only on intellectual and spiritual perfection.

Few religions can be found with this advantage. Look how the Brahman religion divides men into four classes—first the Brahmans, second the Kshatriyas, third the Vaishyas, and fourth the Shudras—and reserves the highest degree of natural nobility to the Brahmans and the next to the Kshatriyas, while the fourth class is considered the lowest of all in all human distinctions. This may be considered one of the main causes for the lack of proper progress among the followers of this religion in the sciences, knowledge, and the arts, despite the fact that they are the most ancient of peoples.

The Christian religion, according to the Gospel, affirms nobility for the race of the sons of Israel, and refers to other races in contemptuous terms. The followers of that religion, however, refused this rule and denied race distinctions, but they gave so much honor to the class of priests that it became a cause for lowering others. For the priests were given control over the acceptance of belief and the forgiveness of sins. They said that other men, even if they had reached the highest degree of perfection, did not have the power to present their own sins before the divine threshold and seek forgiveness. This has to be achieved through the mediation of priests.

Similarly they said that the acceptance of faith in the eyes of God Almighty depends on the acceptance of a priest. They took this rule, which debases people, from the Gospel, since in it was written: "Whatever you unbind on earth will be unbound in heaven, and whatever you bind on earth will be bound in heaven."[20] As long as this debasing belief was firm and well established among the Christian community in European lands no progress was achieved among that community.

Luther, the leader of the Protestants, who rejected this rule, in opposition to the Gospels, was following the example of the Muslims.

[The third foundation of human virtues] is that the members of each community must found their beliefs, which are the first things written on the slates of their minds, on certain proofs and firm evidence. In their beliefs they must shun submission to conjectures and not be content with mere imitation (taqlīd) of their ancestors. For if man believes in things without proof or reason, makes a practice of following unproven opinions, and is satisfied to imitate and follow his ancestors, his mind inevitably desists from intellectual movement, and little by little stupidity and imbecility overcome him—until his mind becomes completely idle and he becomes unable to perceive his own good and evil; and adversity and misfortune overtake him from all sides.

It is no wonder that Guizot, the French minister who wrote the

---

[20] Matt. 16:19. As Afghānī implies, this passage is part of one that has been taken as legitimizing the Catholic church, though this is unclear without the full passage. Christ says to Peter: "And I say also unto thee, that thou art Peter, and upon this rock I will build my church; and the gates of hell shall not prevail against it. And I will give thee the keys of the kingdom of heaven: and whatsoever thou shalt bind on earth shall be bound in heaven; and whatsoever thou shalt loose on earth shall be loosed in heaven."

history of *civilisation*,* that is, civilization, of the European peoples,[21] said as follows: One of the greatest causes for European civilization was that a group appeared, saying: "Although our religion is the Christian religion, we are seeking the proofs of the fundamentals of our beliefs." The corpus of priests did not give permission, and they said that religion was founded on imitation. When the group became strong their ideas spread; minds emerged from their state of stupidity and dullness into movement and progress; and men made efforts to achieve the attributes of civilization.

The Islamic religion is the only religion that censures belief without proof and the following of conjectures; reproves blind submission; seeks to show proof of things to its followers; everywhere addresses itself to reason; considers all happiness the result of wisdom and clearsightedness; attributes perdition to stupidity and lack of insight; and sets up proofs for each fundamental belief in such a way that it will be useful to all people. It even, when it mentions most of its rules, states their purposes and benefits. (Refer to the Holy Koran.)

There is no other religion having this excellence. I believe that the non-Muslims will also acknowledge these distinctions. It is no secret that the foundation of the Christian religion is the worship of the Trinity. All Christians confess that it is not possible for reason to understand it, which means that one must abandon reason in order to comprehend it.

As to the principles of the Brahman religion, it is clear to everyone that most of them are contrary to plain reason, whether the followers of that religion acknowledge it or not.

.   Fourth, there must be in each community a group of people who are constantly occupied with teaching the others, who do not shirk from adorning their intellects with true knowledge, and who do not fail to teach the ways of felicity. And there must be another group that always strives to straighten and rectify souls; to explain virtuous qualities and describe their benefits; and explain wicked manners and elucidate their harm and injuries. They should not neglect to enjoin the good and forbid the evil.[22] For naturally all man's knowledge is acquired, and if man does not have a teacher he will not

---

[21] The reference is to Guizot's *History of Civilization in Europe*, which assigns to the Reformation a key role in the progress of freedom of thought and of civilization. This book had recently been translated into Arabic.

[22] A Koranic phrase found, with some variation, in several different passages in the Koran.

derive advantage or benefit from his reason. And he will live in this world like the animals and will leave this world barred from the happiness of both this world and the next.

Thus a teacher is indispensable. And since the lust and desires of man have no limit or measure, if there is no straightener and adjuster it will inevitably result in transgressions and oppression, and the possessor of those desires will deprive others of tranquillity and safety, and even burn himself on the fire of his passions. Man will then go to the abode of misfortune in the greatest wretchedness. Thus an enjoiner of the good, a forbidder of evil, and a rectifier of morals are indispensable.

The greatest duties and obligations of the Islamic religion are these two matters. (Refer to the noble Koran.)

In other religions there has not been such concern for these two matters, and since there are many pillars of the Islamic religion, and to explain the benefits of each one for civilization and to describe how each of them is the source of perfect felicity would cause me to go beyond the subject of my discourse, I have considered it incumbent on me to write a separate treatise on this matter; in that treatise I will explain why the virtuous city for which philosophers have died hoping will only be achieved by man with the Islamic religion.[23]

If someone says: If the Islamic religion is as you say, then why are the Muslims in such a sad condition? I will answer: When they were [truly] Muslims, they were what they were and the world bears witness to their excellence. As for the present, I will content myself with this holy text:

"Verily, God does not change the state of a people until they change themselves inwardly."[24]

---

23 This is the third approving reference to the "virtuous city," the others being on pp. 110 and 144 above. The phrase is part of the title of a popular work of political philosophy by al-Fārābī, and was used also by later philosophers.

24 Koran 13:11. Since Afghānī first used it, this has become a favorite passage for modernists exhorting the Muslims to self-improvement. According to a statement by Professor H. A. R. Gibb in the autumn of 1963, however, the verb used for "change," ghayyara, had, at that time, the sense of "to change for the worse." This is certainly its sense in this Koranic passage, which reads (in 'Abdallāh Yūsuf 'Alī's translation): "Verily never will God change the condition of a people until they change it themselves. But when God willeth a people's punishment, there can be no turning it back, nor will they find, besides Him, any to protect." In Afghānī's brief citation here it is unclear whether he is thinking of the Muslims' past decline, their future improvement, or, most likely, both.

This is a summary of what I wished to explain about the evils and corruption of the *neicheri* path for civilization and the social order, and the benefits of religions and of Islam.

Completed by the writer Jamāl ad-Dīn Husainī.

The
Materialists
in India

al-'Urwa al-Wuthqā,
August 28, 1884[1]

Tʜᴇ English entered India and toyed with the minds of her princes and kings in a way that makes intelligent men both laugh and cry. They penetrated deeply into India's interior, and seized her lands piece by piece. Whenever they became lords of the land they took liberties with its inhabitants, and showed anger and contempt regarding their stay among them, saying that the English are occupied only with commercial affairs. As for tending to administration and politics, that is not their business. However, what calls them to bear the burdens [of administration and politics] is pity for the kings and the princes who are incapable of governing their dominions. When the kings or princes are able to control their land, no Englishmen will remain there [they said], because they have other important affairs that they have abandoned out of sheer compassion. With this the English stole property from every owner on the pretext that work on property is oppressive to a person and fatiguing for mind and body. It is better for the owner of the property to relax and to die poor and humble, free of the pains of management. [The English] declare that when the opportunity presents itself, and the time comes when the affairs of this world and the hereafter will not influence bodies and thoughts, they are prepared to leave the country (on the Day of Resurrection!). And today they are saying the very same words in Egypt!!

When [the English] entrenched themselves in India, and effaced the traces of Moghul rule, they gave the land a second look, and found within it fifty million Muslims, each of whom was wounded

---

1 From the Cairo, 1958, ed., pp. 382–387.

in heart by the extinction of their great kingdom. They were connected with many millions of Muslims in the East and West, North and South. [The English] perceived that as long as the Muslims persisted in their religion, and as long as the Koran was read among them, it would be impossible for them to be sincere in their submission to foreign rule, especially if that foreigner had wrested the realm from them through treachery and cunning, under the veil of affection and friendship. So they set out to try in every way to weaken belief in the Islamic faith. They encouraged their clergymen and religious leaders to write books and publish tracts filled with defamation of the Islamic religion, and replete with abuse and vilification for the Founder of Islam (may God free him of what they said!). From this abominable activity resulted what is intolerable to human nature, and what would prevent an honorable man from remaining in a land where such books are published or from living under a sky whose sun shines on the perpetrators of that great slander. With that they aimed only, on the one hand, at weakening the beliefs of the Muslims, and at inducing them to profess the English religion. On the other hand, they began to restrict the means of livelihood available to the Muslims, and to intensify their oppression and disadvantages in every respect. They hurt their interests regarding public works, and plundered *waqfs*[2] set aside for mosques and *madrasas*, [3] and exiled their ulama and leaders to the Andaman and *Filfilān* [?] Islands, hoping to use this means, if the first one did not work, to alienate the Muslims from their religion, and to reduce them to the depths of ignorance concerning their faith, so that they would neglect what God had ordained for them. When the hopes of those tyrannical rulers for the first means failed, and the period of profiting from the second one seemed too long, they resorted to another policy for the limitation or weakening of the Islamic religion in the land of India, because they fear only the Muslim possessors of that plundered realm and usurped right.

It happened that a man named Aḥmad Khān *Bahādūr* (an honorary title in India) was hovering around the English in order to obtain some advantage from them. He presented himself to them and took some steps to throw off his religion and adopt the English religion. He began his course by writing a book demonstrating that the Torah and the Gospel were not corrupted or falsified, in order

---

2 *Waqf*: an inalienable endowment, a pious foundation.
3 *Madrasa*: a higher religious school.

to ingratiate himself with the English. Then he considered, and saw that the English would not be satisfied with him until he said, "I am a Christian," and that this vile deed would not bring him a large reward, especially since thousands of clergymen and priests had produced books like his and they had [only] converted a few Muslims from their religion. So he took another road in order to serve his English masters, by sowing division among the Muslims and scattering their unity.

He appeared in the guise of the naturalists [materialists], and proclaimed that nothing exists but blind nature, and that this universe does not have a wise God (This is a clear error), and that all the prophets were naturalists who did not believe in the God taught by the revealed religions (We take refuge in God!). He called himself a *neicheri* or naturalist, and began to seduce the sons of the rich, who were frivolous young men. Some of them inclined toward him, escaping from the bonds of the Law of Islam, and pursuing bestial passions. His doctrine pleased the English rulers and they saw in it the best means to corrupt the hearts of the Muslims. They began to support him, to honor him, and to help him to build a college in Aligarh, called the Muhammadan College, to be a trap in which to catch the sons of the believers in order to bring them up in the ideas of this man, Aḥmad Khān Bahādūr.

Aḥmad Khān wrote a Commentary on the Koran and distorted the sense of words and tampered with what God revealed. He founded a journal called *Tahdhīb al-Akhlāq* which published only what would mislead the minds of the Muslims, cause dissension among them, and sow enmity between the Muslims of India and other Muslims, especially between [the Indian Muslims] and the Ottomans.

He called openly for the abandonment of all religions (but he addressed only the Muslims), and cried, "Nature, Nature," in order to convince people that Europe only progressed in civilization, advanced in science and industry, and excelled in power and strength by rejecting religions and returning to the goal aimed at by all religions (according to his claim), which is the explanation of the ways of nature. ("He invented a lie against God.")[4]

When we were in India we learned of certain weak intelligences misled by the hoaxes of this man and his disciples. We wrote a treatise exposing their corrupt doctrine and the ruin that arose from it. We established that religion is the foundation of civiliza-

---

4 Koran 6:21.

tion and the pillar of culture. Our treatise was printed in two languages, Hindustani and Persian.

Aḥmad Khān and his followers took off the garb of religion and publicly called for its abandonment, desiring discord among the Muslims and seeking to divide them. They compounded their error, sowing discord between the inhabitants of India and the other Muslims. They wrote a number of books in opposition to the Islamic caliphate.

Those materialists are not like the materialists of Europe; for whoever abandons religion in Western countries retains love for his country, and his zeal to guard his country from the attacks of foreigners is not diminished. He gives freely of his most precious possessions for its advancement, and will sacrifice his life for its sake. But Aḥmad Khān and his companions, just as they invited people to reject religion, [also] disparaged to them the interests of their fatherland, and made people consider foreign domination over them a slight thing, and strove to erase the traces of religious and patriotic zeal. They breach those national resources that perhaps the English have neglected to plunder, in order to call the government's attention to them, so that they should not neglect them. They do this not for a considerable reward or an exalted honor, but for a vile piece of bread, a paltry gain. (Thus the Oriental materialist is distinguished from the Western materialist by baseness and vileness in addition to unbelief and impiety.)

The English did well by Aḥmad Khān, by appointing his son Maulavī Maḥmūd member of the council of an Indian village no larger than Shubrakhit in the Buhaira region [in Egypt].

One of the snares for the hunting of weak Muslims was to promise and raise their hopes that if they followed him, he would bring them into government service, thanks to his position with the English tyranny. But the English government named only four of his companions to village councils, and no native Indian is found in such positions except they. This is the glory bestowed on Aḥmad Khān as the price for his religion and fatherland. As Ṣiddīq Nawwāb Ḥasan Khān, King of Bhopal and the author of famous works, has said: "Aḥmad Khān is the Arch Deceiver of the Day of Judgment."[5]

---

[5] The Arabic is *dajjāl*, a figure in Muslim eschatology comparable to the Antichrist—the archvillain who prefigures the End of Time. Aziz Ahmad informs me that Afghānī has confused the title and rank of this author, who correctly was Ṣiddīq Ḥasan Khān, Prince-Consort of Bhopal.

The English authorities helped him to employ some to whom they gave preference, but not in the British Indian Government, and not in the English Treasury. Rather, the ruler obliged one of the princes remaining in formal independence to employ them in certain inferior functions.

[Aḥmad Khān's] doctrine was pleasing to the eyes of the English rulers and they were delighted with it. They considered it a means to their goal of obliterating the Islamic religion in Indian territory.

These materialists became an army for the English government in India. They drew their swords to cut the throats of the Muslims, while weeping for them and crying, "We kill you only out of compassion and pity for you, and seeking to improve you and make your lives comfortable." The English saw that this was the most likely means to attain their goal: the weakness of Islam and the Muslims.

The most faithful disciple of Aḥmad Khān, his chief assistant and administrator in all his affairs, is a man named Samī'allāh Khān. Samī'allāh Khān is the cleverest and most diligent of the materialists in misleading the Muslims, the most subtle in tricks, and the most cunning in creating means to split the unity of the believers and to strengthen the English government in India. This swindler sets himself up as a preacher at Muslim gatherings, and his tears precede his words. He brings forth the utmost of his eloquence in order to destroy the pillars of the Islamic religion and nullify its fundamental beliefs. He even turns on the divine presence, and finds fault with the prophetic mission and its bearer, all this while he weeps, as if he were mourning the religion and its adherents.

When he enters a land in order to carry out this service, he continues for days to enter the mosques and attend religious gatherings; to entice people with agreeable words and charming promises; and to attract them to him without their knowing it. When some of the people assemble around him, blinded by his pleasing exterior, he proceeds to call them to his turbid doctrine of the abandonment of religion.

This evident enemy of Islam and the Muslims has already been given for these efforts the post of judge (in the English law) in the town of Agra, a town no bigger than Dasuq in the Gharbiyya province [in Egypt]. The newspaper, the *Times*, after highly praising Samī'allāh Khān, said that this post, a judgeship in a small town, was the highest post conferred on a native Indian. (Is there any need, in order to demonstrate English justice, for more evidence than this?)

Northbrook, the English lord, one part of whose history in India we referred to in the last issue, fully recognized Samī'allāh Khān as soon as he became the ruler in India, and he understood that he was the most faithful of men in service to the English, and the most capable of serving them. Therefore, that lord asked him to be private secretary in Egypt, in order to use him to alienate the Egyptians from the Ottoman Government; to persuade the Egyptians that the government of England wished them well; and to employ him to win over the hearts of the ulama, since he was one of them (according to his claim). Perhaps he intends to enter the mosques and to preach and give sermons, and to relate regarding English justice what has no truth and what is belied by reality. However, we have hope, because of the intelligence of the Egyptians, the correctness of their religious beliefs, and the strength of their ties to the Ottoman Government, that they will not be deceived by this Indian *Rākis*. (*Rākis* in the Sanscrit language is the Devil's disciple. May God not grant success to his goals, and may he not bestow on him his desires!)

Answer of
Jamāl ad-Dīn
to Renan

Journal des Débats,
May 18, 1883

Sir,

I have read in your estimable journal of last March 29 a talk on Islam and Science, given in the Sorbonne before a distinguished audience by the great thinker of our time, the illustrious M. Renan, whose renown has filled the West and penetrated into the farthest countries of the East. Since this speech suggested to me some observations, I took the liberty of formulating them in this letter, which I have the honor of addressing to you with a request that you accommodate it in your columns.

M. Renan wanted to clarify a point of the history of the Arabs which had remained unclear until now and to throw a live light on their past, a light that may be somewhat troubling for those who venerate these people, though one cannot say that he has usurped the place and rank that they formerly occupied in the world. M. Renan has not at all tried, we believe, to destroy the glory of the Arabs which is indestructible; he has applied himself to discovering historical truth and making it known to those who do not know it, as well as to those who study the influence of religions in the history of nations, and in particular in that of civilization. I hasten to recognize that M. Renan has acquitted himself marvelously of this very difficult task, in citing certain facts that have passed unnoticed until this time. I find in his talk remarkable observations, new perceptions, and an indescribable charm. However, I have under my eyes only a more or less faithful translation of this talk. If I had had the opportunity to read it in the French text, I could have penetrated better the ideas of this great thinker. He receives my humble salutation as an homage that is due him and as the sincere expression of my admiration. I would say to him, finally, in these circumstances, what al-Mutanabbi, a poet who loved philosophy wrote several centuries ago to a high personage whose actions he celebrated: "Receive," he said to him, "the praises that I can give you; do not force me to bestow on you the praises that you merit."

M. Renan's talk covered two principal points. The eminent philosopher applied himself to proving that the Muslim religion was by its very essence opposed to the development of science, and that the Arab people, by their nature, do not like either metaphysical sciences or philosophy. This precious plant, M. Renan seems to say, dried up in their hands as if burnt up by the breath of the desert wind. But after reading this talk one cannot refrain from asking oneself if these obstacles come uniquely from the Muslim religion itself or from the manner in which it was propagated in the world; from the character, manners, and aptitudes of the peoples who adopted this religion, or of those on whose nations it was imposed by force. It is no doubt the lack of time that kept M. Renan from elucidating these points; but the harm is no less for that, and if it is difficult to determine its causes in a precise manner and by irrefutable proofs, it is even more difficult to indicate the remedy.

As to the first point, I will say that no nation at its origin is capable of letting itself be guided by pure reason. Haunted by terrors that it cannot escape, it is incapable of distinguishing good from evil, of distinguishing that which could make it happy from that which might be the unfailing source of its unhappiness and misfortune. It does not know, in a word, either how to trace back causes or to discern effects.

This lacuna means that it cannot be led either by force or persuasion to practice the actions that would perhaps be the most profitable for it, or to avoid what is harmful. It was therefore necessary that humanity look outside itself for a place of refuge, a peaceful corner where its tormented conscience could find repose. It was then that there arose some educator or other who, not having, as I said above, the necessary power to force humanity to follow the inspirations of reason, hurled it into the unknown and opened to it vast horizons where the imagination was pleased and where it found, if not the complete satisfaction of its desires, at least an unlimited field for its hopes. And, since humanity, at its origin, did not know the causes of the events that passed under its eyes and the secrets of things, it was perforce led to follow the advice of its teachers and the orders they gave. This obedience was imposed in the name of the supreme Being to whom the educators attributed all events, without permitting men to discuss its utility or its disadvantages. This is no doubt for man one of the heaviest and most humiliating yokes, as I recognize; but one cannot deny that it is by this religious education, whether it be Muslim, Christian, or pagan, that all nations have emerged from barbarism and marched toward a more advanced civilization.

If it is true that the Muslim religion is an obstacle to the development of sciences, can one affirm that this obstacle will not disappear someday? How does the Muslim religion differ on this point from other religions? All religions are intolerant, each one in its way. The Christian religion, I mean the society that follows its inspirations and its teachings and is formed in its image, has emerged from the first period to which I have just alluded; thenceforth free and independent, it seems to advance rapidly on the road of progress and science, whereas Muslim society has not yet freed itself from the tutelage of religion. Realizing, however, that the Christian religion preceded the Muslim religion in the world by many centuries, I cannot keep from hoping that Muhammadan society will succeed someday in breaking its bonds and marching resolutely in the path of civilization after the manner of Western society, for which the Christian faith, despite its rigors and intolerance, was not at all an invincible obstacle. No, I cannot admit that this hope be denied to Islam. I plead here with M. Renan not the cause of the Muslim religion, but that of several hundreds of millions of men, who would thus be condemned to live in barbarism and ignorance.

In truth, the Muslim religion has tried to stifle science and stop its progress. It has thus succeeded in halting the philosophical or intellectual movement and in turning minds from the search for scientific truth. A similar attempt, if I am not mistaken, was made by the Christian religion, and the venerated leaders of the Catholic church have not yet disarmed so far as I know. They continue to fight energetically against what they call the spirit of vertigo and error. I know all the difficulties that the Muslims will have to surmount to achieve the same degree of civilization, access to the truth with the help of philosophic and scientific methods being forbidden them. A true believer must, in fact, turn from the path of studies that have for their object scientific truth, studies on which all truth must depend, according to an opinion accepted at least by some people in Europe. Yoked, like an ox to the plow, to the dogma whose slave he is, he must walk eternally in the furrow that has been traced for him in advance by the interpreters of the law. Convinced, besides, that his religion contains in itself all morality and all sciences, he attaches himself resolutely to it and makes no effort to go beyond.

Why should he exhaust himself in vain attempts? What would be the benefit of seeking truth when he believes he possesses it all? Will he be happier on the day when he has lost his faith, the day when he has stopped believing that all perfections are in the religion he practices and not in another? Wherefore he despises science. I know all this, but I know equally that this Muslim and Arab child whose portrait M. Renan traces in such vigorous terms and who, at a later age, becomes "a fanatic, full of foolish pride in possessing what he believes to be absolute truth," belongs to a race that has marked its passage in the world, not only by fire and blood, but by brilliant and fruitful achievements that prove its taste for science, for all the sciences, including philosophy (with which, I must recognize, it was unable to live happily for long).

I am led here to speak of the second point that M. Renan treated in his lecture with an incontestable authority. No one denies that the Arab people, while it was still in the state of barbarism, rushed into the road of intellectual and scientific progress with a rapidity only equaled by the speed of its conquests, since in the space of a century, it acquired and assimilated almost all the Greek and Persian sciences that had developed slowly during several centuries on their native soil, just as it extended its domination from the Arabian peninsula up to the mountains of the Himalaya and the summit of the Pyrenees.

One might say that in all this period the sciences made astonishing progress among the Arabs and in all the countries under their domination. Rome and Byzantium were then the seats of theological and philosophical sciences as well as the shining center and burning hearth of all human knowledge. Having followed for several centuries the path of civilization, the Greeks and Romans walked with assurance over the vast field of science and philosophy. There came, however, a time when their researches were abandoned and their studies interrupted.

The monuments they had built to science collapsed and their most precious books were relegated to oblivion. The Arabs, ignorant and barbaric as they were in origin, took up what had been abandoned by the civilized nations, rekindled the extinguished sciences, developed them and gave them a brilliance they had never had. Is not this the index and proof of their natural love for sciences? It is true that the Arabs took from the Greeks their philosophy as they stripped the Persians of what made their fame in antiquity; but these sciences, which they usurped by right of conquest, they developed, extended, clarified, perfected, completed, and coordinated with a perfect taste and a rare precision and exactitude. Besides, the French, the Germans, and the English were not so far from Rome and Byzantium as were the Arabs, whose capital was Baghdad. It was therefore easier for the former to exploit the scientific treasures that were buried in these two great cities. They made no effort in this direction until Arab civilization lit up with its reflections the summits of the Pyrenees and poured its light and riches on the Occident. The Europeans welcomed Aristotle, who had emigrated and become Arab; but they did not think of him at all when he was Greek and their neighbor. Is there not in this another proof, no less evident, of the intellectual superiority of the Arabs and of their natural attachment to philosophy? It is true that after the fall of the Arab kingdom in the Orient as in the Occident, the countries that had become the great centers of science, like Iraq and Andalusia, fell again into ignorance and became the center of religious fanaticism; but one cannot conclude from this sad spectacle that the scientific and philosophic progress of the Middle Ages was not due to the Arab people who ruled at that time.

M. Renan does do them this justice. He recognizes that the Arabs conserved and maintained for centuries the hearth of science. What nobler mission for a people! But while recognizing that from about A.D. 775 to near the middle of the thirteenth century, that is to say during about five hundred years, there were in Muslim countries very distinguished scholars and thinkers, and that during this period the Muslim world was superior in intellectual culture to the Christian world, M. Renan has said that the philosophers of the first centuries of Islam as well as the statesmen who became famous in this period were mostly from Harran, from Andalusia, and from Iran. There were also among them Transoxianan and Syrian priests. I do not wish to deny the great qualities of the Persian scholars nor the role that they played in the Arab world; but permit me to say that the Harranians were Arabs and that the Arabs in occupying Spain and Andalusia did not lose their nationality; they remained Arabs. Several centuries before Islam the Arabic language was that of the Harranians. The fact that they preserved their former religion, Sabaeanism, does not mean they should be considered foreign to the Arab nationality. The Syrian priests were also for the most part Ghassanian Arabs converted to Christianity.

As for Ibn-Bajja, Ibn-Rushd (Averroes), and Ibn-Tufail, one cannot say that they are not just as Arab as al-Kindi because they were not born in Arabia, especially if one is willing to consider that human races are only distinguished by their languages and that if this distinction should disappear, nations would not take long to forget their diverse origins. The Arabs who put their arms in the service of the Muslim religion, and who were simultaneously warriors and apostles, did not impose their language on the defeated, and wherever they established themselves, they preserved it for them with a jealous care. No doubt Islam, in penetrating the conquered countries with the violence that is known, transplanted there its language, its manners, and its doctrine, and these countries could not thenceforth avoid its influence. Iran is an example; but it is possible that in going back to the centuries preceding the appearance of Islam, one would find that the Arabic language was not then entirely unknown to Persian scholars. The expansion of Islam gave it, it is true, a new scope, and the Persian scholars converted to the Muhammadan faith thought it an honor to write their books in the language of the Koran. The Arabs cannot, no doubt, claim for themselves the glory that renders these writers illustrious, but we believe that they do not need this claim; they have among themselves enough celebrated scholars and writers. What would happen if, going back to the first period of Arab domination, we followed step by step the first group from which was formed this conquering people who spread their power over the world, and if, eliminating everything that is outside this group and its descendants, we did not take into account either the influence it exercised on minds or the impulse it gave to the sciences? Would we not be led, thus, no longer to recognize in conquering peoples other virtues or merits than those that flow from the material fact of conquest? All conquered peoples would then regain their moral autonomy and would attribute to themselves all glory, no part of which could be legitimately claimed by the power that fructified and developed these germs. Thus, Italy would come to say to France that neither Mazarin nor Bonaparte belonged to her; Germany or England would in turn claim the scholars who, having come to France, made its professorships illustrious and enhanced the brilliance of its scientific renown. The French, on their side, would claim for themselves the glory of the offspring of those illustrious families who, after [the revocation of] the edict of Nantes, emigrated to all Europe. And if all Europeans belong to the same stock, one can with justice claim that the Harranians and the Syrians, who are Semites, belong equally to the great Arab family.

It is permissible, however, to ask oneself why Arab civilization, after having thrown such a live light on the world, suddenly became extinguished; why this torch has not been relit since; and why the Arab world still remains buried in profound darkness.

Here the responsibility of the Muslim religion appears complete. It is clear that wherever it became established, this religion tried to stifle the sciences and it was marvelously served in its designs by despotism.

Al-Siuti tells that the Caliph al-Hadi put to death in Baghdad 5000 philosophers in order to destroy sciences in the Muslim countries down to their roots. Admitting that this historian exaggerated the number of victims, it remains nonetheless established that this persecution took place, and it is a bloody stain for the history of a religion as it is for the hisory of a people. I could find in the past of the Christian religion analogous facts. Religions, by whatever names they are called, all resemble each other. No agreement and no reconciliation are possible between these religions and philosophy. Religion imposes on man its faith and its belief, whereas philosophy frees him of it totally or in part. How could one therefore hope that they would agree with each other? When the Christian religion, under the most modest and seductive forms, entered Athens and Alexandria, which were, as everyone knows, the two principal centers of science and philosophy, after becoming solidly established in these two cities its first concern was to put aside real science and philosophy, trying to stifle both under the bushes of theological discussions, to explain the inexplicable mysteries of the Trinity, the Incarnation, and Transubstantiation. It will always be thus. Whenever religion will have the upper hand, it will eliminate philosophy; and the contrary happens when it is philosophy that reigns as sovereign mistress. So long as humanity exists, the struggle will not cease between dogma and free investigation, between religion and philosophy; a desperate struggle in which, I fear, the triumph will not be for free thought, because the masses dislike reason, and its teachings are only understood by some intelligences of the elite, and because, also, science, however beautiful it is, does not completely satisfy humanity, which thirsts for the ideal and which likes to exist in dark and distant regions that the philosophers and scholars can neither perceive nor explore.

Reference Material

Bibliography

Items containing significant primary material or analysis of Afghānī are starred.

UNPUBLISHED DOCUMENTS

Browne, Edward G. Correspondence with Mīrzā Āqā Khān Kirmānī. *Oriental Manuscripts*, vol. 60. Edward G. Browne collection. Cambridge University Library. Cambridge, England.

France, Archives du Ministère des Affaires Étrangères. Perse, 1888–*1896.

*Great Britain. Commonwealth Relations Office. Government of India, Foreign Department. *Narrative of Events in Cabul from the Death of Dost Mahomed to the Spring of 1872. . . . Cabul Précis 1863–74*. Simla, 1874.

*Great Britain. Commonwealth Relations Office. Government of India, Foreign Department. *Proceedings of the Government of India in the Foreign Department, Political*. Calcutta, 1869; "Cabul Diary," Dec., 1868, and Jan., 1869.

Great Britain. Public Record Office. Documents in the following series: *F.O. 60: original despatches to and from Persia, especially *F.O. 60/594, Djemal ed-din; proceedings of, and expulsion from Persia, 1883–1897. F.O. 65: original despatches to and from Russia. *F.O. 78: original despatches to and from Egypt. *F.O. 248: archives of the British Embassy in Tehran.

*Malkam Khān Manuscripts, Supplement Persan, no. 1995 (containing two letters from Abū al-Hudā to Afghānī, 1892); Supplement Persan, no. 1996 (correspondence of Mīrzā Āqā Khān Kirmānī with Malkam Khān).

*Sayyid Jamāl ad-Dīn al-Afghānī's Personal Books and Papers. Majlis Library. Tehran, Iran. (Catalogued in Afshār and Mahdavī, eds., *Documents*; reference given below.)

BOOKS AND ARTICLES BY SAYYID JAMĀL AD-DĪN AL-AFGHĀNĪ

*al-Afghānī, Sayyid Jamāl ad-Dīn. "Al-Afghānī on Types of Despotic Government." Trans. L. M. Kenny. In *Journal of the American Oriental Society*, 86, 1 (1966), 19–27.

*———. "Les Anglais en Égypte," *La Justice* (Paris), March 27, 1883. (Reprinted in Pakdaman, "Notes sur le séjour . . . "; see reference below.)

*———. *Ārā' va muʿtaqadāt-i Sayyid Jamāl ad-Dīn Afghānī*. Ed. Murtaẓā

Mudarrisī Chahārdihī. Tehran, 1337/1958–59. (Includes Afghānī's Persian articles and the text of the "Refutation of the Materialists.")

*———. Ḥaqīqat-i mazhab-i naichirī va bayān-i ḥāl-i naichirīyān. Hyderabad, 1298/1881. ("Refutation of the Materialists," original Persian ed. Majlis Library, Tehran.) Another edition, Tehran, 1303/1924–25.

*———. "Lettre sur l'Hindoustan," L'Intransigeant (Paris), April 24, 1883. (Reprinted in Kedourie, Afghani and ʿAbduh, and in Pakdaman, "Notes sur le séjour . . . ," both cited below.)

*———. "Le Mahdi," L'Intransigeant (Paris), Dec. 8, 11, 17, 1883. (Reprinted in Kedourie, Afghani and ʿAbduh, and in Pakdaman, "Notes sur le séjour. . . .")

*———. Maqālāt-i jamāliyyeh. Tehran, 1312/1933–34.

*———. Articles in Muʿallim-i Shafīq (Hyderabad), nos. 1–10, Dec., 1880– Oct., 1881. (Persian journal, Majlis Library, Tehran.)

*———. "Pages choisies de Djamal al-din al-Afghani: La Nationalité (djinsiya) et la religion musulmane," trans. M. Colombe (from al-ʿUrwa al-Wuthqā, no. 2, March 20, 1884), Orient, 22 (1962), 125–130. Also, Orient, 21 (1962), 87–115; 22 (1962), 125–159; 23 (1962), 169–198; 24 (1962), 125–151; and 25 (1963), 141–152.

*———. "Pages peu connues de Djamal ad-Din al-Afghani," trans. Mehdi Hendessi, Orient, 6 (1958), 123–128.

*———. al-Radd ʿala al-dahriyyīn. Trans. into Arabic from the Persian by Muḥammad ʿAbduh. Cairo, 1955.

*———. Réfutation des matérialistes. Trans. A. M. Goichon. Paris, 1942.

*———. "The Reign of Terror in Persia," Contemporary Review, LXI (Feb., 1892), pp. 238–248.

*———. Tatimmat al-bayān fī tārīkh al-Afghān. Ed. ʿAlī Yūsuf al-Kirīdlī. Cairo, 1901.

*———, and Muḥammad ʿAbduh. al-ʿUrwa al-Wuthqā. Cairo, 1958. Originally published as a periodical in Paris, 1884. (Original ed., Public Record Office, London, F.O. 78/3682.)

*———. Several articles in Ḍiyāʾ al-Khāfiqain (The Eastern and Western Review) (London), I (1892). (Arabic-English journal, at the British Museum.)

NEWSPAPERS AND JOURNALS

*Abū Naẓẓara (Paris, Arabic), Jan., Feb., 1883. Several issues contain items by or concerning Afghānī.

*al-Baṣīr (Paris, Arabic), nos. 66, 67, 68, 74, 75, and 77 (Feb. 8, 15, 22; April 5, 12, 26) and May 3, 1883. These issues contain articles by Afghānī, and other early issues of 1883 contain comments about him.

al-Hilāl (Cairo), 1897.

Kābul (Kabul, Persian), Dec., 1939–Jan., 1940.

La Turquie (Istanbul), Dec. 9, 1870.

Le Monde Maçonnique (Paris), 1867–1882.

Le Temps (Paris), May 6, 7, 8, 9, 16, and 26, 1896.

Levant Times (Istanbul), Nov. 15, 1870.

*Qānūn (London, Persian), 1890–1896. (Cambridge University Library, Cambridge, England.)

Sirāj al-Akhbār (Kabul, Persian), VI, nos. 3, 5 (1916).

The Times (London), Aug. 30 and Sept. 8, 1879.

Türk Yurdu (Istanbul), I (1327–28/1911–12), 200–201.

BOOKS IN WESTERN LANGUAGES

Abdel-Malek, Anouar. Anthologie de la littérature arabe contemporaine. Vol. 2: Les essais. Paris, 1965.

*'Abduh, Muḥammad. Rissalat al Tawhid. Trans. B. Michel and M. Abdel Razik. Paris, 1925.

Adams, Charles C. Islam and Modernism in Egypt. London, 1933.

Afnan, Soheil M. Avicenna, His Life and Works. London, 1958.

Ahmad, Aziz. Studies in Islamic Culture in the Indian Environment. Oxford, 1964.

Ahmed, Jamal Mohammed. The Intellectual Origins of Egyptian Nationalism. London, 1960.

*Alexander, J. The Truth about Egypt. London, 1911.

Algar, R. F. [Hamid]. "The Political and Social Role of the 'Olamā in Qajar Iran." Unpublished Ph.D. dissertation. Trinity College, Cambridge, England, 1965.

Ameer Ali, Syed. The Spirit of Islam. London, 1922.

Amin, Osman. Muḥammad 'Abduh: Essai sur ses idées philosophiques et religieuses. Cairo, 1944.

———. Muḥammad 'Abduh. Trans. Charles Wendell. Washington, D.C., 1953.

Anonymous. Eminent Mussalmans. Madras, 1926.

Averroes (Ibn Rushd). Averroes' Tahafut al-Tahahfut. Trans. and ed. S. van den Bergh. London, 1954.

———. On the Harmony of Religion and Philosophy. Trans. and ed. George F. Hourani. London, 1961.

Avicenna (Ibn Sīnā). Avicenna on Theology. Trans. A. J. Arberry. London, 1951.

———. Livre des directives et remarques (Kitāb al-išārāt wa al-tanbīhāt). Trans., intro., and notes by A. M. Goichon. Beirut and Paris, 1951.

Baljon, J. M. S. The Reforms and Religious Ideas of Sir Sayyid Ahmad Khan. Leyden, 1949.

Bausani, Alessandro. Persia religiosa. Milan, 1959.

*Berkes, Niyazi. The Development of Secularism in Turkey. Montreal, 1964.

Binder, Leonard. Religion and Politics in Pakistan. Berkeley and Los Angeles, 1961.

———. The Ideological Revolution in the Middle East. New York, 1964.

*Blunt, Wilfrid S. India under Ripon. London, 1909.

*———. Gordon at Khartoum. London, 1912.

*———. Secret History of the English Occupation of Egypt. New York, 1922.

*———. My Diaries. London, 1932. Vol. I.

Browne, Edward G. *A Traveller's Narrative: Written to Illustrate the Episode of the Bāb*. Cambridge, 1891. 2 vols.
———. *A Year amongst the Persians*. London, 1893.
*———. *The Persian Revolution of 1905–1909*. Cambridge, 1910.
———. *Materials for the Study of the Bābī Religion*. Cambridge, 1918.
Corbin, Henry. *Avicenna and the Visionary Recital*. Trans. Willard R. Trask. New York, 1960.
Cottam, Richard W. *Nationalism in Iran*. Pittsburgh, 1964.
Cromer, Lord (Evelyn Baring). *Modern Egypt*. London, 1908. 2 vols.
Curzon, George N. *Persia and the Persian Question*. London, 1892. 2 vols.
Davison, Roderic. *Reform in the Ottoman Empire, 1856–1876*. Princeton, 1963.
Douin, G. *Histoire du règne du Khédive Ismaïl*. Rome, 1933–1941. 3 vols.
Encyclopaedia of Islam. Leyden and London, 1913–1938; new ed., 1960–1967. Referred to below as *EI¹* and *EI²* respectively.
Fabunmi, L. A. *The Sudan in Anglo-Egyptian Relations: 1800–1956*. London, 1960.
al-Fārābī. *Alfarabi's Philosophy of Plato and Aristotle*. Trans. and intro. by Muhsin Mahdi. New York, 1962.
Faruqi, Ziya-ul-Hasan. *The Deoband School and the Demand for Pakistan*. London, 1963.
Feuvrier, Dr. (Jean-Baptiste). *Trois ans à la cour de Perse*. New ed. Paris, 1906.
Gardet, Louis. *La pensée religieuse d'Avicenne*. Paris, 1951.
Gendzier, Irene L. *The Practical Visions of Ya'qub Sanu'*. Cambridge, Mass., 1966.
al-Ghazālī. *The Confessions of al Ghazzali*. Trans. Claud Field. London, 1909.
Gibb, H. A. R. *Modern Trends in Islam*. Chicago, 1947.
Gobineau, Comte (J. Arthur) de. *Les religions et les philosophies dans l'Asie centrale*. Ninth ed. Paris, 1957.
*Gordon, Sir Thomas Edward. *Persia Revisited*. London, 1896.
Gould, Robert F. *The History of Freemasonry*. New York, 1889. 4 vols.
Greaves, Rose Louise. *Persia and the Defence of India, 1884–1892*. London, 1959.
Guizot, François Pierre Guillaume. *History of Civilization in Europe*. Trans. William Hazlitt. New York, n.d.
Habberton, William. *Anglo-Russian Relations concerning Afghanistan, 1837–1907*. Urbana, Ill., 1937.
*Haim, Sylvia, ed. *Arab Nationalism*. Berkeley and Los Angeles, 1962.
Hanna, H. B. *The Second Afghan War*. London, 1899. Vol. I.
Hartmann, Martin. *The Arabic Press of Egypt*. London, 1899.
Hodgson, M. G. S. *The Order of the Assassins*. 's-Gravenhage, 1955.
Holt, P. M. *The Mahdist State in the Sudan, 1881–1898*. Oxford, 1958.
*Hourani, Albert. *Arabic Thought in the Liberal Age: 1798–1939*. London, 1962.
Hunter, W. W. *The Indian Musalmans: Are they Bound in Conscience to Rebel against the Queen?* London, 1871.

Kazemzadeh, Firuz. Advance copy of MS on Anglo-Russian relations in Iran. [New Haven: Yale University Press, 1968.]

*Keddie, Nikki R. *Religion and Rebellion in Iran: The Tobacco Protest of 1891–1892.* London, 1966.

*Kedourie, Elie. *Afghani and 'Abduh: An Essay on Religious Unbelief and Political Activism in Modern Islam.* London, 1966.

Kerr, Malcolm H. *Islamic Reform: The Political and Legal Theories of Muḥammad 'Abduh and Rashīd Riḍā.* Berkeley and Los Angeles, 1966.

Kirkpatrick, F. A. *Lectures on the History of the 19th Century.* Cambridge, 1904.

*Kosogovskii, V. A. *Iz tegeranskogo dnevnika polkovnika V. A. Kosogovskogo.* Moscow, 1960.

Lambton, Ann K. S. *Islamic Society in Persia.* London, 1954.

Landau, Jacob. *Parliaments and Parties in Egypt.* Tel Aviv, 1953.

Landes, David S. *Bankers and Pashas.* London, 1958.

Lasswell, Harold. *Psychopathology and Politics.* New ed. New York, 1960.

Lerner, Ralph, and Muhsin Mahdi, eds. *Medieval Political Philosophy.* Toronto, 1963.

Lewis, Bernard. *The Emergence of Modern Turkey.* London, 1961.

———. *The Middle East and the West.* London, 1964.

Long, Col. C. Chaillé-. *The Three Prophets.* New York, 1886.

Mackey, Albert G. *Encyclopedia of Freemasonry.* Chicago, 1929. 2 vols.

Mahdi, Muhsin. *Ibn Khaldûn's Philosophy of History.* London, 1957.

Mahomed Khan, Mir Munshi Sultan, ed. *The Life of Abdur Rahman, Amir of Afghanistan.* London, 1900. Vol. I.

Malet, Edward. *Egypt, 1879–1883.* London, 1909.

Mardin, Şerif. *The Genesis of Young Ottoman Thought.* Princeton, 1962.

Marlowe, John. *Anglo-Egyptian Relations, 1800–1953.* London, 1954.

*al-Mujāhid, Sharif. "Sayyid Jamāl al-Dīn al-Afghānī: His Role in the Nineteenth Century Muslim Awakening." Unpublished M.A. thesis, McGill University. Montreal, 1954.

Nasr, Seyyed Hossein. *Three Muslim Sages.* Cambridge, Mass., 1964.

Nicolas, A. L. M. *Le Beyan arabe de Seyyed Ali Mohammed.* Paris, 1905.

———. *Seyyed Ali Mohammed, dit le Bab.* Paris, 1905.

———. *Essai sur le Cheikhisme.* Paris, 1910–1914. 4 pts.

———. *Le Beyan persan.* Paris, 1911–1914. 4 vols.

Ninet, John. *Arabi Pacha.* Berne, 1884.

Novikoff, Olga. *The M. P. for Russia: Reminiscences and Correspondence of Madame Olga Novikoff, 1878–1908.* London, 1909. Vol. II.

Ohrwalder, Father Joseph. *Ten Years' Captivity in the Mahdi's Camp.* London, 1892.

Pakdaman, Homa. Advance copy of manuscript on Sayyid Jamāl ad-Dīn al-Afghānī.

Razi, G. H. "Religion and Politics in Iran: A Study of Social Dynamics." Unpublished Ph.D. dissertation, University of California. Berkeley, 1954.

Renan, Ernest. *L'Islamisme et la science.* Paris, 1883.

*———. *Oeuvres complètes.* Paris, 1947. Vol. I.

*Rochefort, Henri (Marquis de Rochefort-Luçay). *The Adventures of My Life*. Trans. by author and Ernest W. Smith. London, 1897. 2 vols.

Rodinson, Maxime. *Islam et capitalisme*. Paris, 1966.

Rosenthal, E. I. J. *Political Thought in Medieval Islam*. Cambridge, 1958.

*Sabry, M. *La genèse de l'espirit national égyptien (1863–1882)*. Paris, 1924.

——. *L'empire égyptien sous Ismail et l'ingérence Anglo-Française (1863–1879)*. Paris, 1933.

*Safran, Nadav. *Egypt in Search of a Political Community*. Cambridge, Mass., 1961.

Sammarco, A. *Histoire de l'Égypte moderne*. Cairo, 1937. Vol. III.

Sayyid Aḥmad Khān (Syed Ahmad Khan Bahadur). *Review on Dr. Hunter's Indian Musalmans*. Benares, 1872.

——. *Essay on the Question whether Islam has been Beneficial or Injurious to Human Society in General and to the Mosaic and Christian Dispensations*. Lahore, 1954.

Sharif, M. M., ed. *A History of Muslim Philosophy*. Wiesbaden, 1963, 1966. 2 vols.

Shibeika, Mekki. *British Policy in the Sudan, 1882–1902*. London, 1952.

Slatin, Rudolf C. *Fire and Sword in the Sudan*. London, 1896.

Smith, Wilfred Cantwell. *Modern Islām in India*. London, 1946.

*——. *Islam in Modern History*. Princeton, 1957.

Strauss, Leo. *Persecution and the Art of Writing*. Glencoe, Ill., 1952.

Terentyef, M. A. *Russia and England in Central Asia*. Trans. F. C. Daukes. Calcutta, 1876. 2 vols.

Von Grunebaum, G. E. *Modern Islam*. Berkeley and Los Angeles, 1962.

Walzer, Richard. *Greek into Arabic*. Oxford, 1962.

Watson, Robert Grant. *A History of Persia: From the Beginning of the Nineteenth Century to the Year 1858*. London, 1866.

Watt, W. M. *Islamic Philosophy and Theology*. Edinburgh, 1962.

Wheeler, Stephen. *The Ameer Abdur Rahman*. New York, 1895.

Wingate, Major F. R. *Mahdism and the Egyptian Sudan*. London, 1891.

Wittlin, Alma. *Abdul Hamid: The Shadow of God*. Trans. Norman Denny. London, 1940.

Wyllie, J. W. S. *Essays on the External Policy of India by J. W. S. Wyllie*. Ed. Sir William Wilson Hunter. London, 1875.

ARTICLES IN WESTERN LANGUAGES

*Ahmad, Aziz. "Sayyid Aḥmad Khān, Jamāl al-dīn al-Afghānī and Muslim India," *Studia Islamica*, XIII (1960) 55–78.

Anonymous (Mīrzā Āqā Khān Kirmānī). "Controverses persanes," trans. A. L. M. Nicolas, *Revue du monde musulmane*, XXI (Dec., 1912), 238–260.

Auriant. "Un emir afghan, adversaire de l'Angleterre en Orient; Djemmal ed Dine, ténébreux agitateur," *Mercure de France*, 288 (Dec. 1, 1938), 316–330.

Avicenna (Ibn Sīnā). "Ibn Sina: Treatise on the Secret of Destiny," trans. George F. Hourani, *Muslim World*, LIII, 2 (April, 1963), 138–140.

*Baidar, Abid Raza. "Jamāl al-Dīn al-Afghānī: A Bibliography of Source

Materials," *International Studies*, III, 1 (July, 1961), 99–108.

*Basetti-Sani, G. "Sayyid Jamâl el-Dîn al-Afghânî: Saggio sul suo concetto della religione," *Orientalia Christiana Periodica*, XXV, 1–2 (1959), 5–43.

Becker, C. H. "Panislamismus," *Archiv für Religionswissenschaft*, VII (1904), 169–192.

Browne, Edward G. "Pan-Islamism." In *Lectures on the History of the Nineteenth Century*. Ed. F. Kirkpatrick. Cambridge, 1904. pp. 306–330.

——. "Bāb, Bābīs." In *Encyclopedia of Religion and Ethics*. New York, 1926. Vol. II, pp. 299–308.

Corbin, Henry. "Confessions extatiques de Mīr Dāmād," *Mélanges Louis Massignon*, I (Damascus, 1956), 331–378.

——. "L'École Shaykhie en Théologie Shi'ite," École Pratique des Hautes Études, Section des Sciences Religieuses, *Annuaire 1960–1961*, Paris (1961) pp. 3–59.

Dawn, C. Ernest. "From Ottomanism to Arabism: The Origin of an Ideology," *Review of Politics*, XXIII, 3 (July, 1961), 378–400.

*Federmann, Robert. "Scheik Djemaleddin el Afghan: Ein Lebensbild aus dem Orient," *Beilage zur Allgemeinen Zeitung*, no. 144 (Munich), June 24, 1896.

Gardet, Louis. "Le problème de la 'Philosophie Musulmane.'" In *Mélanges offerts à Étienne Gilson*. Paris, 1959. pp. 261–284.

Goldziher, I. "Djamāl al-Dīn al-Afghānī," *EI*[1]. Vol. I, pp. 1008–1011.

——, and J. Jomier. "Djamāl al-Dīn al-Afghānī," *EI*[2]. Vol. II, pp. 416–419.

Haim, Sylvia G. "Blunt and al-Kawākibī," *Oriente Moderno*, XXXV, 3 (1955), 132–143.

——. "Islam and the Theory of Arab Nationalism." In *The Middle East in Transition*. Ed. Walter Z. Laqueur. New York, 1958.

Hanna, Sami A. "Al-Afghānī: A Pioneer of Islamic Socialism," *The Muslim World*, LVII, 1 (Jan., 1967) 24–32.

Hourani, G. F. "Ibn-Rushd's Defence of Philosophy." In *The World of Islam*. Ed. James Kritzeck and R. Bayly Winder. London, 1960.

——. "Averroes on Good and Evil," *Studia Islamica*, XVI (1962), 13–40.

*Keddie, Nikki R. "The Pan-Islamic Appeal: Afghani and Abdülhamid II," *Middle Eastern Studies*, III, 1 (Oct., 1966), 46–67.

*——. "Religion and Irreligion in Early Iranian Nationalism," *Comparative Studies in Society and History*, IV, 3 (April, 1962), 265–295.

*——. "Symbol and Sincerity in Islam," *Studia Islamica*, XIX (1963), 27–63.

*——. "Afghani in Afghanistan," *Middle Eastern Studies*, I, 4 (July, 1965), 322–349.

——. "The Origins of the Religious-Radical Alliance in Iran," *Past and Present*, 34 (July, 1966), 70–80.

*——. "Sayyid Jamāl al-Dīn al-Afghānī's first Twenty-seven Years: The Darkest Period," *Middle East Journal*, XX, 4 (Autumn, 1966), 517–533.

*Kedourie, Elie. "Further Light on Afghani," *Middle Eastern Studies*, I, 2 (Jan., 1965), 187–202.

Key, Kerim Kami. "Jamal ad-Din al-Afghani and the Muslim Reform Movement," *Islamic Literature* (Oct., 1951), 5–10.

Kudsi-zadeh, A. Albert. "Jamal ad-Din al-Afghani: A Select List of Articles," *Middle Eastern Studies*, II, 1 (Oct., 1965), 66–72.

Lambton, Ann K. S. "Secret Societies and the Persian Revolution of 1905–6," *St. Antony's Papers*, no. 4 (London, 1958), 43–60.

———. "Persian Society under the Qājārs," *Journal of the Royal Central Asian Society*, XLVIII, Pt. II (1961), 123–139.

———. "Dustūr: iv. Irān." In *Encyclopaedia of Islam*. New ed. Leyden and London, 1965. Vol. II, pp. 649–657.

Landau, Jacob M. "Al-Afghani's Panislamic Project," *Islamic Culture*, XXVI, 3 (July, 1952), 50–54.

———. "Prolegomena to a Study of Secret Societies in Modern Egypt," *Middle Eastern Studies*, I, 2 (Jan., 1965), 135–186.

Lee, Dwight E. "The Origins of Pan-Islamism," *American Historical Review*, XLVII, 2 (Jan., 1942), 278–287.

Lewis, Bernard. "The Ottoman Empire in the Mid-Nineteenth Century: A Review," *Middle Eastern Studies*, I, 3 (April, 1965), 283–295.

Mackey, Albert G. "Egypt." In *Encyclopedia of Freemasonry*. Chicago, 1929. Vol. I, pp. 315–316.

Malcom Khan. "Persian Civilization," *Contemporary Review*, LIX (Feb., 1891), 238–244.

Malik, H. "The Religious Liberalism of Sir Sayyid Aḥmad Khān," *Muslim World*, LIV, 3 (1964), 160–169.

Massignon, L. M. "De Jamal oud Din au Zahawi," *Revue du monde musulmane*, XII, 12 (Dec., 1910), 561–570.

Minorsky, Vladimir. "Iran: Opposition, Martyrdom and Revolt." In *Unity and Variety in Muslim Civilization*. Ed. G. E. von Grunebaum. Chicago, 1955.

Ninet, John. "The Origin of the National Party in Egypt," *Nineteenth Century*, XIII (Jan., 1883), 117–134.

*Pakdaman, Homa. "Notes sur le séjour de Djamâl al-dîn al-Afghânî en France," *Orient*, 35 (1965), 203–207.

Rossi, Ettore. "Il centenario della nascita di Gemal ud-Din el-Afghani celebrato a Kabul," *Oriente Moderno*, XX, 5 (May, 1940), 262–265.

Scarcia, Gianroberto. "Kermān 1905: La 'guerra tra Šeiḫī e Bālāsarī,' " *Annali del Istituto Universitario Orientale di Napoli*, n.s., XIII (1963), 195–238.

Smith, Wilfred C. "The 'Ulamā' in Indian Politics." In *Politics and Society in India*. Ed. C. H. Philips. London, 1962.

Snouck Hurgronje, C. "Les confréries religieuses, la Mecque et le panislamisme," *Revue de l'histoire des religions*, 44 (1901), 262–281.

———. "Over Panislamisme," Haarlem, Musée Teyler, *Archives*, 3d ser., I (1912), 87–105.

Thornton, A. P. "Afghanistan in Anglo-Russian Diplomacy, 1869–73," *Cambridge Historical Journal*, XI, 2 (1954), 204–218.

———. "The Reopening of the Central Asian Question, 1864–69," *History*, XLI, 141–143 (Feb.–Oct., 1956), 122–136.

Toynbee, Arnold J. "The Ineffectiveness of Panislamism." In *A Study of History*. London, 1954. Vol. VIII, pp. 692–695.

BIBLIOGRAPHY

199

Vambery, Arminius. "Pan-Islamism," *The Nineteenth Century*, LX (Oct., 1906), 547–558.

Wirth, Albrecht. "Panislamismus," *Deutsche Rundschau*, CLXIII (June, 1915), 429–440.

"X" (Sayyid Ḥasan Taqīzādeh). "Le panislamisme et le panturquisme," *Revue du monde musulmane*, XXII (March, 1913), 179–220.

Books and Articles in Arabic, Persian, Turkish, and Urdu (Unless otherwise indicated, the language is that of the country of publication.)

*'Abbās Mīrzā Mulk Ārā. *Sharḥ-i ḥāl-i 'Abbās Mīrzā Mulk Ārā.* Ed. 'Abd al-Ḥusain Navā'ī. Tehran, 1325/1946–47.

*'Abd al-Ghaffār, Qāẕī Muḥammad. *Āṣār-i Jamāl ad-Dīn Afghānī.* Delhi, 1940.

*'Abduh, Muḥammad. *Risālat al-wāridāt.* Cairo, 1925.

*Abū Rayya, Maḥmūd. *Jamāl ad-Dīn al-Afghānī.* Cairo, 1961.

*Afshār, Īraj, and Aṣghar Mahdavī. *Documents inédits concernant Seyyed Jamāl-al-Dīn Afghānī (Majmū'eh-yi asnād va madārik-i chāp nashudeh dar bāreh-yi Sayyid Jamāl ad-Dīn mashhūr bi Afghānī).* Tehran, 1963.

*Amīn, Aḥmad. *Zu'amā' al-iṣlāḥ fī al-'aṣr al-ḥadīth.* Cairo, 1949.

*Amīn ad-Dauleh. *Khāṭirāt-i siyāsī-yi Mīrzā 'Alī Khān-i Amīn ad-Dauleh.* Ed. Hafez Farman-Farmaian. Tehran, 1962.

*Anonymous (Mīrzā Āqā Khān Kirmānī and Shaikh Aḥmad Rūḥī). *Hasht Bihisht,* N.p., n.d. (An Azalī Bābī text published in Iran.)

*Arslān, Shakīb. *Ḥāḍir al-'ālam al-Islāmī.* Cairo, 1343/1924–25.

*Asadābādī, Mīrzā Luṭfallāh. *Sharḥ-i ḥāl va āṣār-i Sayyid Jamāl ad-Dīn Asadābādī ma'rūf bi "Afghānī."* Tabriz, 1326/1947–48.

—— (Author listed as Mīrzā Luṭfallāh Khān). *Jamāl ad-Dīn al-Asadābādī, al-ma'rūf bi al-Afghānī.* Arabic trans. and introduction by Ṣādiq Nash'at. Cairo, 1957.

*Asadābādī, Ṣifātallāh Jamālī. *Asnād va madārik dar bāreh-yi Īrānī al-aṣl būdan-i Sayyid Jamāl ad-Dīn Asadābādī.* Tehran, n.d.

al-Bustānī, Buṭrus, ed. *Dā'ira al-Ma'ārif (Encyclopedie Arabe).* Vol. V. "Bābī." Beirut, 1881.

Canib, Ali. "Cemaleddin Afghanî," *Hayat* (Ankara), III, 77 (May, 1928).

Ergin, Osman. *Türkiye maarif tarihi.* Vol. II. Istanbul, 1939.

Karbalā'ī, Shaikh Ḥasan. *Qarārdād-i rizhī 1890 m.* Ed. and intro. by Ibrāhīm Dihgān. Arāk, Iran, ca. 1955.

al-Kawākibī, 'Abd ar-Raḥmān. *Ṭabā'i' al-istibdād.* Cairo, n.d.

*Keskioğlu, Osman. "Cemâleddin Efgânî," *İlâhiyat Fakültesi Dergisi,* X (1962), 91–102.

Khūgiyānī, Muḥammad Amīn. *Ḥayāt-i Sayyid Jamāl ad-Dīn Afghānī.* Kabul, 1318.

Kirmānī, Nāẓim al-Islām. *Tārīkh-i bīdārī-yi Īrānīyān.* 2d ed. Tehran, 1324/1945–46.

Madkūr, Muḥammad Salām. *Jamāl ad-Dīn al-Afghānī.* Cairo, 1937.

*al-Maghribī, 'Abd al-Qādir. *Jamāl ad-Din al-Afghānī.* Cairo, 1948.

Makāryūs, Shāhīn Bey. *Kitāb al-ādāb al-māsūniyya.* Cairo, 1895.

al-Makhzūmī, Muḥammad. *Khāṭirāt-i Sayyid Jamāl ad-Dīn Asadābādī.*

Trans. into Persian by Murtaẓā Mudarrisī Chahārdihī. Tabriz, 1328/ 1949–50.

———. Khāṭirāt Jamāl ad-Dīn al-Afghānī. Beirut, 1931. 2d ed.; Damascus, 1965.

*Malikzādeh, Mahdī. Tārīkh-i inqilāb-i mashrūṭiyyat-i Īrān. Tehran, 1328/ 1949–50. Vol. I.

Mudarrisī Chahārdihī, Murtaẓā. Zindiganī va falsafeh-yi ijtimā'ī va siyāsī-yi Sayyid Jamāl ad-Dīn Afghānī. Tehran, 1334/1955–56.

*Muḥammad Ḥasan Khān I'timād aṣ-Ṣaltaneh. al-Ma'āṣir va al-āṣār. Tehran, 1889.

*Pâkalïn, Mehmed Zeki. Son sadrâzamlar ve başvekiller. Vol. IV. Istanbul, 1944.

*Qāsim, Maḥmūd. Jamāl ad-Dīn al-Afghānī, ḥayātuhu va falsafatuhu. Cairo, n.d.

*Rāfi'ī 'Abd ar-Raḥmān. Jamāl ad-Dīn al-Afghānī. Cairo, 1957.

*Riḍā, Muḥammad Rashīd. Tārīkh al-ustādh al-imām ash-shaikh Muḥammad 'Abduh. Vol. I, 2d. ed. Cairo, 1931.

Ṣafā'ī, Ibrāhīm. Rahbarān-i mashrūṭeh. Tehran, 1344/1965–66.

*Sāsānī, Khān Malik. Siyāsatgarān-i daureh-yi Qājār. Tehran, 1338/1959–60.

*Shafīq, Aḥmad. Mudhakkirātī fi niṣf qarn. Cairo, 1934.

Shīrāzī, Furṣat ad-Dauleh. Dīvān-i Furṣat. Tehran, n.d.

Ṣifat 'Alī Shāh Ẓahīr ad-Dauleh. Tārīkh-i bī durūgh. Tehran, 1334/1955–56.

Ṭabāṭabā'ī, Muḥammad Muḥīṭ. Majmū'eh-yi āṣār-i Mīrzā Malkam Khān. Tehran, 1327/1948–49.

Taimūrī, Ibrāhīm. Taḥrim-i tanbākū. Tehran, n.d.

*Taqīzādeh, Sayyid Ḥasan. "Sayyid Jamāl ad-Dīn," Kāveh (Berlin, Persian), II, 3 (1921), 5–11; and "Takmileh," Kāveh, II, 9 (1921), 10–11.

———. "Sayyid Jamāl ad-Dīn ma'rūf bi Afghānī," Mardān-i khudsākhteh. Ed. Ibrāhīm Khājeh Nūrī. Tehran, 1947.

Zaidān, Jurjī. Tārīkh al-māsūniyya al-'āmm. Cairo, 1889.

———. Tarājim mashāhīr ash-sharq. Cairo, 1922. 2 vols.

Index

Persian, Afghan, and Indian names are as in the text—without consonantal diacriticals unless taken from a footnote or an Arabic text. All references beginning with page 101 are to works by Afghānī.

(All references beginning with page 101 are to works by Afghānī.)

(All references beginning with page 101 are to works by Afghānī.)

(All references beginning with page 101 are to works by Afghānī.)

(All references beginning with page 101 are to works by Afghānī.)

(All references beginning with page 101 are to works by Afghānī.)